Practical
Software Factories
in .NET

Gunther Lenz and Christoph Wienands

with contributions by Jack Greenfield and Wojtek Kozaczynski

Foreword by Douglas C. Schmidt, Jack Greenfield,
Jürgen Kazmeier and Eugenio Pace

Apress®

Practical Software Factories in .NET

Copyright © 2006 by Gunther Lenz, Christoph Wienands

ISBN-13: 978-1-4302-1175-4

ISBN-10: 1-4302-1175-X

Lead Editor: Jim Sumser
Technical Reviewer: Erik Gunvaldson
Editorial Board: Steve Anglin, Ewan Buckingham, Gary Cornell, Jason Gilmore, Jonathan Gennick, Jonathan Hassell, James Huddleston, Chris Mills, Matthew Moodie, Dominic Shakeshaft, Jim Sumser, Keir Thomas, Matt Wade
Project Manager: Richard Dal Porto
Copy Edit Manager: Nicole LeClerc
Copy Editor: Ami Knox
Assistant Production Director: Kari Brooks-Copony
Production Editor: Katie Stence
Compositor: Susan Glinert
Proofreader: Kim Burton
Indexer: Broccoli Information Management
Artist: April Milne
Cover Designer: Kurt Krames
Manufacturing Director: Tom Debolski

For information on translations, please contact Apress directly at 2560 Ninth Street, Suite 219, Berkeley, CA 94710. Phone 510-549-5930, fax 510-549-5939, e-mail info@apress.com, or visit http://www.apress.com.

The source code for this book is available to readers at http://www.apress.com in the Source Code section.

To Okson for inspiring me. ☺
—Gunther

Dedicated to April for making every day a happy day.
—Christoph

Contents at a Glance

Contents

Foreword

Douglas C. Schmidt
Professor of Computer Science,
Associate Chair of Computer Science and Engineering
Vanderbilt University

The evolution of software technologies over the past five decades has involved the creation of languages and platforms that help developers program more in terms of their design intent, such as architectural concepts and abstractions, and shield them from the complexities of the underlying computing substrate, such as CPU, memory, and network devices. After years of progress, many projects today use third-generation programming languages, such as Java, C++, and C#, and middleware runtime platforms, such as service-oriented architectures and web services. Despite these improvements, however, the level of abstraction at which software is developed still remains low relative to the concepts and concerns of the application domains themselves. As a result, too much time and effort is spent manually rediscovering and reinventing solutions to common domain requirements, which has led to the situation where the majority of software projects are late, over budget, and defect ridden.

These problems occur for various reasons. For example, most application and platform code is handcrafted using third-generation languages. This manual approach incurs excessive time and effort due to complexity stemming from the semantic gap between the design intent and the expression of this intent in third-generation languages, which convey domain semantics and design intent poorly. This semantic gap is particularly noticeable and problematic for integration-related activities, such as system deployment, configuration, and quality assurance that software developers perform when assembling applications using off-the-shelf components. Third-generation languages also force developers to focus on numerous tactical imperative programming details that distract them from strategic concerns, such as satisfying user needs and meeting quality requirements.

A related set of problems stem from the growth of platform complexity, which has evolved faster than the ability of third-generation languages to mask this complexity. For example, popular middleware platforms, such as J2EE, .NET, and CORBA, contain thousands of classes and methods with many intricate dependencies and subtle side effects that require considerable effort and experience to program, tune, and maintain properly. Moreover, since these platforms often evolve rapidly—and new platforms appear regularly—developers expend considerable effort manually porting application code to different platforms or newer versions of the same platform. Due to these types of problems, platform technologies have become so complex that developers spend years mastering—and wrestling with—platform APIs and usage patterns, and are often familiar with only a small subset of the platforms they use regularly.

Without significant enhancements in our languages, platforms, and development processes, therefore, we will be unable to meet increasing customer demands for large quantities of quality software. Achieving the necessary levels of productivity and quality requires a movement away from today's guild-based software paradigm, where applications are largely handcrafted as "one-off" custom artifacts using third-generation languages and general-purpose middleware platforms. We instead need to shift closer to a manufacturing paradigm, where applications are assembled from configurable software components using domain-specific tools and automated quality assurance processes.

Various efforts in the past several decades have attempted to address the problems just described. An effort begun in the 1980s was Computer Aided Software Engineering (CASE). One goal of CASE was to enable developers to write programs more quickly and correctly by using general-purpose graphical notations, such as state machines, structure diagrams, and dataflow diagrams. In theory, these graphical notations are more effective at expressing design intent than using conventional third-generation programming languages. Another goal was to synthesize implementation artifacts from graphical representations to reduce the effort of manually coding, debugging, and porting programs.

Although CASE tools attracted considerable attention in the research community and trade literature, they weren't adopted widely in practice for various reasons, including the following:

- Early CASE tools tried to generate entire applications, including the business logic and the software substrate, which led to inefficient, bloated code that was hard to optimize, validate, evolve, or integrate with code from other sources.

- It was hard to achieve round-trip engineering that moves model representations back and forth seamlessly with synthesized code.

- Due to the simplicity of the notations for representing behavior, CASE tools have largely been applicable to a few domains, such as telecom call processing, that map nicely onto state machines.

- Due to the lack of powerful and common middleware, CASE tools targeted proprietary execution platforms, which made it hard to integrate the code they generated with other software languages and runtime environments.

Practical Software Factories in .NET focuses on a more practical and effective approach to address problems resulting from the complexity of platforms—and the inability of third-generation languages to alleviate this complexity and express domain concepts effectively. This approach is called *Software Factories* and is based on four core concepts that are well established in today's leading software organizations and projects: architectural frameworks, context-based guidance, domain-specific languages, and product line architectures. Software Factories combine and extend related technologies associated with these four core concepts, including patterns, models, object-oriented frameworks, and tools, to help industrialize the development of software. In particular, Software Factories enable the rapid assembly and configuration of separately developed, self-describing, location-independent components to produce families of similar but distinct software systems.

At the heart of the Software Factory paradigm are product line architectures, which consist of object-oriented frameworks whose designs capture recurring patterns, structures, connectors, and control flow in application domains, along with the points of variation explicitly allowed among these entities. Product line architectures are typically designed using common/variability analysis, which captures key characteristics of software product lines, including

- *Scope*, which defines the domains and context of a product line

- *Commonalities*, which describe the attributes that recur across all members of a family of products

- *Variabilities*, which describe the attributes unique to different members of a family of products

- *Extension points*, which can be used to add new features to product variants and accommodate features outside the scope of the product line

Although product line architectures are a powerful technology, they have historically been hard to use and even harder to develop and evolve using conventional third-generation languages and runtime platforms. A key contribution of this book is therefore its focus on developing Software Factories with a high degree on automation using model-driven development and context-based guidance. Model-driven development helps raise the level of abstraction and narrow the gap between application and solution domains by combining

- Metamodeling and model interpreters to create domain-specific languages that help automate repetitive tasks in product line architectures that must be accomplished for each product instance, such as generating code to glue components together or synthesizing deployment artifacts for middleware platforms.

- Commonality/variability analysis and object-oriented extensibility capabilities to create domain-specific frameworks that factor out common usage patterns in a domain into reusable middleware platforms, which help reduce the complexity of designing domain-specific languages by simplifying the code generated from models.

Automated context-based guidance provides product developers with suggestions on what activities to perform in a particular context, such as changing the solution structure, providing custom activities in the context they are applicable, and displaying context-specific help and guidance to developers. This guidance can be created by domain experts, systems engineers, and software architects to convey best practices and semantic constraints to developers using tools that help automate these activities and integrate them into products.

Although the concepts underlying Software Factories have been published before, this book breaks new ground by showing detailed examples of how model-driven development tools and context-based guidance can be used in software projects today. The book presents a case study using the Microsoft .NET Framework, C#, and other .NET-related tools to specify, analyze, optimize, synthesize, validate, and deploy Software Factories that can be customized for the needs of a wide range of software systems. The case study covered in the book includes desktop applications based on the Smart Client Software Factory from the Microsoft patterns & practices group, local services, and third-party services that are accessed via the Internet.

The book covers the entire process of specification, design, implementation, deployment, and use of a Software Factory. It also shows how Software Factory schemas and templates can be used to combine separate software technologies into a coherent application development paradigm. In addition, the book shows how to develop domain-specific languages and guidance packages that incorporate best practices to help eliminate common errors when developing systems, in particular application domains. The entire case study can be downloaded and used as a comprehensive reference. While the Software Factory paradigm can be used with any language and platform, these working examples are invaluable to reinforce key concepts and principles when implementing your own Software Factories.

It's been my experience developing and applying advanced software technologies over the past two decades that mastering the concepts and technologies described in this book is hard without effective guidance from experts who can guide you step by step. We are therefore fortunate that Gunther and Christoph have found time in their busy lives to write a book on practical Software Factories in .NET. If you want thorough coverage of the technologies that will shape the next generation of software applications, read this book. I've learned much from it, and I'm sure you will too.

Jack Greenfield
Architect, Enterprise Tools
Microsoft Corporation

Since Keith Short and I first published our book on Software Factories with Steve Cook and Stuart Kent about eighteen months ago, there has been a tremendous amount of interest, excitement, and activity around the ideas put forward there, both in the academic community and among practitioners. Systems integrators and enterprise IT organizations, in particular, have taken a keen interest the methodology.

With so many practitioners seeking to apply the concepts, requests for better tools and examples quickly became a daily occurrence, and continue to grow in volume and frequency. While the tools are probably the responsibility of software vendors, examples can and should come from the community. *Practical Software Factories in .NET* is exciting because it presents an example from the community.

The book is also exciting because it is part of the forward-thinking research at Siemens AG, one of the world's largest software companies. I've known Gunther Lenz since early 2004, when we were introduced by Carolin Dhaens. We knew about the pioneering work that Siemens had done with patterns, but prior to that introduction, we were not aware of their work in model-driven development, or their experience in software product line engineering. It quickly became clear to both companies that Software Factories were a good fit for Siemens, and that Siemens would become an important partner in refining and applying the methodology.

Gunther took an immediate interest in Software Factories, and quickly became an authority on the topic. In addition to teaching about Software Factories within Siemens, he has presented a number of papers on Software Factories and related topics at workshops and conferences. It was at one of those conferences, UML World in Austin, that I met Christoph Wienands, as he joined Gunther in comparing Software Factories with Model-Driven Architecture (MDA).

What I most appreciate about this book is its focus on reducing theory to practice. The authors may have adopted this focus in order to make the methodology more accessible to others, but in the process they have also contributed significantly to our understanding of Software Factories.

Through our correspondence and occasional meetings about the book and its underlying example, many opportunities arose to discuss some key principle in depth, and then to consider how best to apply it in the context of the example. They have undertaken a useful exercise and produced a valuable resource for the Software Factories community.

Eugenio Pace
Product Manager, pattern & practices Team
Microsoft Corporation

Enterprise architects and developers face many challenges as they address technical scenarios in their enterprise solutions. For the last few years, the Microsoft patterns & practices Team has been developing design and architecture guidance to address the most challenging technical scenarios. The response has been favorable, but has led to a new request: give us guidance on how to build end-to-end solutions. Using a cooking metaphor, the members of the enterprise development community like the ingredients, but what they really want are the instructions and kitchen supplies required to create a complete meal, all put into one elegant box. Software Factories are an answer to this request.

The Software Factory is an approach to solving the problem of packaging reusable assets, tools, and guidance for developing instances of solutions that share common architecture and features. It is an approach to reliably and effectively develop applications that belong to the same family. The concept of the Software Factory integrates the principles of product line architectures, model-driven development, contextual and automated guidance, and reusable software assets such as application blocks and frameworks.

Despite Software Factories' conceptual clarity, they are not easy to build. They require careful and often difficult analysis and development. They must address common scenarios and integrate existing assets (both code and documentation), yet remain extensible to be useful across the target application family. Considering these difficulties, our team worries about the feasibility, cost, and complexities of building anything larger than simple Software Factories. *Practical Software Factories in .NET* directly addresses those concerns.

This book is a pragmatic description of what Software Factories are and how to build them, illustrated with a concrete example. The authors and contributors of the book come from companies with a wealth of experience developing software. Gunther Lenz and Christoph Wienands, the authors, are both software researchers and software practitioners. They come from Siemens, a company that pioneered research and application of software patterns, and that has a real need for Software Factories. Siemens builds all kinds of software ranging from medical devices, to industrial processes control systems, to hospital management systems, to list a few. Many of the systems developed by Siemens are naturally members of product families.

The contributors of the book, Jack Greenfield and Wojtek Kozaczynski, work for Microsoft. Jack defined the original Software Factory concept, and Wojtek architected the first patterns & practices Software Factory for smart client application development, which is reused by Gunther and Christoph in the book.

Development of a Software Factory will remain an inherently complex undertaking. This book, however, makes a great step in the direction of providing concrete, exemplified guidance on how to build one. If you are developing your own Software Factory, converting existing software assets into a factory, or considering building a Software Factory, you will find this book informative and useful.

Jürgen Kazmeier
Department Head, Software Engineering
Siemens Corporate Research

Within the last decade, we could see a rapidly growing demand for software. At the same time, software systems have become larger as well as more and more complex. While we see productivity gains through new development tools and languages, and better processes, these improvements are not enough to keep up with the growing challenges. Therefore, we need urgent improvements in the area of software development in order to satisfy the market demand for software. We think that the Software Factory approach is an emerging and very promising pattern to shorten development time, to reduce cost, and to increase software quality.

Microsoft and Siemens are the largest software companies in the world; both employ around 30,000 software developers. Because Siemens is not selling shrink-wrapped software but rather provides software as embedded systems in their products, Siemens is not perceived as a software company. Nevertheless, the software produced can be found in a lot of different domains, e.g., industrial automation, automotive electronics, medical devices, and communication solutions. At the same time Siemens, as a global player in the field of electrical engineering, is also one of the largest customers of Microsoft.

The goal of Siemens Corporate Research is to explore new technologies and techniques that promise to ensure the competitiveness of Siemens in the marketplace. We think that the Software Factories methodology has the potential to lead software development into a true engineering discipline. That's the reason why we started a research program on Software Factories two years ago. Our goal at Siemens Corporate Research is to support other Siemens divisions in adopting the concepts of Software Factories to gain a competitive advantage. Building on top of experience with product lines within Siemens, we see a great potential in using domain-specific languages and automation in addition to the traditional tools and techniques.

Fortunately, *Practical Software Factories in .NET* could be worked out in close collaboration with Microsoft. In particular, Jack Greenfield and the patterns & practices group for the Smart Client Software Factory generously supported the entire process of writing the book. This can be seen by contributions and reviews of the book and the support of the case study implementation. Furthermore, the collaboration with Professor Douglas C. Schmidt, Vanderbilt University, has proved very fruitful in this research program.

This book not only gives a pragmatic introduction to the topic of Software Factories, but also guides you, the reader, by using a general example throughout the book. The four pillars of Software Factories—product line practices, model-driven development, guidance in context, and architecture frameworks—are known concepts in software engineering. New is the approach of combining these concepts into a holistic and coherent methodology so that we now can make a step forward from craftsmanship to industrialization in software development as it was done previously in other engineering disciplines.

Big thanks to everybody involved for the open communication and great contributions to make this book possible. We hope not only that you enjoy the book, but also that it helps you to kick off the next steps in implementing your own Software Factory.

About the Authors

 **GUNTHER LENZ** is a pioneer in the field of Software Factories. He received a master's degree (Dipl. Ing. Univ.) in electrical engineering from the Technical University of Munich, Germany. He spent five years working on research and product development of a high-performance medical image-processing system, under FDA regulation. In addition to his project experience, Gunther was also a core member of the Software Engineering Process Group (SEPG), which defined, implemented, and optimized the software development process.

In 2002, Gunther joined Siemens Corporate Research in Princeton, New Jersey, where he is a program manager in the Software Engineering department. His current research activities focus on Model-driven Software Development (MDSD), model evolution, and Software Factories. Within Siemens Corporate Technology, Gunther leads the global research efforts in the areas Software Factories and Microsoft technologies.

Gunther is the author of the book *.NET—A Complete Development Cycle* (Addison-Wesley, 2004) and has published many articles in different software development magazines, focusing on a variety of software engineering topics. Furthermore, Gunther has received the Microsoft Most Valuable Professional (MVP) Solution Architect award and is an invited member of the Microsoft Software Design Review Team. He frequently presents at international conferences on subjects related to his research area. Gunther can be reached at gunther@ispysoft.net.

 **CHRISTOPH WIENANDS** received his Diplom-Informatiker (FH) in general computer science at the Furtwangen University of Applied Sciences, Germany. Before he joined Siemens Corporate Research as a software engineer in 2003, he worked as an independent consultant in Germany and as an IT systems analyst with SS White Burs, New Jersey. As part of his responsibilities in the Software Engineering department at SCR, Christoph gets to apply the latest Microsoft technologies, for example, in proof-of-concept applications and in consulting projects to other Siemens business units.

Together with Gunther, Christoph's current research activities focus on Software Factories, model-driven development, and domain-specific languages. In 2005, he became a Microsoft Certified Solution Developer. Due to his research activities, he is a frequent speaker at conferences such as UML World, SD West, and others. Christoph can be reached at christoph@ispysoft.net.

About the Technical Reviewer

ERIK GUNVALDSON is a technology development manager within Microsoft's Enterprise Partner Group, where he is focused on driving Software Factories with Global System Integrators (GSIs). Before this position, Erik was a technical evangelist, in which capacity he managed Microsoft's Technology Adoption Program (TAP) for Visual Studio 2005 Team System. Other roles enjoyed at Microsoft include program managing the Natural Language SDK and managing the enterprise knowledge management system for application development. Before coming to Microsoft nine years ago, Erik was a software architect at Fidelity Investments and a C++/UNIX software developer and manager at a large telecommunications company. Erik is passionate about software industrialization and looks forward to the day when software development is 90% inspiration and 10% perspiration. Erik enjoys spending time with his wife, Anna, and daughter, Katrina, and when time affords, playing golf and tennis.

Acknowledgments

Taking this book from the initial idea and the first proposal and turning it into the physical entity in front of you now required almost a year of hard work. We wouldn't have been able to achieve this without the generous help of many other people. Therefore, we would like to take this opportunity to thank all those who made this book possible. First, there is Jürgen Kazmeier, who supports not only our research in the areas of Model-driven Software Development and Software Factories, but also the undertaking of writing this book.

A very special thank you goes to Jack Greenfield, who guided us in our quest to understand and apply the Software Factories paradigm to our case study. Jack provided us with valuable advice, many hours of discussions and reviews, and, last but not least, his contributions to this book.

We would also like to express our gratitude to Eugenio Pace and Wojtek Kozaczynski from the Microsoft patterns & practices group for the great collaboration in the areas of software architecture and Smart Client Software Factory. In addition, Wojtek also contributed to the book and took the time to review the key chapters; to him a big thanks.

Furthermore, we would like to thank our editor, Jim Sumser; the book's project manager, Richard Dal Porto; the copy editor, Ami Knox; the production editor, Katie Stence; and the entire Apress team for the excellent cooperation and support during the entire time we have worked on the book. We owe our gratitude also to Erik Gunvaldson, our tech reviewer, who provided us with great ideas and suggestions to improve the book from its first draft to the final version.

Also we would like to thank Paul Clements for the interesting discussions regarding product line architectures. For the implementation of our custom Software Factory tools, much thanks goes to Benjamin Kohler, who wrote his master's thesis at Siemens Corporate Research.

Last but not least, we would like to thank our parents and families for their continuous advice and gracious support during these very busy and oftentimes hectic months of writing this book. There are way too many people to list who helped us through great discussion, interesting questions, ideas, suggestions, and mental support to make this book happen: our friends, colleagues, former colleagues, and all others who encouraged and supported us. Therefore, *thank you*, to all of you. ☺

Introduction

Now that you're past all the forewords and prefatory material, we would like to express our reasons and motivation for writing this book. Furthermore, we will tell you a little bit about what this book is about and how we envision you will use it to get the most benefit from it.

In 2004, we heard about *Software Factories: Assembling Applications with Patterns, Models, Frameworks, and Tools*, written by Jack Greenfield and Keith Short; we immediately thought that the Software Factories paradigm, as proposed, could have great potential within Siemens, where we already had many product lines. We met with Jack many times and discussed the tools and techniques that were proposed to complement the theory described in that book. Based on these discussions, we decided to develop a prototype of a Software Factory to experience the pros and cons first hand. Trying to translate the theory from Jack's and Keith's book into real implementation, we realized that there exists a need for a practical guide about how to develop Software Factories, and so the idea of *Practical Software Factories in .NET* was born. This led us to propose our book idea to Tony Davis, at the time an editor at Apress, who thought it was a great idea, thus the beginning of the book you have before you.

Throughout this book, we will follow an imaginary company, ISpySoft, through the planning, design, implementation, and deployment of a Software Factory. The ISpySoft company sells custom software systems to private investigators, aka "private eyes." The book shows the practical application of the Software Factories paradigm and explains the basic theory behind it. In order for you to navigate through the book more easily, we provide little icons indicating which parts are related to the theory (book symbol icon) and which parts are related to the case study (hammer symbol icon) that we develop.

When you read through the book, keep in mind that although this book is built pretty much linearly, the Software Factories methodology is not. Rather than applying waterfall methods, it proposes iterative development and continuous refinement. In the Appendix, we provide a complete checklist of the activities and work products that you typically will see during Software Factory development, which quickly lets you look up important sections of the book.

Last of all, the entire source code of the case study is available from the Apress web site (http://www.apress.com) in the Source Code section. We also provide general information about the book and the case study at the ISpySoft web site (http://www.ISpySoft.net). In addition, we also started a community project on CodePlex to evolve the tools and implementation introduced in the book in the future. If you are interested in helping us to improve the tools and reference implementation, please join the ISpySoft workspace at http://www.codeplex.com/Wiki/View.aspx?ProjectName=ISpySoft. OK, enough small talk, let's get started...

CHAPTER 1

Software Factories Overview

Our goal is to make this book as practical as possible. Therefore, we will start with a short, and hopefully pragmatic, overview of the Software Factories to establish a common vocabulary of terms and concepts that you will encounter throughout the remainder of the book.

In this chapter you will learn

- The rationale for Software Factories

- What makes Software Factories an emerging pattern of software development

- The building blocks of Software Factories

- The Software Factories development process

If you are familiar with the high-level concepts of Software Factories, or you are simply eager to get right into the discussion of our example Software Factory, you may skip this chapter and come back to it later in case questions arise.

The Rationale for Software Factories

Before we start diving into theory, we start this chapter with a little anecdote, "a typical day in a software developer's life," that probably sounds all too familiar to many of us:

It is Tuesday morning. John comes to work around 7:30 a.m., and after he gets his coffee and checks his e-mails, he continues working on a functional requirements document, which is due for review by his fellow software developers, the quality guy, and a customer representative later today.

Around 10 a.m., John gets a call from his manager, who tells him to stop working on whatever he is doing because a high-priority defect was reported by an important customer. John shelves the requirements document in Visual Studio 2005 Source Control and switches context. He retrieves the defect report in Visual Studio 2005 Team System and manages to reproduce the defect. He then tries to isolate it. It turns out that the defect is only occurring sporadically and seems to be located in a component that was developed by a contractor who no longer works with John's company.

Because of this, John decides to get the functional and design specification from the Visual Studio Version Control system. While reading through the functional description attached to the work item, John realizes rather quickly that the document is not complete, and the description of the functionality he is interested in is vague to say the least. Nevertheless, he moves on to the design document. After analyzing the design document, John believes he has a good grip on the overall architecture of the component. When he goes back to Visual Studio 2005 and browses through the Class Designer, he realizes that the description in the design document was not only outdated, but even wrong.

In the meantime, it is 11:30 a.m., and the review of the requirements document, the one he stopped working on, is scheduled for 2:30 p.m. John is starving, but he figures lunch is out of the question, so he gets some crackers and soda from the vending machine and continues to work through lunch in order to give feedback to his manager (or possibly fix the problem) before the document review.

Since the documents proved pretty much useless, John starts debugging the problem, which puts him in a bad mood because there are no unit tests in place for this part of the code. In his quest to identify the problem, he realizes that some basic functionality of the system is implemented at least three times in different components with slightly different behaviors. However, he decides not to refactor the source code at this point because the philosophy of the team is "If it ain't broke, don't fix it."

Debugging takes some time because John ends up creating some unit tests, doing some static analysis, and executing performance tests to find out that the error is caused by a race condition in the multithreaded part of the program, which is unpredictable and appears in different flavors. John eventually finds the source of the problem and has an idea how to fix it. Since it is already 1:30 p.m., he decides to call his manager to update him on the progress and to see whether he should reschedule the document review in order to fix the bug or finish the document and leave the bug fix for later.

John's manager decides that the document review should not be rescheduled since a customer representative is already on his way. Again, John shelves the bug fix, unshelves the requirements he was working on before, and rushes to finish it. Just before 2:30 p.m. he commits the changes to Team Foundation Server together with the updated work item, takes the laptop, and goes to the conference room. By 2:47 p.m., all the review participants arrive and the review takes place. A lot of time in the review is spent on issues not related to the functionality but rather style and formatting (even though John used the mandatory document template).

By 5:34 p.m., John finally gets back to his desk. He unshelves the changes from before, continues working on fixing the high-priority defect, and ultimately fixes the problem a few hours later (so he thinks). He runs his unit test against his fix, and whoopy doo!, the test passes. Just to be on the safe side, he decides to run the unit test suite for the entire system to make sure nothing else broke before he commits the changes. Sure enough, a whole bunch of other tests now are failing. John investigates the problem and realizes that several other parts of the system are dependent on the functionality just fixed.

John continues to work furiously. It is 9:45 p.m., and John made changes to five other source files within three different components, and still a few tests are failing. John now gets somewhat desperate because the company closes at 10 p.m. Finally, John shelves his changes and leaves to grab a beer and get something to eat, setting aside the bug for the next day.

Many problems that John encountered during his workday are similar to the ones that each one of us struggles with. Statistics about the software industry over the last ten years provide factual backing to the picture we just painted: while new and improved life-cycle tools certainly help, the main problems in software development—poor quality, poor predictability, and poor collaboration—still remain unsolved to a large degree.

Research from different groups like the CHAOS Report from the Standish Group,[1] which is published every year, shows that in 1994 only about 20% of all projects were considered a success by achieving the project goals within budget and time initially estimated. About another 50% of the projects were considered challenged, which means they were either fully functional but over budget, or delivered fewer features than initially planned. The remaining projects, roughly 30%, were considered a failure, which means they were canceled at some point during the development.

We can certainly argue about how exact these numbers are and that there were many innovations over the last decade that improved that situation. However, a similar study shows that in 2004 about 30% of all projects were considered a success, around 20% failed, and the other 50% were considered challenged. The improvement can be attributed to better tooling, more mature processes, and other new technologies and techniques used in software development. However, the number of successful projects still only grew by 10% in 10 years. These numbers show that there are still some fundamental issues with today's approaches to software development. Why is software development still so unpredictable?

To answer this question, it helps to look at other mature engineering disciplines like civil engineering or electrical engineering. After comparing software development with these other engineering disciplines, Jack Greenfield and Keith Short[2] identified the following main reasons for the lack of predictability in software development:

- One-off development

- Monolithic systems and increasing systems complexity

- Working at low levels of abstraction

- Process immaturity

- Rapidly growing demand for software systems

Let's take a brief look at each one of these reasons and how these problems manifest in practice.

One-off Development

We refer to one-off development when a software system (or software product) is developed independently from other similar systems and does not leverage the knowledge gained and the assets produced for those other systems. One-off development often results in systems that are not designed for reuse, and neither do they make considerable reuse of existing components. There are a several reasons for this:

---

1. The Standish Group, *CHAOS Report* (West Yarmouth, MA: The Standish Group, 1994–2004. http://www.standishgroup.com)
2. Jack Greenfield and Keith Short, *Software Factories: Assembling Applications with Patterns, Models, Frameworks, and Tools* (Indianapolis, IN: Wiley, 2004)

- Developing systems in a relative isolation from other systems and projects does not encourage identifying similarities to other systems.

- Even with access to similar systems, it may be difficult to identify matching and reusable assets; sometimes because the information is not available (e.g., an undocumented in-house product) and other times because the selection is overwhelming (e.g., with certain third-party products). If people cannot identify matching reusable assets quickly enough, they usually begin developing them from scratch (ultimately reinventing the wheel).

- Assets that only partially match the requirements and were developed without the foresight of reusability may be so difficult to incorporate, that the development team again will rather build their own versions than modify the existing ones.

Our personal observation is that most software is still built more or less in isolation. Even though the products are similar in many cases, reuse mostly happens at a limited scope (if it happens at all) like copy/paste of code snippets or the reuse of a few class libraries. However, if we analyze the produced systems, we can often identify a large amount of similar functionality that was developed from scratch for each product over and over again.

Monolithic Systems

Monolithic software systems go hand in hand with one-off development. Even though monolithic systems usually consist of many different components, these building blocks are strongly interconnected, nonuniform (not adhering to shared standards), and interwoven. This makes it difficult to separate individual blocks from the rest of the system, and therefore renders them pretty much unusable in the context of other systems. Such tight coupling manifests itself in long-reaching dependencies and high system complexity.

The main problem of monolithic systems especially shows over time when these systems need to be maintained, extended, and adapted to changing business requirements. In our work, we encounter the effects of monolithic designs when changes to one part of the system trigger changes to many other parts (cascading changes), making maintenance and extensions cumbersome and expensive.

Working at a Low Level of Abstraction

By "working at a low level of abstraction," we mean working with general-purpose programming languages that enable us to produce any kind of system, but don't help hiding details that are irrelevant to the business problems we are trying to solve.

Figure 1-1 shows the relationship between a language's level of abstraction and its flexibility. While an assembly language is general-purpose and flexible, it also works at a really, really low level of abstraction (try to find the concept of a web service in it). On the other hand, the WinForms editor in the Visual Studio IDE, which is a graphical and textual language, is only applicable to UI development, but works at a much higher level of abstraction and hides the details of the underlying implementation. In between assembly language and GUI designers are the third-generation languages like C# and Java.

Using languages and tools that work at low levels of abstraction creates additional overhead during development (typically tedious and error-prone plumbing work) and results in systems that are difficult to maintain because abstract concepts are hidden somewhere in the code.

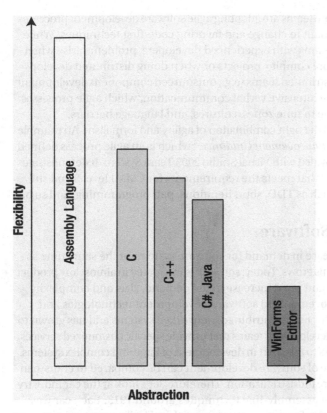

Figure 1-1. *Flexibility versus level of abstraction of programming languages*

Process Immaturity

The statistics of the CHAOS Report we quoted earlier suggests that with only 20% of projects finished on time and within budget, the applied processes do not result in high predictability of software development projects.

Immaturity of software development processes refers to the fact that the software industry still has a long way to go until it will reach the level of engineering process maturity found in, for example, the automotive or medical engineering industries. Unfortunately, many concepts and best practices from these industries' processes cannot be directly transferred to software because of the nature of the software itself (low engineering barrier to change, very low cost of replication and distribution, but practically unlimited variability).

In practice we see two major approaches to software development processes in the industry. On one side, there are projects using formal processes that handle complexity well but sacrifice flexibility for predictability. We usually see this approach in government projects, or projects that need to comply with regulatory requirements (e.g., the Food and Drug Administration [FDA] for medical software). The major problem with this approach is that agility, the ability to adapt the process to the specific needs imposed on the project and to react quickly and efficiently to changes in the requirements, is hard to achieve. Often the result is a 20–100% growth of the project scope due to change requests and additional requirements that were not known at project start but nevertheless are crucial to make the project a success.

On the other hand, more and more teams are adopting agile software development processes optimized to rapidly discover and adapt to change and favoring code-first techniques. While these processes work well in small teams with experienced developers, problems arise when trying to scale them up to larger, more complex projects or when doing distributed development. Furthermore, if we think of distributed teams (e.g., outsourced component development done in other parts of the world), the intensive verbal communication, which agile processes rely on heavily, becomes difficult due to time zones, cultures, and language barriers.

In practice, it is important to find the right combination of agility and formalism. An example for this is the *MSF for CMMI Process Improvement Guidance*,[3] which is an agile process defined through formal project templates provided with Visual Studio 2005 Team System. It demonstrates how a formal process can be defined that meets the requirements for CMMI level 3 and still allows for applying agile methods such as TDD, short iterations, pair programming, and so on.

Increasing Demand for Software

Lastly, we could see continued increase in demand for software systems at the same time as size and complexity of software systems grows. Today, software is integrated in almost any product we can imagine. This simultaneous and rapid increase in the demand, size, and complexity stands in contrast to the slow improvements in software development technologies and techniques. The market today asks for more distributed, networked systems and has grown to include a greater number of smaller development teams that provide specific customized services, which allows smaller software vendors to take part in development of large and complex systems.

To use a metaphor, today's state of software development can be compared to craftsmanship, like other industries were before industrialization. Therefore, let's look at the car industry before Henry Ford's introduction of assembly-line techniques around 1913. Each car was manufactured by hand, and most parts for the car were planned and built as one-off parts, from scratch. This is what we do today in software development. With the industrialization of the car industry, we could see a standardization of parts, a specialization of people and tools, as well as a higher degree of automation. Today, even though two cars look completely different, they might share a large number of parts such as the chassis, engine, etc.

Nevertheless, we need to recognize that software development is different from many other industries. Unlike in other industries, in software development (re)production is a fairly trivial and inexpensive task (e.g., copying CDs), but the development of what other industries would consider a working prototype is complex and expensive (e.g., development of a software application like Microsoft Word).

Our ultimate goal is to learn from other industries while recognizing the unique characteristics of our industry. The idea behind Software Factories is to accomplish exactly that objective. Software Factories do that by identifying, building, and packaging core software assets and prescriptions for developing solutions that share common features, functionality, and architecture. They aim at simplifying and possibly automating common tasks when creating similar yet distinct components and systems.

---

3. MSF = Microsoft Solutions Framework, CMMI = Capability Maturity Model Integration. See
    http://msdn.microsoft.com/vstudio/teamsystem/msf/msfcmmi/default.aspx.

Software Factories in a Nutshell

A Software Factory is an emerging pattern for an approach to software system development when instances of those systems (or their parts) share features, functionality, and architecture. In the context of developing similar yet distinct applications, the problem the pattern addresses directly relates to the ones we described in the previous section:

> *One-off development compounded with immature development processes (inconsistent use of tools, working at low abstraction levels, limited reuse and lack of explicit process structure) lead to cost overruns, delayed deliverables, unimplemented functionality, and even project cancellation.*

SOFTWARE FACTORIES IN THE LATE 1960s TO 1980s

Flashback: if we look back in time, then we realize that the term "Software Factory" was actually introduced by R. W. Bremer of General Electrics and M. D. McIlroy of AT&T in 1968.[4] While Bremer proposed an approach of standardized tools and controls, McIlroy emphasized the systematical reuse of code when creating new software systems. Both approaches can be seen as the ancestors of the Software Factories as proposed by Jack Greenfield et al.

From a practitioner's perspective, Hitachi was the first company to use the word *kojo* (which is Japanese and translates to "factory" or "works") to label a software development facility in 1969. Hitachi Software Factory was founded with two goals in mind: the first was to improve productivity and reliability through process standardization and control, and the second was to transform software into a product with a guaranteed level of quality. These goals reflect the fact that at the time skilled programmers were in high demand in Japan as well as the reality of many customer complaints about software bugs in Hitachi's products in Japan. The implementation of reusability and process standardization over all software products proved to be more difficult than anticipated. Therefore, in 1985, Hitachi split the Software Factory efforts into basic software and application software.

Other Japanese companies like NEC, Toshiba, Fujitsu, and Mitsubishi introduced Software Factories between 1976 and 1987. The first US company to use the term "Software Factory" was the System Development Corp. (which eventually became a Unisys division) in 1975, which was actually the second Software Factory introduced after Hitachi. While the different companies did not adhere to the exact same definition of the term "Software Factory," the efforts were based on the concepts introduced by Bremer and McIlroy and showed a significant improvement in productivity, quality, and process control over what they have done before.

Conceptual Foundation

The recommended solution to this problem is to organize the software development process and environment around the following four concepts, which are known as the four pillars that Software Factories are based on (shown in Figure 1-2):

1. Software product line development

2. Reusable software assets, in particular extensible architecture frameworks

---

4. Michael A. Cusumano, *The Software Factory: A Historical Interpretation* (IEEE Software, March 1989)

3. Contextual and automated guidance

4. Use of higher-level abstractions for code generation (e.g., model-driven development)

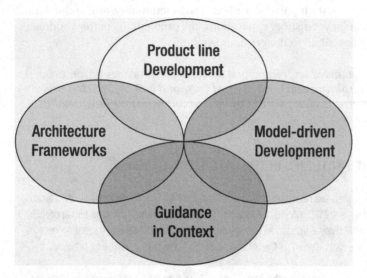

Figure 1-2. *The four pillars of Software Factories*

What follows is an introduction to each of the four pillars.

Software Product Line Development and Reusable Software Assets

The first two concepts are best explained together, as they complement each other. The two core elements of the Software Factory pattern are collections of reusable viewpoints and the definition of their relationship to each other, which is called *Software Factory schema*, and a collection of reusable software assets called the *Software Factory template*. We describe these core concepts in more depth later, but for now the important point is that it is not *any* collection, but a collection of core assets carefully selected and structured following the principles of software product line development (PLD).

The term "software product line" intentionally relates to product lines as we know from other engineering domains (cars, mechanical equipment, TV sets, etc.), but applied to software systems in the following way:

> *A Software Product line is a set of software-intensive systems sharing a common, managed set of features that satisfy the specific needs of a particular market segment or mission and that are developed from a common set of core assets in a prescribed way.*

> —Paul Clements and Linda Northrop, 2002

A product line typically covers a market segment or a domain like, for example, customer relationship management (CRM) software or medical imaging software (you can, for example, find that in x-ray or MRI machines). The three important concepts underlying the software product lines are scope, variability, and extensibility, which are also displayed in Figure 1-3.

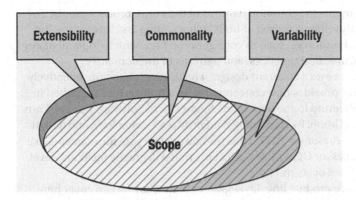

Figure 1-3. *Scope, extensibility, and variability of a product line*

1. *Scope* describes what products (solutions) can be built using the product line assets. Scope is most often represented in the form of a capability or feature model; we discuss them later. Often they are also referred to as the *solution scope*.

2. *Variability* identifies the common and variable features defined in the scope. The parts implementing the common features are often incorporated in architecture frameworks, as discussed later in this section. Variable capabilities are optional features and may be implemented only in some members of a product line (systems created using a product line).

3. *Extensibility* identifies so-called extension points that can be used to add (extend) new features to the products based on a product line. Extensibility is used to incorporate functionality that is outside of the original scope of a product line.

In Figure 1-3, the product line scope (defined by its feature/capability model) is represented by the striped oval. This area represents all the features that can be covered by systems derived from a product line. Variable features, shown in the shaded striped area, are of course also part of the product line scope. On the other hand, some product line members require features that are outside of product line scope, shown as the dark shaded area. A product line may provide extension points where components implementing those features can be integrated with the product line assets. For example, different data storage providers can be plugged into the application framework.

Software product line development also describes a methodical way of requirements analysis, design and development of a flexible product line architecture (PLA) that supports the requirements of the entire product line. Based on that PLA, the product line owner can develop a set of strategically important core assets that implement the identified common features, variable features, and the extension points of out-of-scope features.

The collection of those core assets is the second key concept underlying the Software Factory pattern. We discuss different kinds of assets later in the chapter, but we would like to single one out here: architecture frameworks. An *architecture framework*, sometimes also called the *baseline architecture*, implements the common features of the entire product family. The architecture framework is usually either acquired or built by harvesting and integrating the core reusable classes and related resources, such as configuration files, which implement key components or design mechanisms, best practices, and patterns of the domain.

By tying together components into a coherent design, a baseline architecture effectively raises the level of abstraction and provides new concepts. The example factory described in this book reuses the entire architecture framework of the Smart Client Software Factory from the Microsoft patterns & practices Group. By combining WinForms, OO technology, and design patterns such as the Model-View-Presenter (MVP), this framework can provide concepts like extensible UI shells, UI workspaces, or UI modules; concepts that will greatly facilitate development work through a higher level of abstraction.

There is a lot more to software product line development than what we can cover here. If you are interested in the subject, you might want to take a look at the some of the books that cover it in-depth.[5]

Contextual and Automated Guidance

The third key concept underlying the Software Factory pattern is guidance in context, which has the potential to propel the customization efforts when using an architectural baseline template. Software development guidance takes many different forms. Examples include how-to help pages, developer journal articles, code samples, and patterns (some of them are very well known like those described in the *Design Patterns* book of Gamma et al.[6]). In general, guidance is about helping the developer solve a current design or coding problem.

Within a Software Factory that guidance can be both specialized and contextualized. For example, a general-purpose version of the Model-View-Presenter pattern has to be, well, general to be applicable to a variety of implementation strategies. On the other hand, the version of the same pattern used in the development of a smart-client factory, based on a specific application framework, can be very specific on how to implement it.

Because a Software Factory implies a specific set of development activities and possibly their ordering, guidance can also be provided when needed and where needed. For example, when developing a smart-client composite application, it is strongly recommended to create the container first and put it in the hierarchy before creating views and presenters that will be placed in the container. The reversed order is also possible, but it would lead to an undesirable solution structure. To prevent this, guidance can be contextualized: after creating a new smart-client project, a developer would get the advice to first implement a container before creating modules. At the same time, the how-to for the module's MVP pattern is still "hidden" from the developer until the container is actually created.

Automation is the other important property of guidance in the context of the Software Factory pattern. As we mentioned earlier, a piece of guidance (a *guidance artifact*) is a prescription on how to solve a design or coding problem. In the case of automated guidance, this prescription can be executed by the development environment. For example, a how-to for an MVP

---

5. Jan Bosch, *Design and Use of Software Architecture—Adopting and Evolving a product line Approach* (Boston, MA: Addison Wesley, 2000)
   Paul Clements and Linda Northrop, *Software Product Lines—Practices and Patterns* (Boston, MA: Addison Wesley, 2002)
6. Erich Gamma, Richard Helm, Ralph Johnson, and John Vlissides, *Design Patterns: Elements of Reusable Object-Oriented Software* (Reading, MA: Addison Wesley, 1995)

pattern implementation can be encoded as a script that generates the view and presenter classes from templates on the behalf of the user. In the case of Visual Studio 2005, these scripts are called *recipes* and *automate workflows*, such as creating a project from a template, creating the skeletons of key files within the project that the developer needs to get started, or creating client-side service proxies.

Specialized, contextualized, and automated guidance provides assistance at the right time and the right place when the developer actually needs it. Guidance is provided in a way that helps practitioners understand what to do and then helps implement a solution to the problem at hand.

Model-driven Development

The fourth essential concept behind Software Factories is the use of models to create parts of the software. This concept is known as *model-driven development* (MDD) and is closely related to domain-specific languages (DSL) and graphical designers.

Models have been used to document and communicate software system architectures and structures for a long time. The main idea behind MDD is that models are used not only for documentation, but also to generate source code, validation, tracing, easy navigation, visualization, analysis, and configuration of a system. This has two highly desirable effects:

1. It increases the level of abstraction at which the solution is described. Models are a good mechanism to manage complexity by focusing the user's attention on important aspects by hiding information that is not relevant to solving a particular problem.

2. It bridges the gap between design and coding, as code generation allows for direct transformation of the models into executable code. Models therefore become part of the implementation as first-class life cycle artifacts.

A prominent example of MDD is the Object Management Group's (OMG's) Model-Driven Architecture (MDA). It uses the Unified Modeling Language (UML), which in its current version, 2.0, supports more than 10 different diagram types. Using specialized code generators, UML models can be transformed into executable code, for example, into an EJB application. The most prominent feature of MDA is the platform-independent model where the major part of modeling activity takes place. The idea is that a system can then automatically be generated through transformation into a platform-specific model and through code generation.

An alternative to using a single, general-purpose modeling language is to use a number of specialized, "domain-specific" modeling languages, each describing a different aspect of the solution. Those languages are referred to as *domain-specific languages*, target narrow problem domains and can be optimized for a specific set of design tasks. Table 1-1 shows examples of a few DSLs in common use today.

Many domain-specific languages have graphical notations and designers to create models in these languages. However, having a graphical designer is not a prerequisite for a language to be a DSL. For example, regular expressions have only a textual representation, rather than a graphical one.

Table 1-1. *Examples of Domain-Specific Languages*

DSL	Problem Domain	Language Concepts
WinForms editor	Creating interactive user interfaces	Graphical elements Events Data bindings
SQL	Database queries	Tables, columns Joins, group-bys, expressions Indexes
Regular expressions	Finding patterns in text	Character classes Quantifiers Assertions
Business process modeling language	Modeling business processes	Actors Business objects Transactions
Workflow Foundation (WF) DSL	Workflow modeling	Graphical elements representing workflow C# or VB .NET code
XML Stylesheets (XSLT) expressions Iterators	Transformations of structured documents	Template code XPath

In the context of Software Factories, domain-specific languages are applied in order to do model-driven development. A DSL is typically used to describe a part of an application in a language (notation) that uses domain concepts on different abstraction levels, not only code-level concepts. MDD is then used to transform models into other models or code, to validate designs against deployment topologies, or to configure runtime engines, to name a few examples. This also enables nontechnical domain experts to participate in the software development process more effectively.

A user interface expert can use the WinForms designer shown in Figure 1-4 to design a window and controls without ever looking at a line of code implementing that window. The WinForms designer is a part of the Visual Studio IDE, which transforms the visual window representation to its in-code representation as shown in the figure.

Without a UI "DSL," the alternative is that the UI expert would sketch the window on a piece of paper while the developer would write its implementation directly in code. Without a UI code generator, this would be a tedious and error-prone process consisting of tons of plumbing and wiring code. (Who actually wants to remember the times when we actually DID it this way?)

■**Caution** While DSLs are usually very intuitive for people who are familiar with the target domain of the DSL, this is not the same as to say that nondomain experts would be able to use it to the same degree. In order to use a DSL efficiently, you need to be knowledgeable about the domain, meaning you need to know the semantics that are inherent in the DSL's concepts. For example, the concepts of *flow* and *valve* are used in the medical and engineering domains, and the principle seems clear. However, their semantics, their meaning, is completely different in either domain.

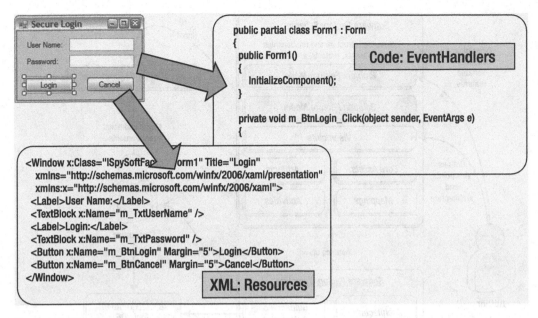

Figure 1-4. *VS .NET WinForms editor as a DSL*

Software Factories Explained

Now that we have described the conceptual foundation of the Software Factory, we can take a high-level look at how Software Factories are built and used. There are two perspectives from which you need to look at a Software Factory:

1. The view of the developer of the factory, often referred to as the *author's view*

2. The view of the developer who instantiates and uses the factory, often referred to as the *consumer's view*

From the author's perspective, a Software Factory is a carefully selected and packaged collection of core software assets and prescriptions for developing instances of a software product line, that is, applications that share features, functionality, and architecture. Furthermore, a Software Factory defines an application development process, a process that application developers (the users of a Software Factory) have to follow when building product line members. The enactment of this process can, for instance, be supported with contextual guidance.

From the consumer's perspective, a Software Factory becomes a part of his development environment that now can be used to develop members of the software product line more effectively and predictably. These two views are illustrated in Figure 1-5, the two key concepts being the Software Factory schema and the Software Factory template. What follows is a quick introduction to each of these concepts. We will cover each in depth in Chapters 5 through 7.

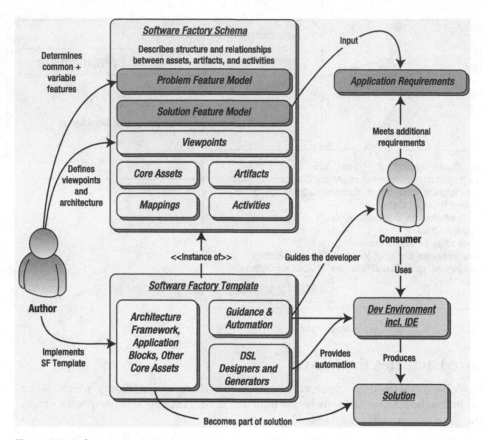

Figure 1-5. *Software Factory overview*

SOFTWARE FACTORIES SUPPLY CHAINS

It is envisioned that in the future third-party vendors will create Software Factories for particular domains like enterprise applications or embedded systems. The base Software Factories can then be used, for example, to assemble larger factories, where the artifacts, the output from one factory, is input to another factory. It also will be possible to derive from a more general Software Factory and specialize and customize it to a narrower domain. While this is a very tempting vision, in this book we will not go into further detail in regards to SF supply chains, as the Software Factory methodology first needs to be better established.

Software Factory Schema

In order to explain the Software Factory schema, we'll present the definition first:

> *The Software Factory schema is a model interpreted by humans and tools that describes work products, workflows used to produce the work products, and assets used in the enactment of the workflows, for a specific family of software products in a given domain.*

——Jack Greenfield and Keith Short

The Software Factory schema is organized around viewpoints, which describe the system from different perspectives such as the runtime behavior, logical and implementation structure, component packaging, or physical distribution across network nodes. Each viewpoint describes certain aspects of a system and how the stakeholders' concerns are addressed. Furthermore, in order to build a system, the combination of all viewpoints onto a system is necessary. The definition of viewpoints in the context of Software Factories is consistent with viewpoints as described in the *IEEE Recommended Practice for Architectural Description of Software-Intensive Systems.*[7]

Each of the viewpoints contains a description of the assets relevant to that viewpoint, which, for instance, means tools, components, libraries, patterns, or even how-to documents that are required to create an implementation. Next, the Software Factory schema defines the relationship between its viewpoints. For example, the logical view represented by an object model is closely related with the physical view of a database schema. Lastly, the schema defines the activities that are necessary to produce the artifacts defined by the viewpoints and to assemble a product.

While the Software Factories methodology prescribes the use of viewpoints to describe a software system, it is up to the factory authors to identify and define the relevant viewpoints for a particular factory under development. This fact is a significant difference between Software Factories and other methodologies. Most other methodologies, outside the software product line community, define a generic one-size-fits-all process with predefined viewpoints. Software factories are unique in creating a custom methodology for a specific family of products with a specific architecture, often in a specific industry domain.

Yet another major difference from other methodologies is that the Software Factory schema in itself represents a model (and of course it has a metamodel, too). Therefore, the knowledge captured inside a schema can be made available for further processing such as model transformations, automatic verification, and others. For example, it is envisioned that in the future, relations between viewpoints will be formally defined, which would allow us to use the output of one viewpoint as input for another viewpoint and generate certain artifacts completely automated.

Software Factory Template

The Software Factory template can be considered the instantiation of the Software Factory schema, just as a model is an instance of a metamodel. The template is basically the collection of all assets defined by the viewpoints of the Software Factory schema. These assets can be broadly divided into the following categories:

---

7. IEEE-SA Standards Board, *IEEE Recommended Practice for Architectural Description of Software-Intensive Systems* (New York, NY: IEEE, 2000. IEEE Std 1471-2000)

- *Libraries and frameworks*, which are the reusable software components employed by the product line architecture. The *Enterprise Library* from Microsoft patterns & practices group is an example of such a library (the p&p libraries are often referred to as *blocks*). The *Composite UI Application Block* from the same group is an example of an application framework.

- *Guidance assets*, which are different forms of prescriptions for developing software solutions with the factory. Some of the guidance assets are automated, as described earlier in this chapter. Examples of those assets are help pages, patterns, how-tos (some of them describing how to implement the patterns), Visual Studio Guidance Automation Toolkit (GAT) templates and recipes, and build scripts.

- *Domain-specific languages and designers*, which provide abstractions of application elements and the code generators for producing code-level implementations of those abstractions. An example is the Microsoft Workflow Foundation designer, which allows for creating workflow models that can directly be executed in a workflow engine.

- *Feature models* (also called *capability models* or *solution capability models*), which describe the scope of the factory. In particular, they define the common and the variable features of the products and the extension points in the factory's application framework and blocks.

While the factory author thinks about the factory primarily in terms of the schema and template, the application developer primarily thinks of the factory as an extension of his development environment, which will give him the following benefits:

- Installs the tools and toolkits necessary to perform the activities as defined in the Software Factory schema

- Gives him the reusable component blocks to assemble the solution

- Provides him with guidance on how to build the solution, which includes the recommended development activities and automation (such as wizards) for recurring development tasks.

Of course, a Software Factory template is only good for building systems within the scope of the underlying product line.

Benefits

By now the benefits of a Software Factory should be pretty clear. A factory facilitates a high degree of reuse, a uniform architecture, automation of error-prone and tedious tasks, and a higher level of abstraction. Combined with guidance in context, it provides the basis for a powerful development paradigm. All the techniques listed above will lead to software projects that have well-defined assets, variability points, behavior, and processes, and are more predictable in regards to quality, performance, maintenance, delivery schedules, regulatory compliance, etc.

Think of a company that invested in creating its software factory. After initially investing into the core assets, the company should see the following results:

- Considerable efficiency gain and shortened time to market with each subsequent version of the product because of the reuse of already existing core assets

- Improved product quality because core factory assets have already been tested and used in previous products and therefore have matured

- Flexibility in addressing the changing market demands because of clear application framework variability and extensibility

These benefits are also called *economies of scope*: producing many similar yet distinct products with a software product line.

■**Note** In contrast to *economies of scale*, where we produce many identical copies of a product (like multiplying a CD with software), we talk of *economies of scope* when we are producing many similar, yet distinct products of a product family. Economies of scale (like in mass production) are usually not of interest in software development because of the relatively low costs of software replication.

Liabilities

The Software Factory pattern is not without liabilities. The stated benefits come at a price, and certain preconditions must be met before it makes sense to invest in a Software Factory:

- Development of a Software Factory, with its reusable assets, takes resources and time. The cost of developing a more complex factory can be significant. This investment needs to be justified by significant savings that occur in development and subsequent maintenance of a number of instances of the product line.

- The domain that a Software Factory is built for should be stable and well understood. A stable domain usually means that there are domain experts with in-depth understanding, which can for example help with designing DSLs, etc. On the other hand, a poorly understood domain increases the risk of building a factory that will not fit customers' requirements (which relates to the last point).

- Development of a Software Factory should be based on previous experience of building software systems for a particular domain. A factory should be a generalization of the assets and the best practices harvested from those instances. It takes the foresight and the discipline to the explicit objective of a project to create assets and guidance for an emerging Software Factory.

- Determining the factory scope is a compromise between opposing goals. A factory that has little variability will have a very limited applicability. On the other hand, adding more variability to broaden applicability will inevitably increase cost. This compromise needs to be made carefully in order to reach the amortization as described in the first point.

- Hand in hand with the previous liability goes the fit between the factory scope and the application requirements. On the consumer side, a misapplied factory can bring more problems than benefits. On the author side, adding variability to a factory adds to its cost.

When considering a Software Factory project, you need to consider these liabilities. While especially the initial investment costs might prove the largest obstacle, we believe that the benefits of lower development and maintenance cost per application outweigh the disadvantages by far. Furthermore, it is possible to introduce product lines incrementally, as, for example, described in *Software Product Lines*.[8] An incremental approach reduces the initial up-front investment, while at the same time it gives more time to gain experience with building product lines (of course, the savings effects also will occur later).

Building a Software Factory: High-level Process

Figure 1-6 shows the basic dependencies when developing a Software Factory.

Usually Software Factories development is, like most development projects nowadays, an iterative process. Furthermore, it is assumed that the development team has already gained the domain knowledge by developing applications in the domain. We could also say that some reference implementations were created. Based on the reference implementations, the factory is developed. The first step is to define the Software Factory schema, as it contains the relevant viewpoints and the relations between viewpoints, and describes the required assets. Based on the schema, the Software Factory template can be implemented.

The template contains different assets, which we refer to as *fixed assets* and *variable assets*. This distinction is based on the variability points we defined using the product line engineering techniques as discussed earlier. Fixed assets refer to common functionality of all products, and variable assets refer to optional functionality of the products developed by the factory.

The Software Factory template bundles all the assets and is installed into the product development environment, thereby configuring and extending a highly customizable development environment. Once configured, these IDEs allow the rapid assembly and construction of products based on the product specification provided by marketing and other stakeholders.

Once the first products are being produced, an iterative process starts. Each product line member will typically have extensions that at development time were out of factory scope. Over time, additional common features can be identified across multiple solutions. Based on these findings, components, guidelines, patterns, code snippets, templates, etc., can be extracted and converted into reusable assets, which then will extend the Software Factory and its scope.

---

8. Clements and Northrop, *Software Product Lines—Practices and Patterns*

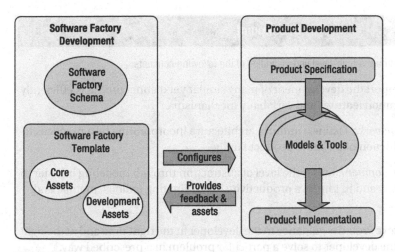

Figure 1-6. *High-level Software Factories development process*

Summary

Software Factories, as introduced by Jack Greenfield and Keith Short,[9] is a paradigm shift that builds on several already established and successfully applied concepts as described in this chapter. What is new is to extend these concepts and to bundle them into a coherent software development pattern.

At this point you might be wondering, reuse in software development has been around for a long time with more or less success; why should it be any different nowadays? The answer why reuse, as defined by Software Factories, is possible today is because tools are much more sophisticated, integrated, and extensible, and we understand the success factors for software development projects much better than in the past.

We would like to point out that the Software Factories concept is not bound to any specific technology or platform. This means that the concepts we discuss throughout the book can be applied to any platform (like Linux or Windows), any technology (like Java or .NET), and even across platforms. Nevertheless, we will show our implementation based on Windows and .NET technology. The reason is that Visual Studio 2005, the Domain-Specific Language Toolkit, and the Guidance Automation Toolkit make up the first set of tools to provide specific support for the successful implementation of a full-fledged Software Factory. There are still many parts missing, though, but we can say that today's tools are the first down payment from Microsoft to create a real Software Factory infrastructure in the future.

Throughout this book, we will walk you through all aspects of this exciting methodology. In each chapter we will present artifacts from our hands-on case study and demonstrate how a Software Factory is built from beginning to end. By the end, you will have practical and in-depth knowledge of what we covered in this chapter at a very high level. Enjoy the ride.

---

9. Greenfield and Short, *Software Factories: Assembling Applications with Patterns, Models, Frameworks, and Tools*

Checkpoint

After this chapter, you should have a high-level understanding of the following concepts:

- *Product lines*: Support the development of many similar yet distinct products efficiently by providing common features and variability mechanisms.

- *Architecture frameworks*: Define a uniform architecture incorporating best practices to support the production of an entire product family.

- *Model-driven development*: Raises the level of abstraction through modeling in order to manage complexity and to improve productivity by eliminating tedious, menial, and error-prone tasks.

- *Guidance in context*: Provides guidance to the developer at the right time and at the right place and helps the developer to solve a particular problem in a prescribed way.

- *Software Factory schema*: The heart of the Software Factory. It defines the relationships between all the ingredients in a Software Factory.

- *Software Factory template*: Instance of the Software Factory schema that customizes the IDE to enable the product developer to produce members of the product family very efficiently by providing reusable assets, tools, and guidance in context.

Software Factory Definition

We kick this chapter off with an introduction to our case study featuring our imaginary company called ISpySoft.[1] Being an independent software vendor (ISV) that is currently facing some challenging and exciting changes, ISpySoft will accompany us throughout the rest of this book to showcase our first Software Factory implementation. As a primer to our Software Factory project, we discuss the following work products in this chapter:

- Software Factory overview

- Software Factory vision

- Software Factory inputs

- Application and Software Factory constraints

- Stakeholder description

- Software Factory context

- Domain glossary

■**Note** We need to mention one thing up front to make sure you get a clear understanding of how to approach Software Factories. For educational purposes, the content of this book is organized in a linear fashion; however, it is important to realize that Software Factory development is typically done in an iterative manner. While we go step by step through the work products for our Software Factory implementation, in an individual iteration of a Software Factory project you would select a number of these work products that fit the particular purpose. Furthermore, we might refine a given work product in more than one iteration. For example, we start with an initial list of stakeholders in the first iteration, and then add, remove, or modify stakeholder descriptions in later iterations.

---

1. The web site for the ISpySoft implementation can be found at http://www.ISpySoft.net.

In our Software Factory development we start with developing the work products listed previously. Later, each of the following chapters will add another piece to the development of our ISpySoft sample Software Factory. In the rest of the book, we will cover the entire cycle from the definition to the implementation of the Software Factory, as well as using the factory to produce an actual product.

The Appendix provides a comprehensive checklist showing all the work products and activities, as described in this book, to define and implement a Software Factory; this checklist is intended to be used as a reference. It maps activities that may be performed during the implementation of a Software Factory to the corresponding sections in the book and to the tools and techniques that are used. For a particular project or iteration of a project, you can select the necessary items and customize them from there.

Software Factory Overview

The overall goal of the Software Factory overview, as described in this chapter, is to explore the vision and constraints, and to provide a high-level description of the Software Factory, as it helps to align the expectations of the different parties involved. Like in any other software development project, we set the stage for our Software Factory project by giving some detailed background information and a solid business case that explains why we conduct this Software Factory project.

A good way to accomplish this is through an analysis of the current situation with regards to business, technical, financial, organizational, political, and strategical aspects. Software Factories are based on software product lines and can only play their advantage if there are a number of similar systems to be developed (see Chapter 1's discussion of economies of scope). They require significant investment, such as harvesting best practices and patterns from the existing one-off projects, and forming them into reusable assets (e.g., templates, class libraries, DSLs) that need to be recouped by savings achieved with each product built with a factory. Therefore, a thorough business case is done in order to calculate the return on investment of building a factory as well as the break-even point. This business case analysis takes into consideration how many assets need to be developed, the scope of the factory, the provided tool support, the market, and the overall business goal, to just name a few items.

Unlike with one-off development projects, with Software Factories we develop a capacity to build a specific type of product. Such an investment makes sense only if we plan to build many instances of that product type. We will therefore use the factory overview not just at a single point in time, but over the course of many projects. Keep in mind that the factory will usually be harvested from existing products. From there, it will continue to evolve as new products are developed.

ISpySoft's target market is mainly private investigators and detectives (aka private eyes). At the current time the company has two sources of income. The first revenue channel is through an online store (based on the very popular ASP.NET starter kit IBuySpy[2]) that offers special equipment such as miniature binoculars, bugs, directional microphones, small cameras, lock pick sets, and many more useful high-tech gadgets. The second source of income, and by far the most important, is through the implementation and maintenance of custom-made software for private eyes' offices. At this point, ISpySoft has sold software solutions to five customers,

---

2. The IBuySpy starter kit and documentation for it can be downloaded from http://www.asp.net.

each tailored specifically to the needs of the individual customer. Figure 2-1 shows the online shop hosted at the ISpySoft location, and two applications installed at customer sites.

Figure 2-1. *Sample of ISpySoft's current range of products*

So far, our company has been pretty successful and has a reliable and satisfied customer base. However, there are some major challenges that ISpySoft faces:

- Because of the high costs involved in the development and maintenance of custom software systems, it is hard to expand the existing customer base. ISpySoft is feeling pressure from software vendors that sell less customized and less powerful, but much cheaper, software packages.

- Developers find it hard when developing to switch from one project to the other, and oftentimes mistakes happen simply through confusion. The reason is not so much the variety of product features but rather that there is not much consistency in design and implementation from one customer to the next. This inconsistency also makes project management very difficult, since patches to the existing software and new features often have to be developed or at least customized for multiple customers. The result is duplication of code for each installation and inefficient maintenance.

- During the past two years, customers have repeatedly asked for many additional features (e.g., integration with the online shop, mobile support for agents in the field, location services, and other value-added services like license plate checks, etc.). ISpySoft's management would like to offer part of these requested features as fee-based services to open up new revenue channels (aka premium services). While there is some variation in the functionalities requested by individual customers, the majority of the requests are very similar, with only minor differences in the requested features. However, since ISpySoft is currently maintaining five similar but distinct instances of essentially the same application, these features probably would have to be developed five times.

Back at ISpySoft, upper management, the software developers, and the marketing folks have been pondering for some time the best way to solve these problems. After doing extensive research and seeking advice from several software specialists, ISpySoft management bought into the suggestion of their software development organization to explore possibilities to restructure the product development. This would mean phasing out the current five variations of basically the same product and implementing in their place a new system using the Software Factories paradigm. The ultimate goal is to solve the current problems and to make software development and maintenance more efficient, and therefore achieve cost savings and become more competitive while giving up little or nothing of the current flexibility.

Following are the reasons why people at ISpySoft believe a transition to Software Factories will be a success:[3]

- A product line approach will allow them to provide the existing customers with customized, individual systems as variants of one system based on a common product line platform, rather than having to support many different systems.

- Additional product variants, for new clients, can be developed much faster by using configuration, orchestration, and custom extensions based on the features provided by the product line approach.

- Product quality will increase because most of the components will be reused and therefore have undergone thorough testing in previous products.

- A common architecture and increased reuse of system components will lead to a more predictable and more uniform user experience.

- ISpySoft has already established a knowledge management system to capture lessons learned from existing development, which is an important prerequisite for adopting the Software Factories approach.

- ISpySoft's architects and developers have gained great expertise and domain knowledge in the field of investigation management systems and therefore feel pretty comfortable with the task of building a product line.

At ISpySoft, the switch to build a Software Factory will be done in an evolutionary and iterative manner. In order to reduce the risk that the new approach brings and to gain experience, the first iteration will be a pilot project. After that pilot, ISpySoft will roll out the Software Factories approach more broadly, as some of the benefits and cost can be better estimated. Management and software developers like the idea because of the anticipated smooth transition. Neither group is happy with the current situation, and both are convinced that the planned changes will improve it in the following ways:

- Management sees the potential to save development costs for future products because of the product line approach. In addition, management hopes to be able to cut the very high maintenance costs drastically by using Software Factories in the future.

- Management and developers are hoping that a more modular architecture will make it easier and more efficient to identify the cause of errors as well as fix them. The current monolithic architecture brought about a lot of finger-pointing and friction between the groups because of tight coupling and the inability to easily identify the actual cause of bugs. The result was a lot of wasted time and energy.

- Software developers are hoping to get more time to do fun stuff like developing new features rather than fixing the same problems repeatedly for each of their customers. Furthermore, they hope to get some relief from the versioning, integration, and maintenance nightmare that currently exists through reuse of one common code base of the factory.

---

3. For more information on product lines, their benefits, and additional references, out SEI's website at http://www.sei.cmu.edu/productlines/index.html.

Software Factory Vision

Behind every major business activity should be a clearly defined goal or a vision (well, at least in theory). The Software Factory vision is a short, precise statement that captures this goal and is the common ground for all participants involved in SF development. In the end, the success of the project will be measured against this vision.

■**Tip** The vision statement is defined as a fundamental deliverable within the Microsoft Solutions Framework (MSF).[4] As a guideline, the vision statement should be less than 25 words. The measure for success of the vision statement is if everyone involved in the project can recite it from memory and relate it to their daily work.

For a common understanding among all participants during SF development, ISpySoft developers and management mutually came up with a concise vision for their undertaking:

> *Develop a Software Factory that enables efficient development and maintenance of high-quality, modular, extensible applications for private investigator offices and field agents, and that allows ISpySoft to also offer new services to its customers.*

To top off the business case analysis and Software Factory vision, Figure 2-2 gives a high-level view of the future ISpySoft unified enterprise application. The new product will be called *ISpySoft Enterprise Suite*, and customers will be able to purchase diverse business modules that provide a wide range of functionality. Additionally, the Enterprise Suite will allow for custom extensions for clients who have specific needs that are not covered by any of the existing modules. Systems installed at client sites will be connected to the ISpySoft Online Shop and the fee-based premium services. Furthermore, to follow requests for more field agent support, the system will provide the ability to integrate mobile devices. Please note that Figure 2-2 only serves as an illustration to visualize the goals of our vision; it is not meant to reflect architectural or technical details.

At ISpySoft, one of the existing development teams is appointed for initiating the Software Factory adoption. Their original product responsibilities are rolled into the other existing development teams. Subsequently, the Software Factory team will work with the other teams to collect existing assets, develop new assets that capture best practices, integrate them into the factory, and make them easy to apply during product development. Once a basic factory is set up, this team pilots the redevelopment of one of the existing customer applications using the factory. It is planned that an early adopter customer will help validating the result of this first transition. If successful, in a phased approach the Software Factory will be extended, variabilities from other products factored in, and other products redeveloped using the factory.

---

4. The Microsoft Solutions Framework can be downloaded from http://msdn.microsoft.com/vstudio/
teamsystem/msf/.

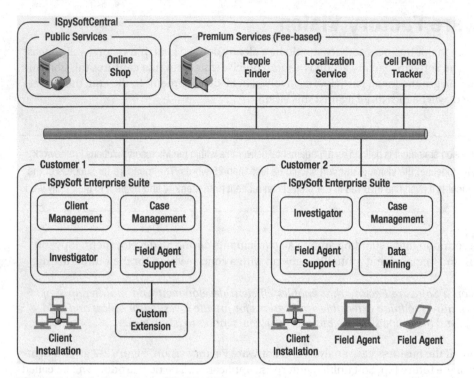

Figure 2-2. *High-level view of ISpySoft Enterprise Suite*

TRANSITION TO SOFTWARE FACTORY DEVELOPMENT

The transition from product development to product line development using a Software Factory is a considerable change to the development process within an organization. The transition needs careful consideration in order to make a successful change. It is outside the scope of this book to cover this in great detail. Generally, there are several requirements to allow for a successful transition:

- There is intellectual property (IP) sharing via a combination of formal training, brown bag lunches, demos, and presentations to make sure all team members understand the changes necessary to successfully implement the product line.

- The domain is stable and well understood, and the customer needs are clear.

- There is experience with one or more software systems in the domain that were previously built.

- The organization has an implemented and mature development process.

Alternatively, there could be a more radical transition. Such a transition would halt most of the current product development, except for high-priority bug fixes and critical maintenance, to make all resources available for the Software Factory development. We see this approach sometimes taken in larger organizations with products that have a rather long life cycle (e.g., ~10 years with medical devices) where larger up-front investments do not have such a huge impact because the release of new products occurs in rather long intervals anyway.

While we are aware of several radical transitions to product lines, most organizations usually prefer a smooth and iterative approach to reduce risk when making the transition to a new paradigm like Software Factories. An excellent reference regarding product line transitions is the *Software Product Lines* book.[5]

Software Factory Inputs

 One of the building blocks for a Software Factory is the set of existing assets that we use as inputs for our Software Factory. As you will see, these assets not only include libraries, components, or frameworks, but also less obvious things like requirements specifications, process definitions, architecture documentation, marketing material, and design patterns.

> *An asset is anything owned which can produce future economic benefit. ... An asset has potential to earn revenue, its value is managed over [its] life cycle, and its failure leads to irrecoverable commercial loss.*

—Wikipedia, http://en.wikipedia.org/wiki/asset, 2005

Because one of the basic principles of the Software Factories paradigm is learning from previous implementations, we feel the definition of assets in the context of Software Factories should be extended to "... Furthermore, an asset is improved over several projects (life cycles)."

We identify the existing assets that we bring into our Software Factory as inputs. This inventory of existing assets will be leveraged to bootstrap the Software Factory and speed up factory development. Here is a (noncomprehensive) list of examples:

- Libraries, components, off-the-shelf software

- Tools: integrated development environments (IDEs), versioning systems (CVS, Team Foundation Server version control, SVN, SourceSafe), build tools (NAnt, MSI Builder), unit test frameworks (NUnit, csUnit), editors

- Platforms: For example, .NET Framework, J2EE, BizTalk

- Architecture: Models, architecture documentation, patterns

- Implementation: Templates, configuration files, executables, scripts, code snippets (e.g., taken from existing applications)

- Best practices, specifications (e.g., the XML specification), applicable laws and regulations (important for FDA)

■**Tip** When looking for existing assets, you should also try to identify and gather all existing information that other people need to participate in the Software Factory development and usage.

---

5. Paul Clements and Linda Northrop, *Software Product Lines—Practices and Patterns* (Boston, MA: Addison Wesley, 2002)

Table 2-1 lists the existing assets for the ISpySoft Factory.

Table 2-1. *ISpySoft Existng Assets*

Asset	Description
Software Factory Assets	
Microsoft Smart Client Software Factory (SCSF)	Collection of integrated assets[a]
Documents and Standards	
ISpySoft functional requirements	Requirements for the current ISpySoft applications
W3C standard	W3C web services architecture document[b]
Architecture and Implementation	
IBuySpy architecture	Documentation about concepts like shopping carts, product catalog, web services, orders, configuration, user controls, user details, and the home page[c]
ISpySoft design specification	Design specification for the current ISpySoft applications
IBuySpy online store	Reference implementation for ISpySoft online shop
Platform	Microsoft Windows and .NET Framework 2.0
Microsoft Web Services Enhancements (WSE)	Add-ons to Visual Studio and .NET to incorporate new features in the evolving Web services protocol[d]
Tools	
Visual Studio 2005	IDE
Visual Studio Team System	Supporting tools like source control and work-item tracking as well as project management
Guidance Automation Toolkit (GAT)	SDK for automating Visual Studio 2005
Domain-Specific Language (DSL) Toolkit	Framework for developing DSLs and code generators (included in VS 2005 SDK)

a. http://www.gotdotnet.com/codegallery/codegallery.aspx?id=941d2228-3bb5-42fd-8004-c08595821170
b. http://www.w3.org/TR/2004/NOTE-ws-arch-20040211/
c. http://www.asp.net/
d. http://msdn.microsoft.com/webservices/webservices/building/wse/default.aspx

Application and Software Factory Constraints

The goal of this section is to identify the outside constraints that are imposed on a Software Factory. In general, we can say that constraints are nonnegotiable standards, rules, or policies that must remain true in order for the system to be considered operational with regards to these standards, rules, and policies. With Software Factories, we differentiate between two types of constraints:

1. *Application constraints*: (Also called *product constraints*) External requirements and restrictions imposed on applications that are developed with a factory

2. *Software Factories constraints*: (Also called *production constraints*) External requirements and restrictions imposed on the application development process that is prescribed by the factory

Constraints in the context of Software Factories refer to external influences such as fixed standard or corporate policies. These constraints typically are general and are valid across many iterations and different applications. Internal influences, such as a team decision to use a certain development platform, are not constraints but rather internal policies.

Application Constraints

As mentioned previously, application constraints are often imposed by policies and regulations. An example might be that, in the course of a government project, a multiserver system needs to provide a logging mechanism that cannot be tampered with, even while withstanding a hacking attack. This is a hard requirement that needs to be fulfilled; otherwise the software contract might get cancelled.

A possible solution to the previous example of a constraint could be a separate logging server placed on the network that is secured by a separate firewall and only allows for adding log entries but not manipulating them.

The application or product constraints do not constrain the way the application is developed. They constrain the application itself. Frequent application constraints are technology constraints, for example, the system must be developed using .NET Framework, or components must communicate using web services.

■**Note** We can compare the application constraints to common application requirements. Requirements against the products may be either common or variable. The variable requirements may vary from one member of the product line to another, but the common requirements do not. Similarly, application constraints do not vary. We can say that application constraints are not negotiable, while the application requirements are negotiable.

 The application constraints of the ISpySoft factory are listed in Table 2-2. This list is relatively short because the software that ISpySoft is building does not need to conform to any governmental or other regulations. Furthermore, ISpySoft's customers did not put up any other technological constraints except the given ones.

Table 2-2. *ISpySoft Application Constraints*

Application Constraint	Description
.NET Framework 2.0 and .NET Compact Framework	The system will completely run on the .NET platform except for eventual legacy components.
Unauthorized access	Any applications developed by the factory needs to prevent unauthorized access to confidential information.
Data security	Confidential data stored on nonvolatile media always needs to be encrypted by applying state-of-the art cryptography standards (e.g., 128-bit encryption).
Web service standards	Any web service exposed by an ISpySoft application will conform to the SOAP/1.1 standard (http://www.w3.org/TR/soap/) to enable interoperability with other technologies and platforms.

Software Factories Constraints

 Process, or Software Factory, constraints must hold for the way we work in this factory, even if we change the kinds of applications that we build. Most factory constraints come from corporate or governmental requirements, and often are about ensuring compliance through process maturity, such as well-defined and repeatable development processes. In addition, there are market or customer constraints forced on the factory, like Sarbanes-Oxley compliance, which prescribes how the software development process is managed and accounted for on the books. Often, they can be imposed by methodologies, e.g., FxCop and unit tests with at least 50% coverage must be run before any code is checked in. Technology constraints can also be factory constraints, and when they are, they usually concern tooling (e.g., Visual Studio must be used for development). The following list contains several categories of Software Factory constraints:

- *Project constraints*: In this category, we find constraints levied by our own company or customer, such as CMMI compliance. This type of constraint often applies to the development process. It should be clear that over time these process constraints can undergo improvement.

- *Policies*: These are outside compliancy requirements such as governmental regulations like Sarbanes-Oxley (SOX) or regulations from the Food and Drug Administration (FDA). This is a growing concern for many companies, and Software Factories will directly deal with helping customers implement compliancy measures in an affordable way.

- *Technology constraints*: This refers to vendor or platform preferences that dictate how to build applications, development tools, process tools, configuration management, hardware requirements, and many more.

■**Tip** For an easy distinction between application and factory constraints, think of the following: if you're limited in "what" you build, it's an application constraint. If you're limited in "how" you build, it's a factory constraint.

What follows in Table 2-3 are the factory constraints for the ISpySoft factory classified according to the preceding schema.

Table 2-3. *ISpySoft Factory Constraints*

Factory Constraint	Description
Project	
Schedule and budget	First release within 6 months. One project manager. One software architect. Three software developers. One test engineer.
Development process	Carry forward elements of the existing process, such as quality gates, review policies, exit criteria, coverage requirements, etc.
Reporting structure	See organizational chart in Figure 2-3.
Policies	
Testing	Unit tests run automatically after each nightly build.
Build	Automatic nightly builds to test integration.
Technology	
Visual Studio Development Environment	Microsoft Windows XP SP2 or higher. Microsoft .NET Framework 2.0. Microsoft Visual Studio 2005. Microsoft Visual Studio 2005 VSIP package. Microsoft Visual Studio 2005 DSL Toolkit. Development language: C#, Microsoft Guidance and Automation Toolkit (GAT), Microsoft Guidance Automation Extensions (GAX).
Source Control Management	Team Foundation Server Version Control.

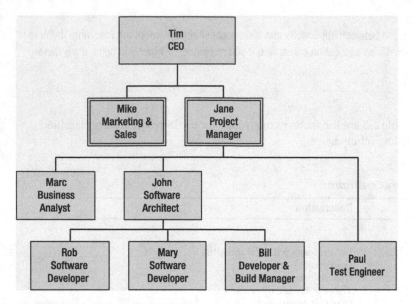

Figure 2-3. *Development organization for the ISpySoft Software Factory*

Stakeholder Description

 In our quest to develop a factory, we need to identify the different stakeholders on the products of the factory. This is an iterative task, and often the stakeholders are not clearly known until after many iterations. What we show here is the start of this activity as it is continued throughout the factory development process.

Stakeholders are any kind of person or organization that has some kind of interest in a system. Examples are the client, who will pay for the system; the client's employees, who will use your software; your CEO, who wants to make money by selling product line members; your project manager, who wants to deliver on time and in budget; and, of course, the developers implementing the software. Each stakeholder makes different demands to this system that later need to be addressed during requirements analysis, development, testing, deployment, maintenance, etc.

 For ISpySoft, the stakeholders and their main concerns are shown in Table 2-4. This list briefly outlines each stakeholder's concerns. We will go into further detail when we introduce viewpoints in Chapter 4, where you can see how these interests manifest in concrete requirements and in the way we organize the Software Factory.

As you can see, about half of the concerns are of a nontechnical nature. This goes along with our project experience, where political, organizational, and social factors on projects are often underestimated. When it comes to a long-term investment like a Software Factory, it is very important to take these soft factors into account.

Table 2-4. *The Stakeholders of the ISpySoft Software Factory*

Stakeholder	Concern
Current and future clients	Need their employees be more productive, want to pay less for acquisition and maintenance
System user	Wants more system customization possibilities and new features to work remotely
ISpySoft CEO	Wants a sustainable solution that will give a competitive advantage to fight pressure from lower-price competitors
ISpySoft Marketing and Sales departments	Plan to introduce fee-based services, aim for a lower retail price and shorter delivery times of new features
ISpySoft project management	Is looking for ways how to make development more predictable (budget- and time-wise) and how to increase quality
ISpySoft business analyst	Hopes to streamline the application definition by using a product line approach
ISpySoft architect	Wants to define and implement a uniform, modular, and extensible architecture that supports all the ISpySoft applications
ISpySoft developer	Wants to spend more time working on essential parts of the system rather than doing repetitive work, bug fixes, and integration
ISpySoft test engineer	Hopes that the factory approach will enable more systematic testing through the use of the common code base for all products and that there will be more time to test the variable features
ISpySoft build manager	Hopes for easier build and versioning of the different applications by using the common code base

■**Tip** The preceding stakeholder list is only an initial list that shows very coarse-grained examples of stakeholders. In practice, a single developer will be a stakeholder on many different decisions or on many different aspects of the factory. For example, the same developer may be a stakeholder on the way web UIs look and feel, and on the way web UIs are developed. Identifying stakeholders at this level of granularity is useful for correctly setting expectations regarding the cost and benefits of building the factory, or regarding the amount of time it will take, or the pace at which productivity gains can be expected to appear, and so on. This is especially true for external stakeholders involved in funding or managing the Software Factory development.

Software Factory Context

 In this section, we define the context in which our Software Factory and its products will reside. More precisely, there are two major contexts: the application context, which defines where the factory's end products will fit in, and the factory context, which defines how the Software Factory fits into the overall development environment. Context diagrams are used to determine high-level interactions between external entities. Furthermore, they help to identify from where constraints might be imposed on factories and products.

Application Context

 The application context diagram in Figure 2-4 shows external entities that interact with the systems that will be built with the ISpySoft Software Factory. From this initial version, you can derive that there will be a number of users of the system that will fulfill different tasks. Furthermore, ISpySoft systems will integrate with a number of other services, such as the online shop hosted at the ISpySoft central.

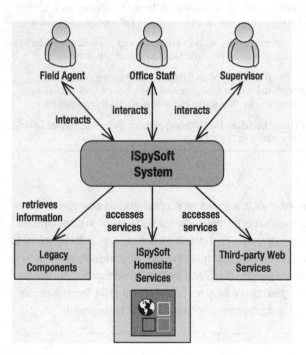

Figure 2-4. *Application context of the ISpySoft Software Factory*

Factory Context

The factory context diagram is shown in Figure 2-5. It displays the different entities that interact with the Software Factory. Note that this is an example typical for the product development phase. Other context diagrams could show the context, e.g., during the phase of Software Factory development, where other stakeholders take part; or during Software Factory improvement, where custom product extensions are fed back into the factory as reusable assets.

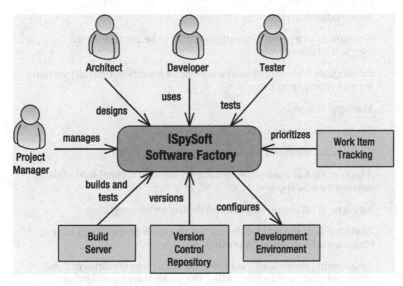

Figure 2-5. *Factory context of the ISpySoft Software Factory*

Domain Glossary

To top off the previous work, we advise creating a domain glossary. This glossary will give a quick and common understanding of the most important terms used throughout the project. It is important to note that a domain glossary does not primarily contain technical terms referring to implementation, but rather terms describing the business domain that the factory will target.

A domain glossary not only ensures everybody is on the same page when talking to customers and defining requirements, but it also is a big help, for example, for people who join a particular Software Factory project later. As the Software Factory gets developed and the team gets a better understanding of it, this domain glossary will be enhanced and refined. Furthermore, the domain glossary in fact is a precursor to a domain model used to support the analysis of the domain that the factory will target.[6]

---

6. Eric Evans, *Domain-Driven Design: Tackling Complexity in the Heart of Software* (Boston, MA: Addison Wesley, 2003)

Table 2-5 shows the domain glossary as the ISpySoft team created it.

Table 2-5. *ISpySoft Software Factory Domain Glossary*

Term	Explanation
PI	Private investigator, investigating on behalf of insurance companies, attorneys, and private persons. ISpySoft's target group.
Case	An investigation case.
Client	A customer of a private investigator (not to be confused with ISpySoft's customers).
Field agent	Investigator who mainly works outside of his office, typically working for an investigation firm.
Supervisor	Manager of agents.
Suspect	Target of an investigation.
Administrative staff	Responsible for client management, finances, IT, etc.
Mobile device	A laptop, PDA or a cell phone (smart phone) that is capable of running custom mobile applications.
Evidence	Any type of information gathered during an investigation.
Information	Evidence is made up of different information pieces, such as text, images, audio or video recordings, etc.
Report	Field agents periodically submit case reports summarizing the collected evidence and reporting the state of an investigation. A special type is the *Case Closed* report, which needs review and approval by a supervisor.
Tip	A piece of secret information passed on to an investigator from someone in favor (voluntarily or for money). Often time-sensitive, requires immediate action.
Expense	Any expenditure that field agents and investigators have in the course of investigating a case.
Bribe	A "special" type of expense (money paid e.g. for a tip), typically needs special approval.
Customer information	Administrative data about clients.
Invoice	Client receives invoice for investigation services rendered.
Reminder	Sent when client does not pay invoice in time.

Summary

The Software Factory definition, which is a major artifact produced during Software Factory development, gives a very high-level overview. It defines the business case that is the foundation for the Software Factory. Furthermore, it provides enough information such that all stakeholders will have a common understanding and accurate expectations of the Software Factory. Now that the stage is set, in the next chapter, we will show how the Software Factory specification builds on top of the Software Factory definition.

Checkpoint

After this chapter, you should be familiar with the following artifacts required for a Software Factory specification:

- *Software Factory overview*: Describes the Software Factory that we want to build from a very high level. This description is the basis for the vision statement and used to communicate the goals of the factory.

- *Software Factory vision*: Communicates the overall goal of the Software Factory between the different stakeholders and relates their daily work to it.

- *Software Factory inputs*: Document existing assets for jump-starting the factory.

- *Application and Software Factory constraints*: Describe the restrictions on the application development process using a Software Factory as well as the external forces on the applications.

- *Stakeholder description*: Documents the interests that each participant in a Software Factory project has.

- *Software Factory contexts*: Display how a Software Factory fits into the overall development environment, and show where the factory's end products will fit in.

- *Domain glossary*: Defines a common, nontechnical vocabulary that helps communication among stakeholders.

CHAPTER 3

■ ■ ■

Software Factory Specification

After two chapters of theory about Software Factories and introduction to our ISpySoft case study, it is finally time to get started doing concrete work. In this chapter, we discuss the Software Factory analysis work. Software Factories use many analysis techniques also used in traditional projects; however, they also use some techniques arising from product line engineering practices, which focus primarily on identifying and separating the requirements common to all members of the product line from those that are unique to only some of its members. These techniques are not commonly used in traditional projects. We have already noted that Software Factories do not necessarily prescribe a certain order of steps. However, at some point, usually as the identity of product line starts to emerge, we start with a *product line analysis* (PLA). Because factory development is iterative, we will not perform product line analysis only once. Rather we will perform it iteratively over time, each time refining our understanding of the problem and solution domains, and consequently refining and extending the artifacts used to support our Software Factory.

■**Caution** At this point we need to emphasize on a very important issue. One of the most radical changes you will face in using Software Factories is the transition from one-off thinking to product line thinking. For the latter, one must always differentiate between the product line (i.e., the Software Factory) and its members (i.e., the products developed using the factory), as well as the individual development cycles for each of them. Therefore, for the rest of the book, we will use the notion of product line, product family, and Software Factory when we are talking about the factory itself, and the notion of application, product, and product family member when we are talking about the members of the product line.

Within PLA, commonality and variability analysis is a powerful concept that will allow us to specify members of the product line by describing only the features that make them unique because the common parts are already provided by the product line. Software Factories are not just about lots of new reusable assets that must be created. They are about the benefits of rapidly building variants by specification, configuration, and assembly rather than hand coding those variants from scratch every time.

The main goals of PLA are to understand the target domain, identify product features, and ultimately scope domain and features to determine the range of products that can be built with a particular Software Factory. The result of the PLA is the *Software Factory specification*, which includes the following artifacts:

- Domain model

- Candidate problem feature matrix

- Feature model for problem domain

- Candidate solution feature matrix

- Feature model for solution domain

- Scoped feature models

The PLA process that we describe in this chapter is based on the one proposed in *Software Factories*.[1] We cross-checked and validated this approach with processes recommended by other institutions (e.g., the Software Engineering Institute at Carnegie Mellon, IEEE standards[2]) and augmented our own software product line development experience. Our ultimate goal was to create an easy-to-understand process that you can follow step by step. Furthermore, it allows for a high degree of requirements traceability, which is important for continuous Software Factory evolution.

This PLA process, of course, is not complete (it could fill a book alone), but we made every effort to point out the aspects that are unique to Software Factory development and to give you a working "base" process that can easily be extended with other proven concepts known from PLA, requirements analysis, and other methods. In our opinion, a process will always have to be adapted to fit a particular project and its organizational environment. Therefore, we recommend you take our approach as a baseline and tailor the PLA process to the specific needs of your Software Factory using your most valuable tool—common sense.

So let's continue with the ISpySoft case study that we kicked off in the last chapter. We need to mention that, because of the amount of documentation, we are only able to show a representative subset of it in this book. Of course, you will get the whole set when you download the case study from the Apress downloads page for our book[3] or from our ISpySoft site.[4]

The ISpySoft factory is tailored to address the problems encountered in private investigation companies. The factory therefore spans three major business domains:

- *Customer relationship management (CRM)*: The CRM system enables the private investigators to manage their client, case, and investigation report information. Besides the capability to manage client data, it also enables the storage of investigation-related information that can be linked to cases and clients. The information that can be stored includes investigation reports and other related digital information (like pictures and videos). In addition, investigators need to search for information by keywords as well as the possibility of sorting by criteria such as open/closed cases, date, or customer name.

---

1. Jack Greenfield and Keith Short, *Software Factories: Assembling Applications with Patterns, Models, Frameworks, and Tools* (Indianapolis, IN: Wiley, 2004)
2. http://standards.ieee.org
3. http://www.apress.com/book/download.html
4. http://www.ispysoft.net

- *E-commerce.* The domain of e-commerce relates to the online store that ISpySoft provides. It should be possible for field agents and administrative staff to procure special equipment and gear as simply as possible. ISpySoft's web-based store, which should be integrated with the ISpySoft desktop solution, gives private investigators the opportunity to easily order investigation gadgets. It offers a catalogue, secure checkout, shopping cart, different payment options, as well as shipping choices.

- *Information services.* These services provide the ISpySoft customers with integrated services that can be used through the web and are charged by amount of usage or on subscription basis. Typically, a private investigator requests information like background check, target location, or records in conjunction with his or her investigation. The requested information is sent back to the requestor depending on the existing contract.

The ISpySoft factory will therefore address a subset of business problems from each one of these domains. This means that we will need to gather knowledge from well-known domains. Chances are that domain analyses have already been performed for the three base domains, either by ISpySoft or other companies, and that we can reuse these. Since we are dealing with specializations of the three domains, we should be able to use the existing analyses, extract relevant parts from them, and tailor the result to the private investigation domain. On top of that, we will need to perform additional analysis work to address the specific needs for the private eye sector, which can be considered an extension to the preceding three domains.

Problem Domain and Solution Domain

Before we undertake the product line analysis, we need to explain the concept of *problem domain* and *solution domain*. The problem domain should be described in business language by stating a number of problems that are common to a family of solutions, whereas the solution domain should be described in mostly technical terms stating concepts available for solving the problems from the problem domain. Table 3-1 gives some example statements from each of these domains and suggests a mapping between the two domains.

Table 3-1. *Example Statements from Problem and Solution Domain*

Problem Domain	Solution Domain
I want to order products easily from home.	An Internet online shop with catalog, products, shopping basket, and credit card payment option.
We need to manage our customer information effectively.	Database for customer information, easy-to-use UI screens and business processes.
Our customers need to pay in a generally accepted and secure method.	Credit card payments and secure SSL connection to credit card processing center.
I need to get from A to B.	Car, train or airplane; streets, tracks, or airway.

Again, the description of the problem domain (as the name indicates) states problems for which the solution domain offers technologies that can be used to provide solutions where these problem statements are formal descriptions of the business problems to be solved. You can also think of a *problem statement* as a *stakeholder request*, which we think is a more intuitive way to describe it. Nevertheless, we will stick to the terms originally used in the Software Factories book, as the term "problem" goes very well along with term "solution." Accordingly, solution statements describe the means provided by an application in order to solve a business problem. Later, these solution statements will be refined into formal requirements.

In an ideal situation, for every problem there would be one or more solutions, and every solution could partially solve one or more problems. We can think of this as a mapping from problem domain to solution domain, as shown in Figure 3-1, where items A through E represent problem statements, and items 1 through 5 represent solutions to these problems.

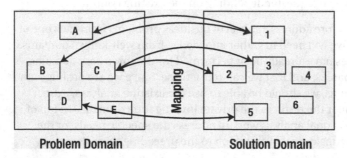

Figure 3-1. *Mapping between problem domain and solution domain*

Domain Model

[Domain analysis is] the process of identifying, collecting, organizing, and representing the relevant information in a domain, based upon the study of existing systems and their development histories, knowledge captured from domain experts, underlying theory, and emerging technology within a domain.

—From the website of the Software Engineering Institute at Carnegie Mellon, 2004

A domain model in the context of PLA is an information model of the business domain that is currently being analyzed. It describes concepts that exist apart from any automation provided by a software system. Furthermore, it is an information model that can be expressed using a variety of notations, such as entity relationship notation or UML static structure notation. Figure 3-2 shows the domain model for ISpySoft's investigation and case management domain. Domain models are used in PLA to get an overview of the business entities that will occur in a product line. It also helps in communicating with other team members and customers.

A good starting point for creating one or more domain models is the domain glossary that was created in Chapter 2 as part of the Software Factory definition. Ideally, all actors, entities, and concepts should already be listed in there (of course, you can also do it the other way around: use the domain model to check whether your domain glossary is complete). The domain model then documents the relations between these concepts and other details that are not captured by the domain glossary, such as properties of information elements.

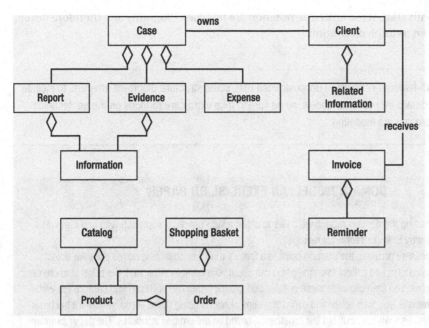

Figure 3-2. *Domain model for product line analysis (taken from ISpySoft)*

Domain modeling differs from requirements analysis in two major ways: first, we model the problem domain, not the requirements of a software; and second, we model all of the concepts in a domain, not just the subset of the concepts that are of interest to the developers of a particular software product.

■**Note** These distinctions from requirements analysis are quite significant. For example, if we only model the concepts used in an application to be developed, we will not be able to use the domain model to support the development of alternative software solutions. Furthermore, if we model only the subset of concepts that are of interest to a particular software product, then we will have no basis for commonality/variability analysis that involves concepts of interest to other software applications targeting the same domain.

Static structure diagrams are good candidates for modeling domains. While domain entities are not classes, they are abstract data types, and the UML static structure notation (class diagrams) is an approximation of what we need to model a domain. Additionally, many software practitioners are familiar with its notation and UML editors, and therefore it seems to be a good choice to bend class diagrams to these purposes. We can do that by applying an informal interpretation to our use of it by saying that a class represents an entity, and that we won't allow any operations to be defined.

Or we can do that formally, in a tool that supports UML extensibility, by defining a stereotype of class called *entity*, applying the constraint that an entity has no operations in the tool, and then attaching that constraint to the stereotype. However, always keep in mind that domain models created with UML static structure notation are not class diagrams and therefore never should be mistaken as implementation.

■**Tip** Using the full-featured richness of unconstrained UML static structure diagrams attempts to include too many technical details into domain models, so be sure to take extra care to focus on the nontechnical aspects of the domain you are modeling.

DOMAIN MODEL: AN EXERCISE ON PAPER

With regards to creating the domain model, we'd like to share a very practical approach with you that was recommended to us by Erik, our technical reviewer:

"A domain glossary provides the starting point to a factory much as collecting nouns does for object orientation. You brainstorm and collect everything you can about your domain. After that, the effort is to create entities and attributes. You then organize these entities into groups (often hierarchical) and capture the verbs possible. Once complete, you then relate and connect groups of nouns using these verbs, which are the basis of the domain model. This will help pull out the constraints, based on the entities attributes. The paper exercise is iterative and may take some time, but often works very well as a collaborative exercise among a group of domain experts before formally capturing this information with the help of a modeling tool.

Use a whiteboard and sticky notes because it is far easier to take a piece of paper and move it next to another than to edit an electronic document as the first draft. The key is having a clear understanding of the domain term (noun) and the domain relationship (verb) up front."

Candidate Problem Feature Matrix

In addition to documenting the main domain concepts, we need to elaborate the high-level features of business problems in a particular domain. A simple but effective method to gather these features is by using a problem feature matrix, and this is typically performed by domain experts together with Software Factory architects. This matrix will give you not only a candidate list of business problem features, but also a first indication of which features are common to all problem statements and which are optional.

There are several ways to create this problem feature matrix. One way is to analyze the business needs of multiple companies in the targeted domain. Another way is to analyze a number of existing applications and examine the business problem statements that the applications are intended to solve. For example, in the domain of private investigation, a common feature in a business problem statement may be capturing and managing information about the person(s) being investigated (Table 3-2, which appears later in this section, shows a simple feature matrix from our case study).

After having kick-started your problem feature matrix, you should ask yourself, "Is this list of possible problem features complete?" Chances are it's not, as there may be problem features of the businesses you are going to target that none of the analyzed applications addresses. Therefore, you will have to discover additional features using other techniques.

The Microsoft Solutions Framework[5] describes several proven techniques for gathering problem statements from stakeholders. These techniques include

- *Shadowing*: Observing users performing their daily work

- *Interviewing*: One-on-one meetings with users or stakeholders

- *Focus groups*: Group interviews through a facilitator

- *Surveys*: Sets of questions answered by users and stakeholders

- *User instruction*: Users training interviewer on tasks

- *Prototyping*: Simulation and verification of production environments

The results, e.g., can be captured and elaborated using UML diagrams, such as use cases or context diagrams. There are many good books available on domain analysis, and we'd like to recommend *Domain-Driven Design*[6] and *Applying Domain-Driven Design and Patterns*[7] to you for additional in-depth information.

In this initial version of the problem feature matrix, some features might be duplicates, as different businesses describe them differently. Therefore, you will need to harmonize the matrix, which means to eliminate duplicate features and align their terminology with your domain glossary. The resulting harmonized version is called the *candidate problem feature matrix*.

■Tip In order to create the first drafts of use cases and context diagrams, we again recommend the "whiteboard and sticky notes" technique described earlier. This will allow stakeholders, domain experts, and technologists to participate. The candidate feature matrix elaboration could be performed even if you were not building any software. For example, say you are a business process reengineering consultant looking to understand the problems that businesses face in a particular domain. You might gather a number of problem statements from the businesses, and look for the common elements. The result would be a problem feature matrix that has nothing to do with software systems (yet).

 The ISpySoft architects analyzed the business problems of the private investigation domain in order to build an initial problem feature matrix, where the outcome is shown in Table 3-2.

---

5. http://www.microsoft.com/technet/itsolutions/msf/default.mspx
6. Eric Evans, *Domain-Driven Design: Tackling Complexity in the Heart of Software* (Upper Saddle River, NJ: Addison Wesley, 2004)
7. Jimmy Nilsson, *Applying Domain-Driven Design and Patterns: With Examples in C# and .NET* (Boston, MA: Addison Wesley, 2006)

Table 3-2. *ISpySoft Problem Feature Matrix*

Business Problem	Features				
	Client Management	Online Store	Case Management	Accounting	Information Gathering
Field agent sends a report			x		
Field agent wants to check license plate					x
Field agent submits expense			x	x	
Field agent wants current location					x
Office agent creates new case	x		x	x	
Office agent maps an address					x
Office agent checks for identity of suspect					x
Office agent orders new equipment		x		x	
Investigator supervisor approves expenses of agent			x	x	
Office agent needs to get a reminder for upcoming appointments	x		x		
Clients access case status online	x		x	x	
Office agent send invoice to client	x		x	x	
Office send payment reminder to clients	x		x	x	
Office agent connects with existing accounting system				x	
Office agent checks on open equipment orders		x			
Office agent browses available equipment		x			
Office agent orders item		x			
Variable workflow	x		x	x	
Office supervisor checks on changes to cases	x		x	x	

Because ISpySoft's architects actually captured nontechnical information about many of the business problems in the investigation domain, they can come up with creative new solutions. For example, Figure 3-3 shows one of the use case diagrams that were produced based on the work of a focus group covering field agent work. There would have been no basis for new innovative solutions if the architects had only captured requirements for a particular application. Requirements for applications do not give you the freedom to explore new ways to solve problems in the business domain, but rather describe a specific negotiated solution to a specific subset of those problems.

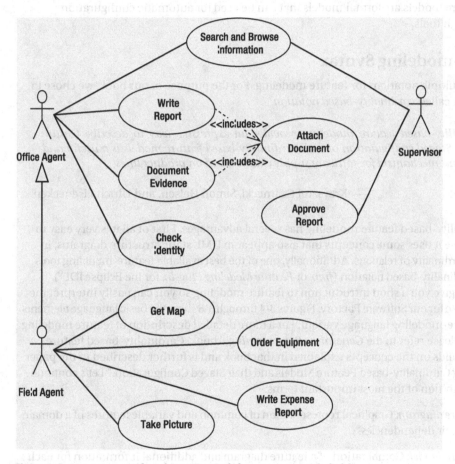

Figure 3-3. *Use-case artifact from ISpySoft focus group with field agents*

Feature Modeling Explained

 While in domain engineering there are multiple ways to perform domain analysis with varying complexity, we chose a simple yet effective one called *feature modeling*. Feature models provide a formal way to capture commonalities and variabilities in features identified during domain analysis. Feature models can easily be derived from feature matrices. So you might ask, "What additional advantages does a feature model bring compared to a feature matrix?" To give you a first idea, these are some benefits of feature modeling:

- Feature modeling enables product line scoping.

- The variations captured in feature models can be mapped to variation points in the architecture.

- Feature models can provide the foundation for defining domain-specific languages.

- Feature models can be used as a basis for estimating development cost and feature prioritization.

- Feature models are formal models that can be used for automatic configuration through tools.

Feature-modeling Syntax

There are multiple notations for feature modeling. For the purpose of our book, we chose to use a variant called *cardinality-based notation*.

> *Cardinality-based feature modeling provides an expressive way to describe feature models. Staged configuration of such cardinality-based feature models is a useful and important mechanism for software supply chains based on product lines.*

> ——Krzysztof Czarnecki, Simon Helsen, and Ulrich Eisenecker[8]

Cardinality-based feature modeling has several advantages. First of all it is very easy to grasp because it uses some concepts that also appear in UML static structure diagrams, in particular cardinality of relations. Additionally, one of the best available feature-modeling tools uses the cardinality-based notation (*fmp*, or *Feature Modeling Plug-in*, for the Eclipse IDE[9]).

We will give you a short introduction to feature modeling so you can easily interpret the models we use for our Software Factory. Figures 3-4 through 3-6 show the basic language elements of this feature-modeling language variant. For a more detailed description of feature modeling in general, please refer to the *Generative Programming*[10] book. Cardinality-based feature modeling builds on the concepts explained in that book and is further described in the paper "Formalizing Cardinality-based Feature Models and their Staged Configuration." Let's continue with the definition of the most important terms:

- *Feature diagram*: Graphical representation of common and variable features of a domain and their dependencies.

- *Feature model*: Combination of a feature diagram and additional information for each feature (e.g., description, stakeholders, etc.).

---

8. Krzysztof Czarnecki, Simon Helsen, and Ulrich Eisenecker, "Formalizing Cardinality-based Feature Models and their Staged Configuration" (OOPSLA'04 Eclipse Technology eXchange [ETX] Workshop, Vancouver, British Columbia, Canada, October 24–28, 2004, ACM 1-58113-833-4/04/0010)
9. The fmp can be downloaded at http://gp.uwaterloo.ca/fmp/.
10. Krzysztof Czarneck and Ulrich W. Eisenecker, *Generative Programming: Methods, Tools, and Applications* (Indianapolis, IN: Addison Wesley, 2000)

- *Concept*: Each feature model has one or more top-level "features" called concepts. Each concept then is described through subordinated features. For example, in Figure 3-4 (shown in the next section), "Computer" is a concept, and "RAM" is a feature.

- *Feature*: Abstract term for an attribute, a property, or a detail that a concept or another feature can have.

Feature modeling allows us to model commonalities and variabilities of features in a particular domain at a very abstract level without specifying any implementation details, which makes this method very suitable for capturing the results of feature analysis for a product line, and for supporting feature-based configuration when developing individual product line members.

Required and Optional Features

A feature model is a hierarchical graph that displays one or more concepts at the top (as *root features*) and subordinated features connected through a line. Each feature has a little circle on top. A black circle means this is a required feature (e.g., no computer can run without RAM), and a white circle means this is an optional feature (e.g., a computer can run with or without a floppy drive). Figure 3-4 shows required and optional features. Furthermore, in a feature model each feature can have additional attributes, such as stakeholders, constraints, and dependencies on other features.

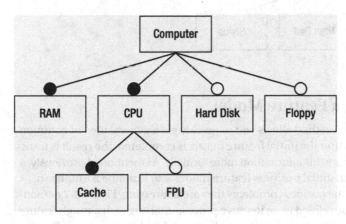

Figure 3-4. *Required and optional features*

Feature Sets

Feature sets are typically used to express two things: a group of similar or interchangeable features and a cardinality constraint. Feature sets are displayed by an arc spanning the subfeatures contained in the feature set. Additionally, the cardinality is shown next to the arc.

If you look at Figure 3-5, you can see that a logical hard disk in a computer can be either an IDE or a SCSI drive (two similar technologies). The *1-1 cardinality* indicates you have to choose exactly one type. In contrast, Figure 3-6 shows *0-n cardinality*, where a computer could have no, one, or even multiple input devices. Features within a feature set do not have a circle on top, since optional/required is determined through the cardinality constraint.

Note A feature set with 0-n cardinality, as shown in Figure 3-6, could also be realized as a feature with only optional subfeatures. Using a feature set instead expresses the similarity amongst the subfeatures.

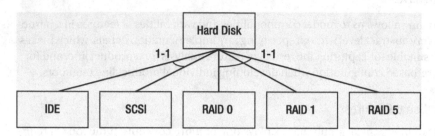

Figure 3-5. *1-1 feature sets*

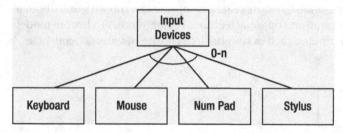

Figure 3-6. *0-n feature set*

Creating and Refining a Feature Model

Using the problem feature matrix method allows you to quickly get a general idea of common and variable high-level features. After the initial feature matrix is completed, the result is transferred into a feature model to capture this information more formally. As mentioned previously, a practical approach for creating an initial business feature model is to examine a number of similar existing applications and the business problems they are addressing. Figure 3-7 demonstrates how a feature model can be refined in an iterative process. Starting with a rough feature model describing the first applications, variabilities are discovered and features are refined.

Throughout the process of creating and refining features, each feature node should be provided with additional data through *parameterization* like the following:

- Detailed description

- Reference to problem statement

- Reference to stakeholders (possibly through problem statement)

- Reference to existing applications that implement this feature

- Constraints and dependencies

- Binding information

- Importance of feature (priority)

This additional information is not only important for the completeness of the model, but can possibly be used for subsequent automation.

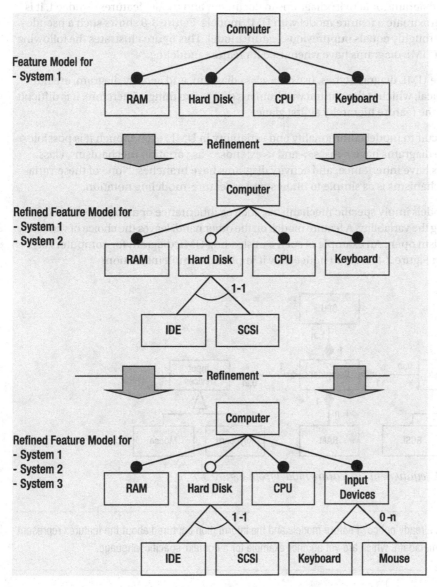

Figure 3-7. *Refining feature models*

Feature Models Compared to UML Class Diagrams

If you look at the example feature models in Figure 3-7, you might argue, "Why don't we just use UML class diagrams or activity diagrams to document and model features?" Indeed, it is possible to approximate a feature model with UML models. Figure 3-8 shows such a pseudo-UML draft that roughly equals our previous feature model. This figure illustrates the following drawbacks that UML diagrams have when used for feature modeling:

- The three UML diagram types, use case, class diagram, and activity diagram, are not hierarchical, which is the natural way humans categorize things. Therefore, it is difficult to grasp the feature hierarchy at first glance.

- It is difficult to model commonality and variability in UML, even though it is possible. Use case diagrams have <<uses>> and <<extends>> as variation mechanisms, class diagrams have inheritance, and activity diagrams have branches. None of these variation mechanisms is as simple to understand as feature-modeling notation.

- UML models imply specific mechanisms, such as inheritance or association, for accommodating the variability. A feature model, on the other hand, leaves the choice of variability mechanism open. An example of such a misleading UML diagram for computers is shown in Figure 3-8. Do you notice how it implies the implementation?

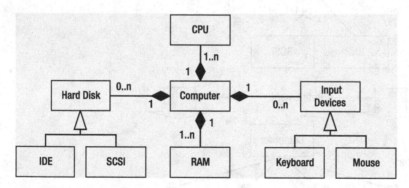

Figure 3-8. *UML "equivalent" to feature model from Figure 3-7*

■**Note** Did you already notice? Feature models and the information captured about the features represent domain-specific metadata, which are yet another example for a domain-specific language.

Configuration Based on Feature Models

In Chapter 1, we discussed the issues of documentation that does not live with the project and gets outdated easily, and loads of paperwork that get created during the initial phase of the project; however, as the project progresses, it often gets too time-consuming to keep this documentation up to date, rendering it basically worthless over time. Following the idea of living documentation, these feature models will be used to rapidly specify the features of the products developed by a factory.

A problem domain feature model can be configured to capture information about specific businesses. The same way you can configure and customize your own PC on a computer manufacturer's website, you can use a feature model to configure an actual product instance. The resulting artifact is called a *configuration*.

Figure 3-9 shows an example of what a configured feature model can look like. This screenshot was taken from our custom feature model configuration tool after configuring the ISpySoft solution feature model, which we present shortly. Variable features are initially represented by a checkbox with a question mark. By setting it to checked or unchecked, features can be selected or deselected.

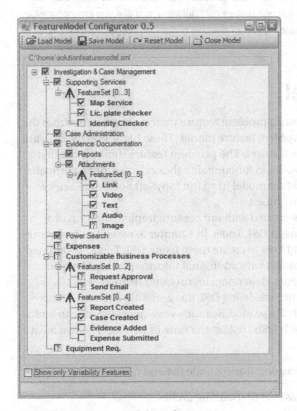

Figure 3-9. *Feature model configuration*

That feature configuration can then be mapped onto a solution domain feature model to create a configuration of solution features that may be appropriate to include in a software product developed for the business to address its problems. Therefore, feature models are first-class development artifacts that become part of the implementation. Also note that every feature identified during PLA could have an associated cost. It is therefore not a foregone conclusion that a customer will opt for all of the suggested features.

In a later stage during application development, it is oftentimes not feasible or desired to completely configure a feature model at once. Initially only a subset of variable features is decided on so that the feature model is only partially configured. The remaining variable features

are configured at a later point during application development. Delaying decisions about variabilities is called *staged configuration*, a technique that can also be useful for agile development
when requirements are discovered throughout multiple iterations.

■**Tip** Each product is a variant that can be fully defined in terms of just the features that make it unique.
Compared to traditional one-off development, where requirements must be exhaustively elicited, captured,
organized, prioritized, and validated for every product, feature configuration is a massive win. In the most
stable portions of some domains, it can be used to drive a build-to-order experience, where users can essentially order the customized application they want through feature configuration, just like you can order a car
or a PC by picking a base model and then configuring it to your specific budget and needs.

Problem Feature Model

A problem feature model can be derived from a problem feature matrix, where items from the
matrix become high-level features in the problem feature model. These high-level features are
then refined and broken down into smaller features. The problem feature model is the first
comprehensive and detailed view on the business functionality that exists within a particular
domain. Figure 3-10 shows a part of the feature model from the ISpySoft Software Factory,
which was derived from Table 3-2 and then refined.

   The model displayed in this figure was created with our custom implementation of a
feature-modeling language based on Microsoft DSL Tools. In Chapter 5, we will go into more
detail about domain-specific languages and how to create them using DSL Tools. As outlined
in the previous section, every node is annotated with additional information like detailed
description, references to problem statements, dependencies on other features, etc.

   As you can see in Figure 3-10, our feature-modeling DSL has a slightly different syntax
than the original notation explained earlier. These modifications were necessary due to limitations in language and editor capabilities with DSL Tools at the time of writing. The two most
noticeable differences are

- The required/optional decorator is inside a feature node instead of attached at the top.

- Feature sets are separate elements instead of spanning arches.

   However, none of these changes should actually affect readability of these diagrams. In
this figure, we show business functionality that is required for investigation and case management. Comparing this model to the previous problem feature matrix, you can see that most
matrix entries were transformed into high-level features in the feature model.

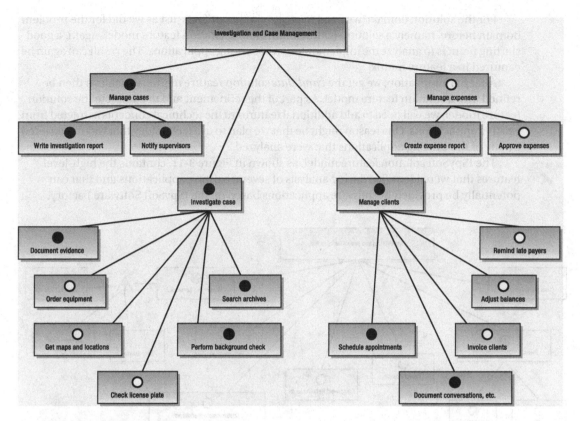

Figure 3-10. *ISpySoft problem feature model*

Solution Feature Matrix and Solution Feature Model

 The solution domain provides solutions to problems from the problem domain. The solution domain can contain technical concepts, but it does not have to. It contains concepts that might be used to address the business problems.

The solution feature model is not just about the technical architecture. It will become the source of requirements, so it may contain very nontechnical terms. Its goal is to describe all the features that members of the target product family can contain. Here, we're talking about features of applications, not about features of the problem domain.

An example of a feature of an application might be a section of a web page containing personalized content based on the application's analysis of my buying habits. The problem domain feature that the solution feature maps to would be the need to cross-sell and up-sell to existing customers.

For the solution domain, we need to create similar artifacts just as we did for the problem domain before, namely a solution feature matrix and a solution feature model. Again, a good starting point is to analyze the implementation of existing applications. The result can again be captured in a feature matrix.

After harmonization, we get the *candidate* solution feature matrix, which can then be refined into a solution feature model. As part of the refinement and to complete the solution feature model, we will need to add additional features to the technical concepts extracted from existing applications. One reason might be that we plan to use technology that was not covered by any of the existing applications that were analyzed.

The ISpySoft solution feature model, as shown in Figure 3-11, contains the high-level features that were identified during analysis of several existing applications and that can potentially be provided by software applications based on the ISpySoft Software Factory.

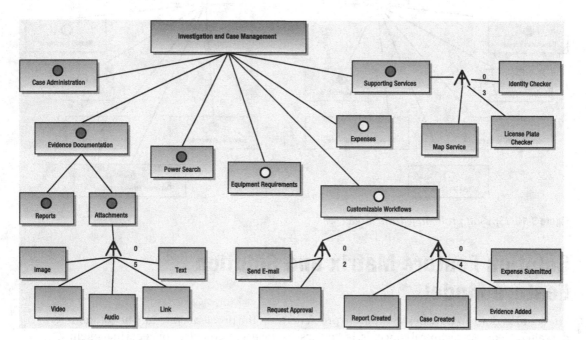

Figure 3-11. *Solution feature model*

At this point you might wonder where the traceability of requirements is that we kept insisting on throughout the Software Factory specification process. In the beginning of this chapter we mentioned a mapping between problem and solution domain. As Figure 3-12 shows, we can create a direct mapping between problem domain and solution domain, or more specifically, we map each problem feature to one or more solution features, and vice versa. That mapping will be the basis for tracing requirements back to business needs.

Furthermore, this figure shows how software architecture provides a mapping between requirements defined in the solution domain and implementation artifacts of a concrete application.

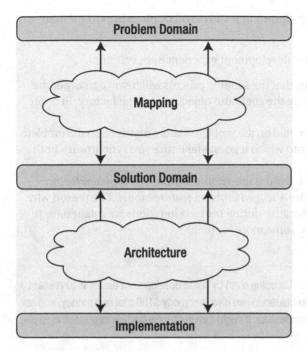

Figure 3-12. *Mapping between problem domain, solution domain, and implementation*

Domain Scoping

The purpose of PLA is to gain a detailed view of the domain for which we plan to develop a product line. Furthermore, PLA teases out what features are common or variable across all members of that product line, what features could reasonably be implemented, and what features should be omitted, e.g., because they are too costly to implement or are only infrequently used. This is called the *domain scoping process*.

As mentioned before, a feature matrix shows all of the features in the target domain, but usually a specific factory will only address a subset of them. In other words, the set of features defined by the feature model must be scoped in order to be used in a specific factory. This scoping process is as critical as the specification process in the previous chapter, where we defined the kind of Software Factory to be built.

The goal is to find the right compromise between a broad Software Factory covering a large market and a narrow Software Factory that is applicable to only a specialized niche, because this compromise determines which products with what functionality can be built by the Software Factory. There are many factors that influence the scoping process, such as

- *Budget*: Sets overall limits to resources and therefore to what can be implemented.

- *Factory constraints*: (Standards, regulations, etc.—see previous chapter.) Can require or prevent certain features.

- *Customer requests*: Top priorities from customers need to be observed.

- *Marketing decisions*: Defines how products from a Software Factory will be placed in the market.

- *Complexity, priority, and relevance*: Common features will be more important than variable features.

- *Experience*: Domain knowledge and development experience are essential.

Having said this, it should be obvious that the scoping process will involve many of the stakeholders in negotiating and prioritizing the goals and objectives for the factory, in order to come up with a compromise.

The scoping process can either be executed on the problem feature matrix or on the problem feature model, depending on the detail into which it goes. Make sure you synchronize both artifacts after scoping.

Scoping turns the candidate problem feature matrix into a *prototype problem feature matrix* and the problem feature model into a *scoped problem feature model*. The reason why these artifacts are labeled prototypes is because during the next iterations we might have to make additional changes and possibly do some more scoping.

Tip A practical technique for prioritization and scoping used by some development teams is to present a list of top-level features to a number of key stakeholders. Then give everybody $100 (not real money) and ask how much each one of them would spend on each feature. It might turn out that nobody is interested in paying for a certain feature.

 In Table 3-3, you can see a selection from the ISpySoft prototype solution feature matrix. These are the features that we scoped from the original candidate solution feature matrix. In order to document the scoping process, each feature has a short explanation about the reason it was excluded.

Table 3-3. *Scoped Solution Features*

Excluded Solution Features	Scoping Reason
Investigation and Case Management	
Access from mobile device	ISpySoft is missing Windows Mobile expert knowledge, and the feature was determined too costly at this point in time. Instead, stakeholders agreed on building a desktop application that allows field agents to work from a notebook in a disconnected manner (without network access).
Customer Relation Management	
Customizable data fields	Low-priority feature, some generic text fields provided instead.
Online self-service for clients (*new*)	Most of ISpySoft's customers don't have the technical means yet (e.g., web hosting) in order to offer online self-service to their clients.

Table 3-3. *Scoped Solution Features (Continued)*

Excluded Solution Features	Scoping Reason
Accounting	
Integration with existing accounting system (*new*)	So far only requested by one customer.
Purchasing	
All purchasing features	No web service integration with online shop at this point. Instead, application will host a web browser running the online shop.
Security	
Fingerprint for access (*new*)	Technology still too expensive.

Elaborating Requirements

The goal of requirements analysis is to come up with a set of requirements for the members of a product line, such that satisfying any given subset of the requirements will solve the associated business problems in a way that meets our goals in terms of cost, time to market, compliance with government regulations, technology choices, etc. According to IEEE standard 1233-1998, a requirement consists of three criteria:

- *Capability*: Describes what a requirement does

- *Condition*: Describes the situation to which the requirement applies

- *Constraint (optional)*: Specifies external boundaries on requirements that limit how a requirement can be implemented.

Looking at a solution feature model, you can see that each feature is in fact a capability that can be provided by a product line member. That means we can evolve a solution feature model into a requirements specification. With one-off applications, a requirements specification targets only a single application, not a family of applications. For product lines we need to combine this requirements specification with a feature model that captures commonality/variability information.

Each feature can have one or more requirements attached to it, together with conditions and constraints. In addition we could attach a scenario to each feature that illustrates the manifestation of the feature in the product. For features that are visible in the UI, the scenario might take the form of a storyboard click-through. For features that are not visible in the UI, the scenario might take the form of a textual narrative. We recommend that you use proven requirements-engineering techniques to gather and harden these functional requirements, e.g., as described in *Software Requirements*.[11]

At this point, we also need to weave in the application constraints documented in the Software Factory definition that are directly related to business requirements. For example, a regulation requires that only authenticated and authorized users can access certain features

---

11. Karl E. Wiegers, *Software Requirements, Second Edition* (Redmond, WA: Microsoft Press, 2003)

of a product. Therefore, we would attach requirements to the affected features with the constraint "User needs to be authorized."

Please be aware that you will not be able to capture all requirements with a feature model, especially when it comes to nonfunctional requirements such as performance. Consequently, you will need additional means of capturing, storing, and versioning requirements.

 Our custom feature-modeling language allows for annotating feature nodes with additional information, such as requirements. However, as this is a proof-of-concept DSL, it only provides a large text field to enter additional information regarding requirements.

Tip Be careful not to falsely specify implementation details as requirements. Requirements will specify "what" has to be implemented, not the "how."

Summary

Herewith we conclude the PLA whose result is the Software Factory specification. This analysis first of all documents what business problems must be solved by the factory. On top of this, it provides an inventory of solutions to these business problems as a starting point for subsequent activities.

Please keep in mind that the techniques that we described in this chapter, such as feature matrices and feature modeling, are nothing set in stone. Feature modeling is especially useful for product line development when you need to determine the common and variable features of a domain. Further down the road, when it comes to actually implementing a product line member, these feature models will not be dry documentation. Instead they will become part of the Software Factory implementation. We recommend that you take these practices as a basis and incorporate them into an analysis process that fits your particular Software Factory and development environment.

Checkpoint

After this chapter, you should be familiar with the following concepts relating to Software Factory specification:

- *Problem and solution domains*: Problem domain is defined in business terms, solution domain mostly in technical terms.

- *Domain model*: Determines the business entities and their relations.

- *Problem feature matrix*: Relates problem statements to high level problem features.

- *Problem feature model*: Refines the problem feature matrix; will be used in later steps for configuration.

- *Solution feature matrix*: Analyzes existing applications and determines technical solutions.

- *Solution feature model*: Refines the solution feature matrix. Provides the basis for a requirements specification.

- *Domain scoping*: Represents a compromise among stakeholders where features that are too costly, low priority, etc., get scoped out.

CHAPTER 4

■ ■ ■

Software Factory Schema: Architecture

 Let's revisit an illustration we first introduced in Chapter 1, repeated here in Figure 4-1, that shows the basic building blocks of Software Factories. Based on our work so far, we may now start working on probably the most important and most complex deliverable of a factory, the *Software Factory schema*.

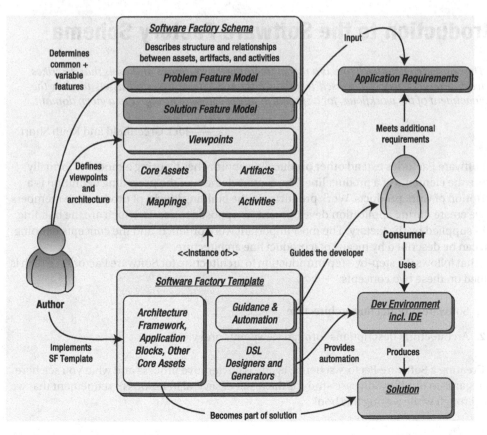

Figure 4-1. *Software Factory building blocks*

The Software Factory schema, with its related concepts and practices, is considered a core part of the methodology. We take a two-step approach to explaining the schema; we focus on product line architecture and the mechanisms to capture it in a schema in this chapter. In the next chapter, we cover the application development process that defines how applications will be built using a Software Factory.

Many of the techniques and principles applied in Software Factory architecture are already well established in product line development. Therefore, we start with a general introduction to product line architecture and then dive into the first part of the Software Factory schema, covering the following concepts:

- Architecture variability

- Product line architecture definition process

- Reference architectures

- Architectural descriptions based on viewpoints and views

- Viewpoints in the Software Factory schema

- Viewpoints and view examples from the ISpySoft Software Factory

Introduction to the Software Factory Schema

The Software Factory schema is a model interpreted by humans and tools that describes work products, workflows used to produce the work products, and assets used in the enactment of the workflows, for a specific family of software products in a given domain.

——Jack Greenfield and Keith Short

Software Factories extend other product line approaches by using a model to formally capture the elements of a product line. The central element of the preceding definition is a description of work products. Work products are the building blocks of product line members that we create during application development, as opposed to assets, which are the building blocks supplied by the factory. The most important work products and the concepts defining them can be described by means of a product line architecture.

What follows is a step-by-step introduction to architecture for Software Factories, which is founded on these two concepts:

1. Software product line architecture

2. Architectural descriptions through viewpoints and views

Creating a Software Factory schema, again, is an iterative process and what you see here, with regards to our ISpySoft case study, is the result of several iterations of refinement that we went through while writing this book.

Note In this book, we provide a high-level overview of software product line architecture principles and focus on issues specific to the Software Factory approach. In-depth information regarding software product line architecture can be found at the Software Engineering Institute (SEI) web site[1] or in *Design and Use of Software Architectures.*[2]

Software Factory Architecture

Let's now discuss the purpose and the goals of software architecture in the context of Software Factories. We will take the definition of architecture provided by SEI as the basis:

> *The software architecture of a program or computing system is the structure or structures of the system, which comprise software elements, the externally visible properties of those elements, and the relationships among them.*

———Len Bass, Paul Clements, Rick Kazman[3]

We also really liked another view on architecture, as we think it gives a different emphasis and brings out the human factor a little bit better:

> *Interface design and functional factoring constitute the key intellectual content of software and are far more difficult to create and re-create than code.*

———Peter Deutsch[4]

Software Factories are based on software product line architectures. Product line architectures are similar to conventional software architectures, but they do have several unique features and additional components that are of interest. Therefore, let's look at two differences that we find most interesting:

- The product line architecture has to support not just one system, but many. It has to be consistent, modular, and extensible for the entire product family.

- The product line architecture must provide configuration and variability mechanisms to satisfy the variation in requirements exhibited by the product family members. If you use feature models to separate common and variable features, as described in Chapter 3, then this variation is expressed by the variable features captured in the solution feature model.

---

1. http://www.sei.cmu.edu/architecture/books.html
2. Jan Bosch, *Design and Use of Software Architectures: Adopting and Evolving a Product-Line Approach* (Boston, MA: Addison Wesley, 2000)
3. Len Bass, Paul Clements, and Rick Kazman, *Software Architecture in Practice, Second Edition* (Boston, MA: Addison-Wesley, 2003)
4. Peter Deutsch, "Design reuse and frameworks in the Smalltalk-80 system," *Software Reusability*, vol. II, eds. T.J. Biggerstaff and A. J. Perlis, (New York City, NY: ACM Press, 1989)

The reasons for investing in a software architecture are somewhat obvious, while each of these reasons accounts for product line architectures equally well:

- A *well-executed* software product line architecture is crucial to the success of software projects, as it allows for quickly reacting to changing requirements.

- A software product line architecture has to *support all of the functional and nonfunctional requirements* for the product line.

- Software product line architecture is an important *communication mechanism* for the different stakeholders on a product line and helps to visualize and identify requirements and resolve conflicting goals. A recommended practice for documenting any software architecture, including a software product line architecture, is to provide different architectural views of different system aspects for different stakeholders. As we will explain shortly, Software Factories are organized around this concept.

But what makes a good architecture? In our opinion, the key attributes of a software product line architecture are the same as the key attributes of any software architecture.

- *Fit for purpose*: A good architecture ensures that known quality attribute goals are met, including those that cut across multiple areas of a system. The behavior (e.g., performance) of the entire system is more important than the behavior of a single component.

- *Pragmatism*: The implementation of a good architecture is achievable within the available schedule, budget, and constraints of the existing investments (people, hardware, and software).

- *Transparency and consistency*: A good architecture provides a clear, consistent, concise, and standard approach to implementation that is apparent throughout.

- *Accessible documentation*: A good architecture is well documented so that all participating stakeholders can quickly achieve the understanding they need to do their jobs. This documentation describes not only the static (structural) and dynamic (behavioral) aspects of a system, but also the process or the steps involved in the construction (or maintenance) of the system.

Architectural Variability

Variability mechanisms in a software product line architecture allow for the customization and extension of the architecture to accommodate the unique needs of each product line member. These variability mechanisms can be classified by their binding time, which is the time when a decision about a particular variable feature is made during development process of a product line member. Table 4-1 shows a number of binding time types.[5]

---

5. http://www.softwareproductlines.com

Table 4-1. *Binding Times*

Binding Time	Decisions Bound...
Source reuse time	...When reusing a configurable source artifact
Development time	...During architecture, design, and coding
Static code instantiation time	...During assembly of code for build
Build time	...During compilation or related processing
Package time	...While assembling binary and executable collections
Install time	...During the installation of the software product
User customizations	...During customization of the end product by the user
Startup time	...During system startup
Runtime	...When the system is executing

As a rule of thumb, the later the binding time, the less needs to be known about a particular product line member in advance. However, typically the later the binding time, the more complex the variation mechanism required to perform the binding. For example, if variability in the form of a customizable workflow is applied at runtime, this requires a complex workflow engine that loads and executes workflow models. On the other hand, the same variability applied at source code reuse time might only require some few manual changes to the code (no complex workflow engine). Therefore, we advise you to bind variabilities as early as possible, unless there is a specific requirement for a later binding time.

In order to support the variability in product lines, we distinguish between different variability mechanisms. They can be classified by the time at which the variability is bound. Table 4-2 provides a list of variability mechanisms and their binding time according to Mikael Svahnberg and Jan Bosch.[6]

Now that we have introduced you to variability mechanisms, we apply these mechanisms to our ISpySoft case study, for which we need to address the variable features described in the solution feature model from Chapter 3. Table 4-3 shows a selection of feature variabilities and the variability mechanism applied to support each one.

---

6. Mikael Svahnberg and Jan Bosch, "Issues Concerning Variability in Software" (Heidelberg, Germany: Proceedings of the Third International Workshop on Software Architecture for Product Lines, Springer LNCS, 2000)

Table 4-2. *Product Line Variation Mechanisms and Their Binding Time*

Mechanism	Binding Time
Inheritance	Development time
Extension and extension points	Customer customizations, installation time
Parameterization	Build time
Configuration and module interconnection languages	Runtime
Code generation	Development time, installation time
Compile-time selection of different implementations	Compile time

Table 4-3. *ISpySoft Variability Points and Variation Mechanisms*

Variable Feature	Variability Mechanism	Variability Type
Configurable and extensible user interface	Microsoft Composite UI Application Block (application shell that loads application modules at runtime using mechanisms like lifetime container, dependency injection, providers, services, and service locator)[a]	Inheritance, configuration
Access of additional ISpySoft services via the web	Web service discovery mechanism (possibly UDDI)	Configuration
Optionally integration with third-party enterprise services	Service adapter implementing standardized interface	Inheritance
Support for multiple databases	Data access layer	Configuration, extension point
Configurable case management workflow	Workflow engine (Windows Workflow Foundation)	Configuration

a. More information about the Microsoft Composite UI Application Block (CAB) appears at
   http://practices.gotdotnet.com/projects/cab.

Please note that we present the end result of an iterative process, architectural decisions that were made over multiple iterations. Often, variability mechanisms for some of the variability points will remain undecided until late in the architecture definition process.

Product Line Architecture Definition Process

When working with Software Factories, we have to differentiate between two architecture definition processes. First, during Software Factory development, we define a product line architecture that provides an abstract basis for building product line members. Later on when building product line members, we need to derive a concrete application architecture from this product line architecture individually for each application. However, at this point we are only concerned about the former, since we are creating a Software Factory schema. Deriving an application architecture will be covered in the last chapter where we use the ISpySoft factory to build our first product line member.

While the points listed previously reemphasize the importance of good product line architecture, they do not make any assumptions about the process used to define it. If you look around, you will see that many different approaches are used in the industry to document software architectures. However, all of these approaches can be classified using two (almost) orthogonal dimensions: direction and emphasis. The alternatives for the direction dimension are *top-down* and *bottom-up*, and the two alternatives on the emphasis dimension are *infrastructure first* and *application first*, as shown in Figure 4-2:

- *Top-down*: Based on the requirements, the architecture is defined in an iterative refinement process. An iteration has to be completed and verified in order for the next iteration to start.

- *Bottom-up*: A bottom-up approach can be used to synthesize the architecture of a software system from selected reference implementations. Once this analysis is complete, the architecture is compared against business requirements to determine matches and mismatches.

- *Application first*: This approach starts with the application architecture first while many infrastructure architecture details are assumed and abstracted. The result is the ability to demonstrate application behavior early on, but without the performance, reliability, or generality that comes from an actual infrastructure.

- *Infrastructure first*: This approach first defines the common infrastructure required by families of applications. On top of the infrastructure, applications can be developed incrementally.

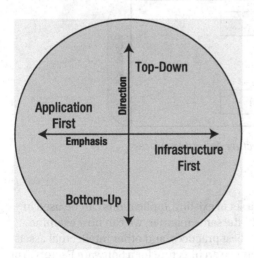

Figure 4-2. *Approaches to architecture definition and discovery*

In reality we often use an iterative "sandwich" approach that switches from top-down to bottom-up and back. By working in both directions we refine an architecture step-by-step until we meet in the middle and bind the results of a top-down analysis to the results of a bottom-up synthesis. Please note that the axes in Figure 4-2 are not perfectly orthogonal as application architecture tends to be top-down whereas infrastructure architecture tends to be bottom-up.

For the ISpySoft case study we first sketch a very high-level application architecture that allows us to look for promising reference implementations. The possible reference implementations are then analyzed bottom-up and matched against the existing requirements.

Figure 4-3 shows the drivers of the architecture definition process. You can see the figure is split into two parts, each relating to chapters of this book. Problem features map to solution features that drive the requirements, as described in the previous chapter, which then drive the architecture of our Software Factory. The architecture specifies the software components, which can be bought, built from scratch, or reused from existing implementations (after making them reusable).

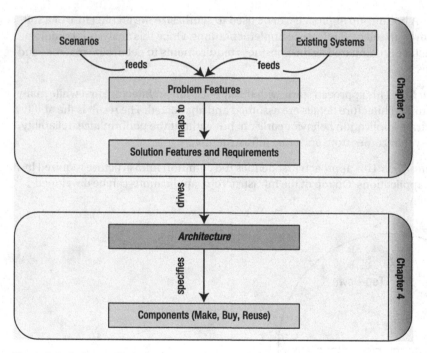

Figure 4-3. *Drivers of a Software Factories architecture definition process*

Reference Architectures

In the previous chapter, we demonstrated how a set of existing applications can be used in order to gather domain concepts and features. In the same manner, we can now examine existing applications in order to extract patterns, best practices, and other intellectual assets. We can then combine these assets to form a reference architecture for a Software Factory. You can think of a reference architecture as an instance of a product line architecture. This reference architecture embodies some or all the common features of the future product line members.

We feel that it is extremely important to emphasize the planned reuse of models, patterns, frameworks, and best practices in this context because successful Software Factory implementation depends heavily on the reuse of these types of assets. Very often we see people struggle only to reinvent an existing solution. In particular, not-so-experienced architects and developers are often unaware of the availability of generic and proven solutions to common problems that encapsulate best practices, experience, and expert knowledge gained over time. We also often see software architects and developers surprised when they hear that there are reference architectures with corresponding frameworks or reference implementations readily available.

> *The software industry has a long history of recreating incompatible solutions to problems that are already solved. [...] If effort had instead been focused on enhancing and optimizing a small number of solutions, developers of [...] software would be reaping the benefits available to developers of hardware.*

——Douglas Schmidt, Michael Stal, Hans Rohnert, Frank Buschmann[7]

In the area of .NET development, you can find plenty of information on patterns, reference architectures, frameworks and best practices published by the *Microsoft patterns & practices group*.[8] Throughout this book, and specifically this chapter, we will use many of the available assets developed by that group. We believe that reusing and adapting proven practices is a key ingredient to successful software development and in particular Software Factory–based projects.

■**Note** In order to avoid confusion, please note that *reference implementation* and *reference architecture* sometimes are used interchangeably. To be 100% correct, a reference implementation is a system that was built to demonstrate best practices or as proof of concept, and this system is based on a reference architecture (doesn't matter whether it's a conventional architecture or an instance of a product line architecture). Analogously, documents about a reference architecture are a *reference architectural description*.

Later on during development of the Software Factory template, we will build a *prototypical application* that is sometimes also called a *reference application*. This prototypical application will be used to harvest more reusable assets, best practices, and patterns, and last but not least it will be used to prove that we can build the type of application that we planned to build using the Software Factory.

 In order to identify reference architectures, patterns, and other reusable assets for the ISpySoft factory, we analyze our solution feature models and compare them with the functionality provided by already existing assets. Very often this analysis goes hand in hand with prototyping to explore parts of the solution for a project at hand that are not covered by the solution feature model. We can also use prototyping in the early stages of factory development when we don't yet have enough knowledge of the solution domain to build solution feature models.

---

7. Douglas Schmidt et al., *Pattern-Oriented Software Architecture*, Vol. 2, *Patterns for Concurrent and Networked Objects* (West Sussex, England: Wiley, 2000)
8. http://msdn.microsoft.com/practices/

As an exercise, we will now compare the ISpySoft requirements to a smart client architecture delivered with the *Smart Client Software Factory* (more on that shortly). Once we identify an initial match, we will refine our discussion further to decide whether a smart client architecture in general is a fitting candidate for the ISpySoft Software Factory.

Smart Client Technology

Before we can begin to analyze any reference architecture in depth, we first need to gather a set of requirements that we think are most relevant and influential in regard to the overall architecture for ISpySoft:

- *Distributed system*: ISpySoft applications are connected in the sense that they use other services over the network (like the ISpySoft-provided premium services) that encapsulate business functionality and make it available to these networked clients.

- *Easy deployment and update*: The client part of ISpySoft applications should support very simple installation on users' machines and automatic update to new versions over the Internet.

- *Offline capability*: The mobile client must support online as well as offline scenarios (at least for short time periods and with limited functionality).

- *Use of local resources*: This allows us to provide, e.g., a rich user experience (compared to web applications), short response times in the UI, locally persisted data (e.g., caching), or access to local operating system services.

 If we compare this list with the choice of available reference architectures and reference implementations, then we come to realize that this feature list is more or less the description of a smart client application as described in the *Smart Client Architecture and Design Guide* from the Microsoft patterns & practices group. Now you might be wondering, "What does 'smart client' actually mean?" Is it only a buzz word, and what are the differences compared to rich and thin clients?

In Figure 4-4, you can see that smart client applications combine the benefits of the rich client and thin client approaches in order to eliminate some of either side's disadvantages. On the one hand, smart clients combine a rich user interface, responsiveness, and flexibility of rich clients, and offline capabilities to reduce network dependency. On the other hand, smart clients also provide typical thin client features such as easy updates and deployment.

In addition to this, smart clients support efficient (or smart) data and connection management, something that neither of the other application types provides. These management features allow smart clients to work either in connected mode by interacting with web services or in disconnected mode by locally caching data and queuing web service requests. Ultimately, this enables seamless integration of online and offline scenarios.

While it is nice to know that we will be building a smart client application, it is more important to know that the Microsoft .NET Framework already provides many features out of the box that enable us to efficiently write smart client applications. For example, the .NET Framework 2.0 provides click-once deployment for easy deployment and update, and many user interface controls to efficiently implement a smart client application. Other features such as smart data handling will require more analysis work. However, the bottom line is that some kind of smart client architecture seems to be a suitable solution for the ISpySoft Software Factory.

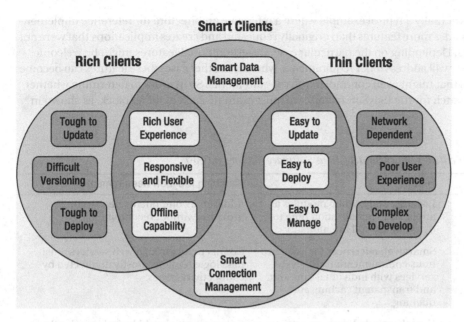

Figure 4-4. *Microsoft's definition of "smart client"*

Smart Client Software Factory (SCSF)[9]

The Smart Client Software Factory provides a range of tools that offer many benefits for architects and developers of smart client applications and components. It is an integrated collection of tools, patterns, source code, and prescriptive instructions that guide developers throughout the development process. Each of the toolkit elements is an expression of recommended practices for smart client application development.

———From SCSF documentation

Only recently, the Microsoft patterns & practices group released the Smart Client Software Factory (SCSF), a new Software Factory that includes an architecture framework for smart clients incorporating existing application blocks like the Composite UI Application Block (CAB) and the Enterprise Library (EntLib). For the purpose of ISpySoft, we will make use of it in several ways:

First of all, SCSF provides an architecture framework that is designed for building smart client applications and that can be integrated into the ISpySoft factory as is. Then, based on this framework, it prescribes a smart client architecture that is well documented and gives architects a great head start. On top of that, it provides a large set of guidance assets that support developers building smart client applications using SCSF.

In order to allow for a quick evaluation of framework features, SCSF comes with a reference implementation that demonstrates important features such as smart web references and the Model-View-Presenter (MVP) pattern. During our evaluation, we came to realize that SCSF provides even more capabilities that we can use for the ISpySoft factory, such as support for an extensible UI.

---

9. http://go.microsoft.com/fwlink/?LinkId=65591

This is actually a typical example where a reference architecture (or reference implementation) provides more features than originally requested and creates implications that were not anticipated. Depending on the particular case, these additional features might be welcome because they will address other requirements, whereas in other cases these features can become limitations that might even contradict other requirements. So in order to determine whether SCSF is a match for the ISpySoft factory, we must examine each building block, as shown in Table 4-4.

Table 4-4. *Matching Features of the Smart Client Software Factory (SCSF)*

Building Block	Feature	Matching ISpySoft Requirement
SCSF	Locating and loading modules at application initialization time to dynamically add functionality.	Additional components need to be provided without recompiling.
SCSF	Smart web references for asynchronous communication with web services with individual time-out, and transparent caching and queuing	Connectivity through web services, business logic remains mostly unaffected by connectivity issues.
SCSF	Loosely coupled components communicating by way of events	Components should be independently developed, tested, and deployed.
Composite UI Application Block	Configurable and extensible UI shell using a plug-in mechanism	Provide flexible UI that adapts to available modules, which can be independently developed, tested, and deployed.
Composite UI Application Block	Model-View-Presenter pattern	Address separation of concerns, e.g., user interface development from pure business logic development.
Enterprise Application Block	Logging and exception handling	Exceptions should be logged in order to trace problems.
.NET Framework 2.0	Click-once deployment and automatic application updates	Provide simple means for deployment of application and future updates.

When matching the features of the SCSF smart client architecture with the ISpySoft requirements, we can see that SCSF seems to be a very good match for ISpySoft. So after analyzing the reference implementation not only can we reuse a proven architecture, but we can also get our hands on a reusable, extensible, and flexible framework that supports this architecture. Not to mention the developer guidance support that we will reuse later in this book. On top of all that, we will show how we can potentially even reuse part of the SCSF schema, or in other words, how we can specialize the horizontal Smart Client Software Factory to create the vertical ISpySoft Software Factory. We basically kill quite a few birds with one stone.

In other cases, you might not be that lucky finding reusable assets with such a good fit. A reference implementation could show architecture design principles without providing a ready-made framework. Or you might actually have a reusable framework available, but without any good architecture guidance incorporating best practices and patterns. Or, a reference architecture might fit for the most part, but contradict some other requirements. Nevertheless, we believe it will always pay off to do a thorough analysis of available reference architectures to prevent reinvention of the wheel.

HORIZONTAL AND VERTICAL SOFTWARE FACTORIES

When talking about the scope of Software Factories, we can distinguish between horizontal and vertical factories. A horizontal factory targets a family of products that have a common architecture and implementation technology, i.e., a common solution domain. In contrast, a vertical factory targets a family of products that have a common industry or business focus, i.e., a common problem domain.

SCSF is a horizontal Software Factory. It delivers reusable assets and prescribes a flexible architecture for building applications in the solution domain of smart clients, or to be more specific, the SCSF is a Software Factory for the horizontal domain of building smart client applications. From the perspective of a developer, SCSF is installed on a developer's computer and extends the integrated development environment (in this case, Visual Studio 2005) by providing reusable assets and guidance. We will specialize this horizontal factory to create the vertical ISpySoft factory, which targets the problem domain of private investigation. This means that we will reuse, specialize, and extend some of the parts provided by SCSF.

Architectural Description

Back in Chapter 1, we first mentioned the IEEE Standard 1471-2000, *Recommended Practice for Architectural Description of Software-Intensive Systems*, a standard that should help us to document the product line architecture. The intent of the standard is described in its abstract as follows:

> *This recommended practice addresses the activities of the creation, analysis, and sustainment of architecture of software-intensive systems, and the recording of such architectures in terms of architectural descriptions.*[10]

Software Factories build on the recommendations of IEEE 1471-2000 by incorporating its two major concepts, viewpoints and views, to support the development of product line members. After a short introduction to viewpoints and views, we will switch to our case study to give you some concrete examples, and we will use architectural viewpoints to describe a product line architecture. In the next chapter, we will then show how the Software Factory schema incorporates and extends these concepts. The viewpoints developed here will be the basis for the factory schema.

Definition of Viewpoint

Viewpoints are used to document the software architecture of a family of software systems in a way that meets the needs of specific stakeholders. The use of different viewpoints to describe different aspects of the architecture provides a separation of concerns. Viewpoints can contain other viewpoints to structure the architecture documentation, and it is the sum of all viewpoints together that describe an architecture sufficiently.

---

10. IEEE-SA Standards Board, *IEEE Recommended Practice for Architectural Description of Software-Intensive Systems* (New York, NY: IEEE, 2000. IEEE Std 1471-2000)

The following attributes specify a viewpoint according to IEEE 1471-2000 recommended practice:

- Viewpoint name

- Stakeholders and their concerns addressed by the viewpoint

- The language, modeling technique, or analytical method that will be used to create views based upon this viewpoint

- Other information about the viewpoint (e.g., source, author, date, references to other literature, etc.)

Definition of View

A view is an instance of a viewpoint that describes certain aspects of a particular software system as defined by the associated viewpoint. Each view is associated with exactly one viewpoint. Furthermore, the view uses the mechanisms (language, model, etc.) defined by the viewpoint to document the relevant aspects of the system.

The following are the attributes of views, based on IEEE 1471-2000:

- Identifier and introductory information

- Representation of the system as defined by the associated viewpoint, e.g., as a model or textual description

- Configuration information

We can compare the relationship of view and viewpoint to that of class and object. A viewpoint is the abstract definition, and a view is the concrete instance of its associated viewpoint. A viewpoint used in an architectural description should have one or more views (otherwise it would be obsolete).

We can use viewpoints to define how an architecture should be documented through views. Specifically, we create views for each of these viewpoints when developing an application.

Viewpoints in the Software Factory Schema

While these attributes of viewpoints and views are the bare minimum required by the recommended practice, the Software Factories methodology extends this recommendation by requiring additional information for each viewpoint, including information about the activities performed to create the views, and the assets supplied by the factory to support those activities. Furthermore, a viewpoint can specify entry and exit criteria for the activities it defines, that is, pre- and post-conditions that apply when an application developer creates work products. This additional information is used to support the application development process.

Later on when we get more into the details of the Software Factory schema, we will refer to views as work products, as this is a more meaningful term in the context of software development.

ISpySoft Viewpoints

Now, before we get lost in the theory of viewpoints and views, let's quickly move on with some practical examples. The following section provides insight into several viewpoints that are used to describe the ISpySoft factory. For easier readability and organizational reasons, we use a hierarchical structure for the ISpySoft viewpoints as shown in the following list (the viewpoints that are shown as examples in this book are in italic):

- Business (problem) viewpoint

- Requirements (solution) viewpoint

- Architecture viewpoint

  - Logical viewpoint

  - Control flow viewpoint

  - *Distributed system viewpoint* (shown later in this chapter)

  - *Component structure viewpoint* (shown later in this chapter)

- Implementation viewpoint

  - *Business workflow viewpoint* (shown later in this chapter)

  - *Data entity viewpoint* (shown later in this chapter)

  - Physical data structure viewpoint

  - User Experience (UX) viewpoint

  - Solution structure viewpoint

- Test viewpoint

  - Unit test viewpoint

  - Integration test viewpoint

  - System test viewpoint

In addition, we show the Smart Client Factory viewpoints, which are provided by SCSF and absorbed and specialized by the ISpySoft Factory. Each viewpoint defines the views derived from it, and defines the context in which the views appear. Some views will actually be provided by the factory as prototypical work products (a certain type of asset), which will be used in the development of each product line member, after being customized to reflect the product line member's specific requirements.

You potentially can reuse some of these viewpoints in your own factories in case they also involve smart clients, tailoring them to your needs as necessary. If your factories do not involve smart clients, then the viewpoints provided by the SCSF may not apply. The other viewpoints are less tied to the smart client architecture, however, and may prove to be more reusable in other factories.

■**Tip** To help you define viewpoints, you can analyze the architectural description (class diagrams, state diagrams, deployment diagrams, etc.) of your existing reference implementations. These artifacts are the views of your existing reference implementations, and you can reverse-engineer from them the viewpoints on which they are based.

Data Entity Viewpoint

Data entities are refined representations of the business entities that were identified during requirements analysis. A typical graphical representation for views conforming to this viewpoint is a class diagram as provided, e.g., by UML. Therefore, the description of the associated viewpoint in Table 4-5 should sound pretty familiar to you. However, instead of using UML for designing class diagrams, for ISpySoft we actually chose to create data entity views with the help of Visual Studio 2005 class diagrams.

Table 4-5. *Data Entity Viewpoint*

Attribute	Description
Name	Data entity viewpoint
Stakeholders	Architects, developers, database designers
Concerns	Static structure of data entities derived from business entities
Language	Visual Studio Class Designer diagrams

Figure 4-5 shows an example of a data entity view as it is used by the server components of ISpySoft applications. It shows several data entities related to case management, such as the Case or the Evidence class. In a factory schema, there can be many other static structure viewpoints like a viewpoint describing service information models and message type definitions.

■**Note** A view does not have to be a graphical model created with a modeling tool. In this particular case, a data entity view represented by class definitions in source code form is a legitimate alternative to a diagrammatic view. Furthermore, we could define several children of the data entity viewpoint, one that describes graphical views based on the Visual Studio Class Designer, and one that describes textual views based on the C# code editor. The Visual Studio Solution Explorer could actually provide a third child of the data entity viewpoint that describes views of the solution structure viewpoint.

VS class diagrams are living documentation. Classes in diagrams correspond one-to-one with class definitions in source code. Since VS class diagrams provide round-trip engineering, the data entity views will automatically change when developers change the definition of an underlying class during implementation.

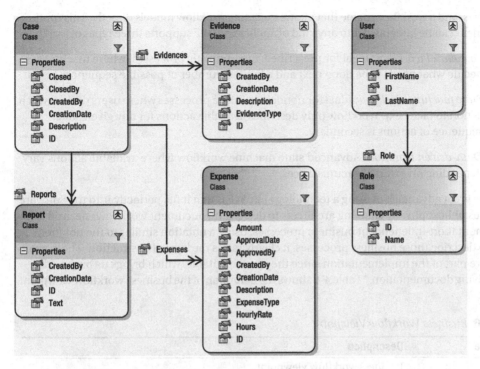

Figure 4-5. *Data entity view for entities related to case management*

Business Workflow Viewpoint

The business workflow viewpoint is one way to document how a system behaves at runtime. Besides workflows, there are other types of dynamic behavior of a system:

- Business processes
- Interaction between components
- Message exchange with a web service
- Data flow between components
- System state change upon events

UML 2.0 provides six diagram types that allow architects and developers to model a system's behavior, such as activity, sequence, or state diagrams. Since we expect most of our readers to be somewhat familiar with UML, we do not dive into theoretical detail here, but rather continue with an exciting new technology that was incorporated in the ISpySoft Software Factory: Workflow Foundation (WF).[11]

A brand new Microsoft technology for workflow modeling, Workflow Foundation consists of two parts: a designer integrated into Visual Studio that allows architects and developers to create

---

workflows, and a workflow engine that allows executing workflow models directly. This runtime component can be integrated into any kind of application. WF supports three types of workflow:

- *Sequential workflow.* Ideal for prescribed, deterministic processes, where machines decide what needs to be done next and a limited number of possible sequences exists.

- *State machine workflow.* Ideal for nondeterministic processes where users decide which action to take next. Workflow only describes available actions for any given state, sequence of actions is secondary.

- *Data-driven workflow.* Advanced state machine workflow where available actions vary depending on external circumstances.

The great advantage of using a technology like WF is that it fits perfectly into the Software Factories philosophy. By enabling architects to design and document workflows derived from implementation-independent business processes, using a notation similar to the notation used to describe those business processes, it clearly raises the level of abstraction. These workflows are part of the implementation since they are executable, which brings us back to the term "living documentation." Table 4-6 shows the definition of the business workflow viewpoint.

Table 4-6. *Business Workflow Viewpoint*

Attribute	Description
Name	Business workflow viewpoint
Stakeholders	Business logic developers
Concerns	Business processes, dynamic workflows of business documents
Language	Workflow Foundation diagrams

The business workflow viewpoint is created during the definition of the ISpySoft architecture. A typical view based on this viewpoint is shown in Figure 4-6. Upon submitting a new expense, the workflow enforces the expense policy, which is twofold: regular expenses will have to be approved only if they are above a certain threshold. In contrast, bribe money paid to informants will have to be approved by a manager in every case. For now, this figure is only for demonstration purposes. Later in Chapter 7, which explores the Software Factory template, we will cover Windows Workflow Foundation in more depth when we actually implement the ISpySoft Software Factory template. As you might have noticed, WF would be an ideal mechanism with which to support the variable feature *Customizable Workflows* from the solution feature model.

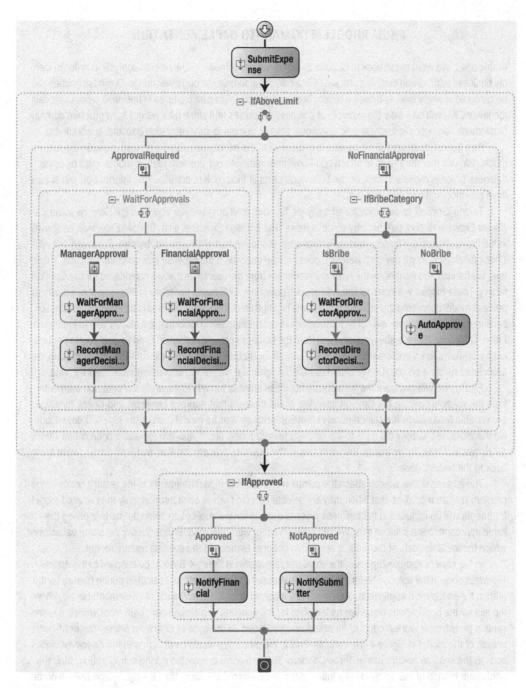

Figure 4-6. *Approval workflow upon submission of a new expense report*

FROM PROBLEM DOMAIN TO IMPLEMENTATION

At this point, we want to cut back to Chapter 3, where we performed a requirements analysis in order to identify business entities and business processes in a particular domain, among other things. Business entities can be captured in entity models (state), whereas business processes can be captured in business process models (behavior). We will now take the example of business processes and show how we got from problem domain (implementation-agnostic business processes) over solution domain to implementation (executable workflows).

As a general rule, we will not be able to capture all of the information about a problem domain in a feature model. We will therefore need to attach additional information to our problem feature model, e.g., by using business process models to capture the behavioral parts in the problem domain. This information will in turn have common and variable elements.

Taking ISpySoft as an example: let's say we found that all private eyes who *Manage Expenses* also *Create Expense Report*, but that only some of those who *Manage Expenses* also *Approve Expenses*, as shown in the ISpySoft problem feature model. Furthermore, we found that of those who *Approve Expenses*, not all *Check for Bribes*. So we need a business process model describing the expense management process. Therefore, we harvest and harmonize the business processes from the examples that we considered for the ISpySoft factory. These models will look a lot like a WF model, but where a WF model describes implementation, a business process model describing the problem domain will be implementation-agnostic. This is an important distinction, because business analysts will not buy into business process modeling tools that are closely tied to implementation. Of course, there is always a mapping from the business process definition used by analysts to the business workflows to be implemented. We would use WF or BizTalk if we plan to execute the diagram using the associated runtime engine. Or, we would use UML diagrams if we plan to implement workflows by hand.

Finally, we will compare the harmonized business process models to separate the common elements from the variable ones. In the ISpySoft case, we would discover that *Approve Expenses* and *Check for Bribes* are variable features. In the comprehensive ISpySoft problem feature model (part of the ISpySoft download), we therefore add an optional node to the problem feature model under *Approve Expenses* node called *Check for Bribes*. But how do we handle the variations in the business process models, and how do we relate them back to the feature nodes?

The answer is that we can attach the common and variable model fragments to the feature nodes in the problem feature model, so that when they are selected during feature configuration, only the required model fragments will be included in the business process models for the application being defined. Applying the same approach to the solution side, we can create a set of workflow models that display the same variability, where the variable parts of the models are tied to optional features in the solution feature model.

In the case of *Approve Expenses*, the entire diagram shown in Figure 4-6 would be attached to the *Approve Expenses* node in the solution feature model. If the *Approve Expenses* feature is selected during feature configuration for an ISpySoft application, then the entire diagram is included in the set of implementable workflow models for the application and serves as template for the concrete implementation, or in other words, it represents a prototypical work product of its associated viewpoint. In the case of *Check for Bribes*, the right-hand branch of the model in Figure 4-6 is variable. This is the piece that would be attached to the *Check for Bribes* node in the solution feature model. If the *Check for Bribes* feature is selected during configuration, then the right-hand branch of the diagram is included. If the feature is not selected, then the right-hand branch of the diagram becomes a pass-through.

Of course, the technique of attaching model fragments to feature models to support variability can be used for other types of information, e.g., for business entities.

Smart Client Software Factory Viewpoints

An essential part of the ISpySoft architecture is the smart client architecture. As mentioned in the introduction to the Smart Client Software Factory, this architecture is mainly prescribed by the smart client framework that we incorporate in the ISpySoft factory. In order to describe a smart client architecture sufficiently, we will need a number of viewpoints, such as viewpoints that describe user experience and flow of control.

We have a special situation here as we will be consuming an existing factory. Therefore, we'd like to perform an experiment that we think will be pretty interesting. Earlier in this book we mentioned that it will be possible in the future to build supply chains of Software Factories where we consume and specialize other Software Factories to build our own. Now we have such a case here, and we want to show how this could work in practice.

At the time of writing, the Smart Client Software Factory is still under development and has no explicit Software Factory schema. But let's assume it has one. In that case, what would this factory specialization look like?

Right now our goal regarding the Software Factory schema is to identify and define viewpoints that are relevant to building ISpySoft applications where the front-end is realized as a smart client.

So here's the clue. If the Smart Client Software Factory had a schema, we might simply copy its viewpoints, and use them in the schemas of other factories, such as the ISpySoft factory, modifying them if necessary by adding, removing, or modifying the descriptions for their work products, activities, and assets.

Now, let's get back to what we have today. While the SCSF does not contain a schema, its documentation does use a set of viewpoints to organize the architecture description. The only information it provides about each viewpoint is the name. However, additional information can be inferred from the views conforming to those viewpoints supplied by the documentation. We have reverse engineered initial definitions of those viewpoints from the documentation, using the format we used for the definitions of the other ISpySoft viewpoints, as shown in Table 4-7. In the next chapter, we will enhance these definitions to support software development, along with the definitions of the other ISpySoft viewpoints, by adding descriptions of work products, activities, and assets, as required by the Software Factories methodology.

Table 4-7. *Consumed Smart Client Software Factory Viewpoints*

Attribute	Description
Smart Client User Experience (UX) Viewpoint	
Name	Smart client user experience viewpoint.
Stakeholders	Users, UI designers, UI developers.
Concerns	Describes the concepts and ways a user interacts with a smart client application, e.g., workspace layout, navigating the UI, and initiating events.
Language	Informal wire frames, working prototype UIs using Rapid Application Development (RAD).

Table 4-7. *Consumed Smart Client Software Factory Viewpoints (Continued)*

Attribute	Description
Smart Client Logical Viewpoint	
Name	Smart client logical viewpoint.
Stakeholders	Architects, developers.
Concerns	Describes the relationships between the logical elements of a smart client application, e.g., classes, interfaces, and patterns.
Language	Class diagrams.
Additional information	This viewpoint will be absorbed by ISpySoft-specific logical viewpoint.
Smart Client Implementation Viewpoint	
Name	Smart client implementation viewpoint.
Stakeholders	Developers.
Concerns	Describes the solution structure of a smart client application project in Visual Studio 2005.
Language	Visual Studio 2005 Solution Explorer.
Additional information	This viewpoint will be absorbed by ISpySoft-specific implementation viewpoint.
Smart Client Control Flow Viewpoint	
Name	Smart client control flow viewpoint.
Stakeholders	Architects, UI developers.
Concerns	Describes the flow of control between different application elements, such as modules, module controllers, service agents, etc.
Language	Sequence diagrams.
Additional information	This viewpoint will be absorbed by ISpySoft-specific control flow viewpoint.
Smart Client Deployment Viewpoint	
Name	Smart client deployment viewpoint.
Stakeholders	Architects, developers, system administrators.
Concerns	Map smart client software components to system configurations.
Language	Deployment diagrams.
Additional information	This viewpoint will be absorbed by the distributed system viewpoint (as shown later in this chapter).

More information on these smart client viewpoints can be inferred from the SCSF Help under "Architectural Views."

Component Structure Viewpoint

The component structure viewpoint now puts the smart client application into an enterprise application context. The viewpoint as defined in Table 4-8 allows for creating rather informal models, as it is used only to support communication among stakeholders, and not to derive an actual implementation.

Table 4-8. *Component Structure Viewpoint*

Attribute	Description
Name	Component structure viewpoint
Stakeholders	Marketing, architects, developers
Concerns	Components and logical distribution of components
Language	Informal view, e.g., use of UML component and deployment diagrams

Figure 4-7 shows the component structure view for a prototypical application built with the ISpySoft factory. The diagram illustrates part of the product line architecture for the factory by describing the component structure that any ISpySoft product line member will have. It is based on the modular three-tiered component architecture for distributed applications in .NET suggested in a Microsoft guide for designing distributed applications[12] and shows the necessary functional components of the system and their relationships. The numbered components in the view are described as follows:

1. *Security, communication, and operation management* are cross-cutting concerns (or aspects) that span the system from front-end to back-end.

2. *Smart client applications* are constructed as described in the smart client viewpoints. The *ISpySoft work item* is the root work item, the lifetime container for the smart client application. A smart client consists of a configurable shell with related components such as workspaces. At runtime the shell loads one or more smart client modules containing additional work items and smart parts (UI controls).

3. Smart client modules are deployment units. Smart parts, presenters, business logic classes, and service agents are hosted in work item containers. *Smart parts* represent viewable components that get loaded into workspaces by the shell. *Presenters* encapsulate the UI logic by wiring smart parts to business logic components. *Service agents* wrap web service references by transparently providing caching and queuing of web service requests.

---

12. http://msdn.microsoft.com/library/default.asp?url=/library/en-us/dnbda/html/distapp.asp

4. All ISpySoft *business logic* is exposed through web services. The two placeholders stand for services such as the case management or the location service. Web services allow easy traversal of firewall boundaries. Furthermore, should ISpySoft decide in the future to support smart clients on additional platforms such as on PDAs running Windows Mobile, the business services ensure interoperability and might not even have to be modified.

5. A layer of *adapters* provides seamless access to data sources such as SQL Server and flat XML files (e.g., with workflow definitions). Furthermore, business logic can access other web services, which are encapsulated by adapters similar to web service agents on the smart client side. Examples of external web services are the ones exposed at the ISpySoft homesite as well as legacy applications that are wrapped and exposed through web services for interoperability.

6. *Data sources* like SQL or Oracle database that store the applications data.

7. *ISpySoft homesite* provides premium services hosted at the central ISpySoft server such as the IDCheck service. These services can be accessed from back-end services at the client site as well as directly from smart clients installed on mobile devices.

■**Note** Premium services running at the ISpySoft location are built exactly the same way as business logic web services hosted at the client site. Since all of these web services follow the same principles, it is irrelevant for smart client developers whether they are developing against a local or a remote web service. Therefore, to reduce the complexity of our case study (e.g., to enable simpler deployment and installation of the solution), we decided to scope out the premium web services because they will not contribute any additional educational value. This means that our actual case study is limited to a back-end server installation with a smart client front-end.

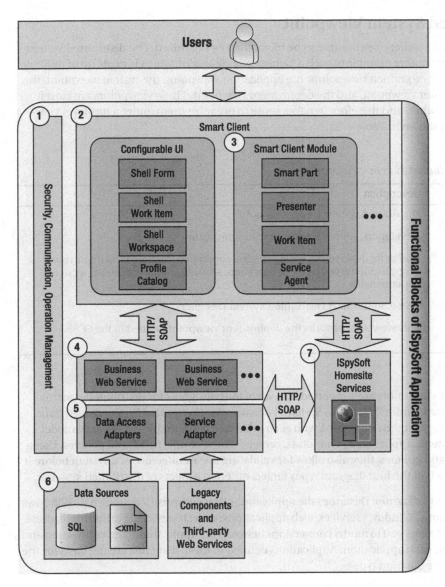

Figure 4-7. *ISpySoft component structure view*

Distributed System Viewpoint

As we mentioned earlier, viewpoints can be hierarchically organized. The distributed system viewpoint is yet another example of such a hierarchical viewpoint, which is made up of multiple subordinated, finer-grained viewpoints: the application viewpoint, the system viewpoint, the logical data-center viewpoint, and the deployment viewpoint. These viewpoints are closely related to each other, and therefore it makes sense to organize them under a top-level viewpoint, which is shown in Table 4-9.

Table 4-9. *Distributed System Viewpoint*

Attribute	Description
Name	Distributed system viewpoint.
Stakeholders	Developers, software engineers, administrators.
Concerns	Design for deployment through logical separation, and physical deployment of applications, policies, configuration, security, communication, service dependencies.
Language	Visual Studio 2005 Distributed System Designers.
Additional information	This viewpoint absorbs the deployment viewpoint defined in the SCSF.

These four viewpoints are supported by a set of four designers for distributed systems included in Visual Studio 2005 Team System, known as the *Distributed System Design Suite*. These designers are tightly integrated with each other and allow architects to easily model distributed systems applications, endpoints, servers, zones, connections, and policies. Using requirements and policies, they also allow for validating the architecture of a system before it is deployed. Each of the four diagram types targets different aspects of distributed systems:

- *Application diagram*: Describes the applications that comprise a system, e.g., Windows applications, Windows services, web applications, or web services. Furthermore, these diagrams allow you to model connections between the applications and connection end points for each application. Applications defined in these diagrams are the basis for the other three diagram types.

- *Logical data-center diagram*: Describes the logical servers in a data-center. Servers can be placed in zones that define policies and in- and outbound connection endpoints. This diagram provides a logical view of the networked environment as it abstracts away technical details such as network protocols, firewalls, and routers. It is also scale invariant, meaning that it depicts the types of servers found in the environment, but not the number of servers of each type.

- *System diagram*: Allows for modeling networked systems and the connections between them. Systems may contain applications and nested systems. This lets architects model large-scale service-oriented systems and create their service contracts, without prior knowledge of the inner workings and content of individual systems.

- *Deployment diagram*: Allows you to describe the deployment of applications onto a data center specified by a logical data-center diagram. These diagrams can be validated against the policies and requirements set for each application, server, and zone, in order to ensure that applications are configured correctly for the servers on which they are deployed, and vice versa. Ultimately, this tool creates deployment reports that are used to support communications between system developers and the administrators who will maintain the deployed system.

We use three of these diagrams to capture the distributed system architecture of the prototypical ISpySoft application. Let's start with the *application view* shown in Figure 4-8, which documents the logical partitioning of the prototypical ISpySoft application into components. The ISpySoft smart client application requires connections to three web applications, each exposing one web service that incorporates the common business logic. All three web applications depend on the ISpySoftDB database.

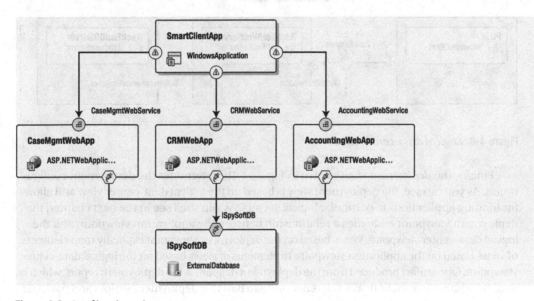

Figure 4-8. *Application view*

One extensibility requirement of the ISpySoft factory is that new business functionality can be provided through additional web services. The application designer lets architects easily model custom extensions for product line members provided by web applications and exposed through web services. The architects can generate partial implementations of these additional web services and the web applications that host them from project templates with the click of a button.

The logical *data-center view* in Figure 4-9 determines which logical servers and client machines are available for a particular system. *Logical* means that each server could in reality be a web server farm, a clustered SQL server, or even a single desktop machine running multiple server applications. The ISpySoftBackEndZone implies that the web and the database server run in an environment with tightened security, as is common for web applications accessible from an intranet or the Internet.

Another extensibility requirement of the ISpySoft factory is that it allows for integrating other web services, such as third-party services or web services encapsulating legacy applications. The logical data-center view lets architects extend the networked environment if required for a particular product line member.

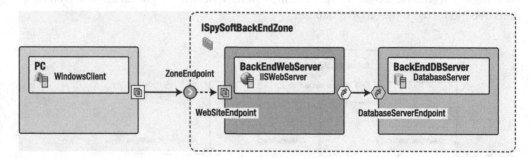

Figure 4-9. *Logical data-center view*

Finally, the *deployment view*, shown in Figure 4-10, determines the deployment configuration. As you can see, the deployment view is based on the logical data-center view and allows for binding applications to particular logical servers. As you shall see in the next chapter, the deployment viewpoint embodies a relationship between the application viewpoint and the logical data-center viewpoint. Views based on the deployment viewpoint explicitly map elements of views based on the application viewpoint to elements of views based on the logical data-center viewpoint. One artifact produced from the deployment diagram is the deployment report, which is used by administrators, both as a reference and as a basis for deployment scripts and packages.

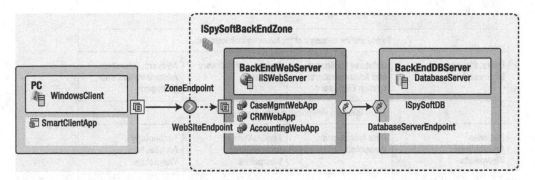

Figure 4-10. *Deployment view*

When deploying a product line member that incorporates additional web services for custom business logic or legacy systems, developers can visually bind these applications to the appropriate servers. These changes then will be reflected in deployment reports.

TAXONOMY OF VIEWPOINTS

The Open Group provides a great article about architectural descriptions on their web site, "Developing Architecture Views—Introduction,"[13] which we'd like to recommend to you. First of all this article provides more in-depth and easy-to-understand information on architectural descriptions using viewpoints and views based on IEEE 1471-2000. Furthermore, it also provides a taxonomy of views, which is a comprehensive collection of views and their respective viewpoints that are widely used to describe software architectures. This taxonomy is shown in Figure 4-11, which is provided courtesy of The Open Group (please note that since we are documenting product lines and not one-off systems, we have adapted the original figure by replacing all occurrences of "View" with "Viewpoint"). This taxonomy provides a great starting point for high-level and more detailed viewpoints that we can include in a Software Factory schema, although in practice, most of the viewpoints used to support software development in a typical software factory will be more fine-grained viewpoints nested within the viewpoints defined by this taxonomy.

---

13. The Open Group, "Developing Architecture Views—Introduction" (The Open Group, 2002. http://www.opengroup.org/architecture/togaf8-doc/arch/p4/views/vus_intro.htm)

To address the concerns of the following stakeholders...			
Users, Planners, Business Management	Database Designers and Administrators, System Engineers	System and Software Engineers	Aquirers, Operators, Administrators and Managers
... the following viewpoints may be developed			
Business Architecture Viewpoints	Data Architecture Viewpoints	Applications Architecture Viewpoints	Technology Architecture Viewpoints
Business Function Viewpoint	Data Entity Viewpoint	Software Engineering Viewpoint	Networked Computing/ Hardware Viewpoint
Business Services Viewpoint			
Business Process Viewpoint			
Business Information Viewpoint			
Business Locations Viewpoint			Communications Engineering Viewpoint
Business Logistics Viewpoint	Data Flow Viewpoint (Organization Data Use)	Applications Interoperability Viewpoint	
People Viewpoint (Organization Chart)			Processing Viewpoint
Workflow Viewpoint			
Usability Viewpoint			
Business Strategy and Goals Viewpoint	Logical Data Viewpoint	Software Distribution Viewpoint	Cost Viewpoint
Business Objectives Viewpoint			
Business Rules Viewpoint			
Business Events Viewpoint			Standards Viewpoint
Business Performance Viewpoint			
	System Engineering Viewpoint		
Enterprise Security Viewpoint			
Enterprise Manageability Viewpoint			
Enterprise Quality of Service Viewpoint			
Enterprise Mobility Viewpoint			

Figure 4-11. *Taxonomy of architecture viewpoints*

Summary

The Software Factory architecture described in this chapter is part of the Software Factory schema and will provide the basis for the Software Factory template. We discussed two very important concepts in this chapter. First, we talked about product line architectures, which support variants of products through variability mechanisms. Second, we talked about how we can describe architectures in a systematic way using views that conform to well-defined viewpoints. The Software Factory schema incorporates both concepts and therefore, among other things, provides the means to document the architecture of products developed using the Software Factory.

Our focus was to showcase modeling techniques, editors, and tools that not only create pretty diagrams, but at the same time create implementation—in other words, living documentation (taken from the ISpySoft prototypical application). When the underlying implementation changes, living documentation should not disconnect from it. However, please keep in mind that nondiagrammatic views (e.g., a set of source code files) are just as valid and due to the lack of "good-enough" modeling tools will make up the major share of the views created for product line members in most factories.

Even though different product lines will have different sets of viewpoints, we are convinced that product lines in similar domains will have similar, overlapping sets of viewpoints (e.g., smart client applications in different business domains). Hopefully in the future there will be libraries of commonly occurring viewpoints that can be used as the basis for rapidly building Software Factory schemas.

Checkpoint

After this chapter, you should be familiar with the following concepts required for the Software Factory design:

- *Software Factory schema*: Core concept of the Software Factories technology, which builds on the concept of architectural description standards based on views and viewpoints defined by IEEE-1471 (we will further elaborate the schema concept in the next chapter).

- *Architecture variability mechanisms and binding time*: Allow for addressing the variabilities in the solution domain where binding times determine when decisions on variabilities are bound.

- *Architecture definition process*: Top-down, bottom-up, application-first, and infrastructure-first approaches that let you iteratively define an architecture through progressive refinement.

- *Reference architectures*: Provide proven solutions to known problems. Reference implementations conform to reference architectures, and act as repositories of reusable assets that can be harvested and used in Software Factories.

- *Architectural description*: Multiple views based on well-defined viewpoints allow for describing an architecture in a structured way.

CHAPTER 5

∎∎∎

Software Factory Schema: Application Development Process

In this chapter, we show how Software Factories extend architectural descriptions based on IEEE 1471-2000, like the one we introduced in the last chapter, with concepts such as work products, activities, assets, and mappings. Furthermore, we show how the Software Factory schema describes, organizes, and interrelates these concepts, providing a model of the solution domain that supports the identification and development of interrelated domain-specific languages (DSLs), and forms the basis of a highly pragmatic approach to model-driven development. Therefore, we discuss in this chapter

- Application development with Software Factories
- Models, model transformations, and generators
- Implementation of a Software Factory schema modeling language

When developing and using a Software Factory, you get in touch with two different development processes: First of all there is the Software Factory development process, which prescribes how the factory is being built. Second, there is the application development process, which we focus on in this section and which defines how a factory is used to build a particular software system.

No matter whether you follow a waterfall, iterative, agile, or other development process, conventional application development and application development using Software Factories have most project phases in common, such as requirements specification, requirements analysis, design, implementation, testing, and deployment. Differences between these forms of application development occur mainly in individual life-cycle activities, such as during requirements analysis. Therefore, we highlight the life-cycle activities that are influenced by our product line approach the most.

■Note In this book, we can merely focus on technical aspects. Organizational and managerial aspects of the application development process are just as important. More information on these aspects together with best practices can be found, e.g., in *Software Product Lines*[1] and to some degree in *Software Architecture in Practice.*[2]

Application Development with Software Factories

The following list of life-cycle activities describes a small subset of the information we can capture in the schema about the application development process to benefit the application developer using a factory. In the context of Visual Studio Team Suite, a factory might, e.g., provide a process template to guide the application development team through the development process:

- *Application requirements analysis*: Determine the specific requirements for an application that will be built using a Software Factory. In a Software Factory environment, this requirements analysis is limited to variable requirements because the common features and some information about the variable features are already provided by the factory.

- *Application feature model configuration (part of requirements analysis)*: Determine for each variable feature provided by the factory whether it is included or excluded.

- *Application implementation*: Beside configuring and assembling common features from existing assets, most effort during this activity goes into implementation of features specific to the application that are not provided by the factory (e.g., extensions, adapters, etc.), and into the implementation of features that are highly variable and therefore not easy to implement using configuration and assembly. A factory often supports the application developer by providing guidance that suggests what to do and how to do it at each point in the development process. Also, it often provides assets, such as examples, patterns, templates, wizards, libraries, and designers, that help the application developer to accomplish what has been suggested. The same is true for testing, where functionality of newly developed components needs to be tested independently and in context of its integration with existing, common components.

- *Software Factory evolution—feedback into the Software Factory*: Each application development cycle poses the opportunity to add additional core assets to the Software Factory, and to refine existing core assets and the application development process.

---

1. Paul Clements and Linda Northrop, *Software Product Lines—Practices and Patterns* (Boston, MA: Addison Wesley, 2002)
2. Len Bass, Paul Clements, and Rick Kazman, *Software Architecture in Practice, Second Edition* (Boston, MA: Addison Wesley, 2003)

Application Requirements Analysis

Using a Software Factory approach greatly facilitates requirements analysis for a particular product. In fact, requirements analysis has already been done for the most part during the creation of the problem and solution feature models and the mapping between them. Figure 5-1 shows the process involved in analyzing the requirements of a specific application in the context of a factory.

- Gather problem statements from the customer (i.e., description of the problems that the application is going to solve), just as we did during Software Factory specification. However, note that the problem statements gathered here are specific to the application being developed. Unlike the problem statements captured during Software Factory specification, they are not required to be representative of problem statements across the entire domain.

- Map application problem statements to the problem statements addressed by the Software Factory: identify the problems to be solved by the application being developed that are addressed by the Software Factory, which at the same time is a harmonization process. The result is a subset of the problem statements solved by the Software Factory, which contains all of the common problem statements and a selection of variable ones. The rest of the problems to be solved by the application do not map to any factory problem statements. The presence of unmapped problem statements indicates that the application requires feature extensions or custom features that must be defined and built specifically for it.

- The problem statements specific to the application are refined into problem features, which then are mapped to solution features and requirements the same way we showed for the Software Factory problem statements in Chapter 3.

■**Note** At the beginning of the application development process, we gather problem statements for the same reason we did so during factory specification. By looking at the problem statements, we can come up with new and innovative ways to solve business problems without implying any specific solution as we would if we focused on requirements instead.

Figure 5-2 shows a small part of the requirements analysis performed during development of the first application based on our ISpySoft Software Factory. During this requirements analysis, problem statements from a fictitious customer were gathered. Out of these, this figure shows how problem statements #27 and #28 were mapped to a Software Factory solution feature, the *Customizable Workflow* feature inside *Investigation and Case Management*.

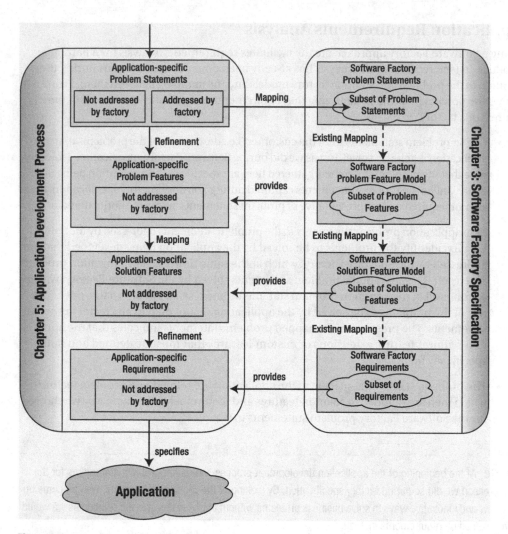

Figure 5-1. *Requirements analysis for applications using Software Factories*

During problem statement verification, it turns out that problem statement #28, *Printing for Archiving*, currently is not supported, a problem statement mismatch. Fortunately, our *Customizable Workflow* supports additional *event handlers* for WF workflows. The result is a variable problem feature, for which we have to perform additional analysis to ensure an accurate understanding of the problem and a valid solution strategy. Finally, these additional requirements need to be documented properly, just as it was done in the specification phase of the Software Factory.

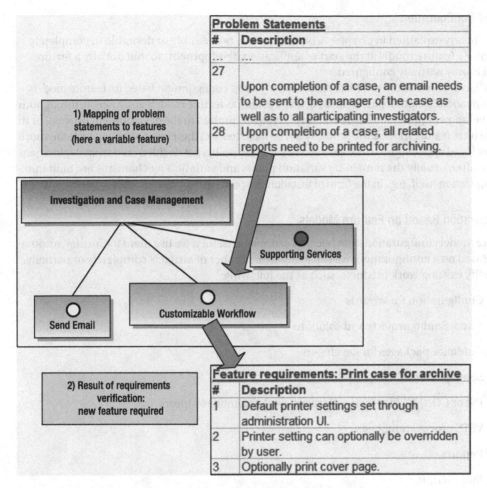

Figure 5-2. *New variable feature discovered during requirements analysis.*

Application Feature Model Configuration

In a Software Factory, a feature model describes the superset of the features of all of the members of a product family. The same way you can configure a new PC on a computer manufacturer's web site, you can configure a feature model to specify a new product family member. The resulting artifact is called a *configuration*, as previously explained in Chapter 3.

Feature model configuration is really a part of application requirements analysis. During feature model configuration, we need to determine for each optional feature whether it is included or excluded by the application. Note that common features, as per definition, will always be part of a configuration and will therefore always be included in the resulting application. In some cases, you may additionally specify property values of variable features.

Staged Configuration

As we already explained in Chapter 3, oftentimes it is not feasible or desirable to completely configure a feature model at the start of application development, so that initially a feature model is only partially configured.

When it comes to the technical realization of staged configuration based on feature models, decisions about variation points can be delayed as long as feature models are available throughout the development process. This availability is typically limited to the development process, or in other words, feature models will probably not be included and therefore not be available anymore in a deployed application. In the case where variation points get decided on during deployment time or after, usually the remaining variation points and variation mechanisms are built into the application itself, e.g., in the form of installation options or application configuration settings.

Configuration Based on Feature Models

Feature model configurations can become especially useful if we use them for further automation. Based on a configuration, we can generate a number of artifacts completely or partially, or modify existing work products, such as the following:

- Configuration for wizards

- Visual Studio projects and solutions

- Guidance packages for developers

- Setup packages

- INI or CONFIG files for deployment, deployment descriptors

- VSTS process templates

- Reports

- Build scripts

- Static analysis rules

- Unit test skeletons

The preceding list shows that configuration can be used at any point in application development. The complexity of configuration can be as simple as setting a couple of ON/OFF flags in an INI file, or as complex as customizing templatized setup scripts.

We also need to mention that it is not necessary, of course, to use feature model configuration at all. An alternative would be to transfer knowledge about variation points into other tools, or just manually perform a series of steps to accomplish the same goal.

■**Tip** The great advantage of using feature models for configuration is that all knowledge about variation points is already captured in feature models, including constraints and dependencies between features (e.g., "Feature 1 requires Feature 2"). Additionally, many people who take part in application development will already be familiar with a particular feature model. The disadvantage of feature models is that they offer access to a relatively limited configuration space, compared with some other mechanisms such as DSLs or coding. In Chapter 7, we will show how a range of these mechanisms can be used to express variability, from raw coding to drop-down lists for individual properties. At this point, it is enough for you to think about feature models as a representation point that ranges between decision tree-based wizards and DSLs.

Application Implementation

Implementation based on a product line architecture is significantly different from implementation of a one-off application. The difference is primarily due to the fact that in the context of product line engineering it makes sense to acquire components that implement key parts of the product line architecture in advance, either by mining, developing, buying, or commissioning them. With one-off application development, you will never have the opportunity to provision these kinds of core assets in advance.

This opportunity is the primary reason for working with product lines in the first place. The goal of working with a product line is to discover commonalities among the product line members, and to exploit them by provisioning core assets that reduce the amount of work that must be done to develop product line members. Therefore, using a Software Factory, the application development part can be described by two major activities:

- Configuring and assembling existing components (core assets)

- Developing additional variable parts and extensions, as determined during requirements analysis and during the process of continuous asset improvement

The focus during implementation is clearly on the latter, developing the variable parts of a system. During application development, Software Factories unleash their full effectiveness because implementation gets reduced to assembling and configuring of core assets for the most part.

■**Tip** The most important benefits of using a factory come from the fact that the common parts are known and in many cases supplied in advance, and from the fact that even where there is variability, a lot is often known about the parameters of variation—i.e., what can vary, how it can vary, when it can vary, why it can vary, etc. It is this knowledge of the common parts and the parameters of variation that make it possible to provide benefits like components that can be assembled and configured to create the solution and a product line architecture that provides the structure of the solution.

One of the most important benefits is information compiled in advance for the product line that can be used to reduce risk during application development, such as cost and schedule information that can be used to form better estimates, and information about performance, security, defect levels, and other operational qualities that can be used to form better insights into architectural trade-offs.

Software Factory Evolution: Feedback into the Software Factory

During successful development and deployment of an application, an important task is improving and evolving our Software Factory. Reusable assets have only a limited shelf life, as requirements in a domain change and new technologies emerge (e.g., new platforms, tools, or process support). Therefore, it is very important to continuously improve these assets and to keep them versioned.

Caution We should mention at this point that keeping applications up to date as the factory evolves is certainly a challenge. The reason is that existing applications continually get out of date because the factory and its core assets are continually evolving. Usually, we can bring the common parts of the application up to date quite easily (e.g., installing a new version of library, converting a file to a new format, etc.), but upgrading the variable parts can present challenges (e.g., a feature used by the application has been deprecated, its configuration parameters have changed, or its implementation involved custom coding that cannot be automatically updated, and perhaps might require significant refactoring to fit into the updated architecture, etc.).

The combination of application development and factory review and assessment forms a feedback cycle. This process of extracting knowledge from application development experience is also called *mining* or *harvesting*. Figure 5-3 visualizes this cycle at the example of core assets.

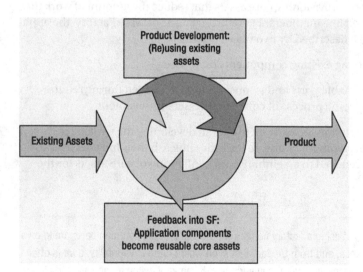

Figure 5-3. *Feedback cycle for core assets*

In this particular example, it was determined through reviews that certain components developed as extensions to a product could potentially be reused in future products. At this point, it does not matter whether these reusable parts will become common or variable features. By extracting these components, preparing them for reuse, and adding them to the other core assets, they become part of the factory and will be available in the next product development cycle.

Components are prepared for reuse by driving generalization into the components over time, as they are used in product line members with differing requirements. Another aspect of preparation involves hardening the components for consumption in new and uncontrolled environments, usually through extended quality assurance (e.g., more rigorous testing, threat modeling, globalization, etc.).

Another aspect of preparation involves making it easy for users to discover, understand, configure, and apply the components. This involves documentation of various forms, such as navigational documentation on web sites that helps users locate components, overview documentation that helps users determine the intended use of a given component, dependency documentation that helps users ascertain the prerequisites for using a given component, and usage documentation that helps users configure and apply a given component. Another aspect of preparation involves providing community support facilities that let users of the components report defects, ask questions, share their expertise with others, request new functionality or changes in existing functionality, and track progress on upcoming releases.

Beside the core assets, a number of other "ingredients" of a Software Factory should be targeted by the feedback process:

- Software Factory scope, e.g., could either be reduced or extended.

- Software Factory architecture, e.g., might have to be modified to support new requirements and features.

- Tooling, e.g., additional tools and guidance in context can be introduced if further need for automation is determined.

- Application development process, e.g., new elements of the architecture might require additional testing.

In any case, any changes and additions to the core assets require structured configuration management and versioning.

Activities and Tools in the Software Factory Schema

The application development process adds several pieces of information to the Software Factory schema beyond the information needed for architectural descriptions. The Software Factory schema uses the viewpoint pattern described by IEEE 1471-2000 to organize information about application development, including information about the work products relevant to each viewpoint, the activities that act upon those work products, and the assets available from the Software Factory to support and perhaps fully or partially automate those activities. The Software Factory schema can also extend beyond the construction phase into the other phases of the software life cycle, including requirements, testing, and deployment.

Because it is specific to the family of products targeted by the Software Factory, this information is generally much more detailed and more concrete than the typical application development process. Also, instead of merely telling the developers how to build the family members, the schema describes the application development process as metadata that can be used to orchestrate its enactment using the core assets, which are made available by the factory. This process enactment is the basis of the Software Factory's promise "to industrialize software development."

The key to accomplishing this goal is to provide as much automation of application development activities as possible using tools. Often these tools use domain-specific languages (see the section "Model-driven Development" in Chapter 1) to reduce the number of tedious and repetitive tasks required of the developer. Table 5-1 gives some examples of such application development activities and possible forms of automation.

Table 5-1. *Activities, Assets, and Work Products in a Software Factory*

Activity	Asset	Work Product
Model workflow.	Workflow designer, workflow engine	Workflow diagram.
Create smart-client module.	GAT, GAX	VS project structure, module source code.
Create new GUI.	WinForms designer	View source code.
Create deployment setup.	Visual Studio 2005	Installer package.
Extend database schema.	SQL management studio	Application-specific DB schema.
Add smart web reference.	GAT, GAX	Smart web reference source code.

A concept closely related to automation is *guidance*. Guidance helps Software Factory users follow an approach prescribed by the Software Factory developers in some part of the application development process. Such prescriptions can address a wide range of concerns, and the guidance that supports them can take many different forms, such as documentation, including guidelines and patterns, code samples, templates, wizards, libraries, frameworks, and designers. For example, the Software Factory might prescribe the use of a certain directory structure within the development environment. The guidance it supplies to partially automate this repetitive task might be a wizard that collects some parameters from a feature model configuration and from the user, and then unfolds a Visual Studio solution template containing the prescribed directory structure, using the parameter values to determine directory names and namespaces.

Microsoft developed the *Guidance Automation Toolkit* (GAT), an extension to Visual Studio 2005, which facilitates the authoring, installation, discovery, and consumption of guidance through the creation of so-called *guidance packages*. We will explain the Guidance Automation Toolkit in depth when we get to the Software Factory template.

At this point, you may be wondering about the relationship between a guidance package and viewpoint. As a good rule of thumb, a guidance package generally maps to a single viewpoint, since it groups related assets that target a specific aspect of the application development process. As you shall see, the guidance package mechanism does not support the Software Factory schema in its current form, and therefore does not support the viewpoint-oriented factory composition and specialization operations described earlier. Still, the GAT is effectively a down payment on the Software Factory vision, a good first step toward the kinds of tools and runtimes required to implement the Software Factory template concept.

For documentation purposes, the automated application development process, with its assets and work products, can be presented as a UML workflow diagram. This diagram is also a good starting point for planning the implementation of the assets. Figure 5-4 shows what the flow-of-control diagram looks like for the ISpySoft Software Factory. Note that this is a simple workflow example, which is completely tied to tools supporting the developer. Each step defines the input in the form of reusable assets and the output in the form of work products. These work products will make up part of the finished application.

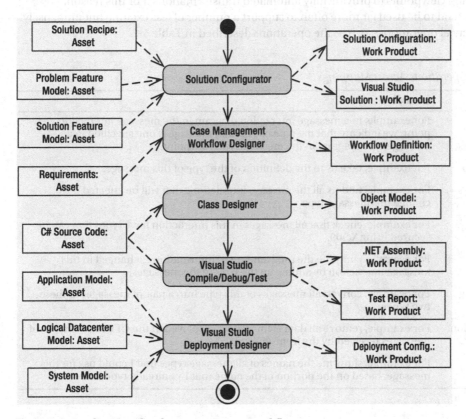

Figure 5-4. *Application development process workflow*

Mappings in the Software Factories Schema

A mapping in the Software Factory schema describes the relationship between two viewpoints. It is possible to formally define mappings so that they can be used to automate operations that cross viewpoints, such as generating work products of one viewpoint from the work products of another viewpoint. However, in most cases we will encounter mappings defined informally, e.g., specified in plain text.

With regard to the development process, let's look at how these mappings help us implement product line members. As mentioned previously, steps taken during development are captured in the Software Factory schema as activities. Activities can use mappings to perform a number of operations. Granted, the most exciting operations are fully automated model-to-model transformations and code generation (which we will explain shortly), and these are the types of operations emphasized by other model-driven development methodologies.

In practice, however, the factory developers have not gained enough experience with the participating viewpoints to provide fully automated transformations. For this reason, mappings tend to be used far more often to support a number of less exciting but immensely more practical operations, such as the operations described in Table 5-2.

Table 5-2. *Operations Across Mappings*

Operation	Example
Reference	For example, in a message interaction diagram in the message interaction viewpoint, we indicate that the type of a certain message is one specified in a message type diagram in the message type viewpoint.
Navigation	For example, take us to the definition of the type of this message.
Trace	For example, find us all the message interactions that will be affected if we change this message type.
Validation	For example, check that all messages in this interaction have types that can be secured using X.509.
Analysis	For example, compute the total amount of information exchanged in this message interaction by adding up the sizes of the messages.
Refactoring	For example, convert all messages of this type into a pair of messages of these two types.
Optimization	For example, remove all data elements not displayed in the UI from the types of messages received by the front-end.
Query	For example, show me the names of all message types that I could use for this message, based on the portion of the name that I've already typed.

We have a model that describes business entities as they are used in most business software. In order to persist business entities, we need a database. If you look at Figure 5-5, you can see that there is a relationship between the business entity model and the database schema that defines the database for these business entities. Both the business entity model and the database schema can be formally modeled using appropriate modeling languages, as defined by their related viewpoints *business entity viewpoint* and *database schema viewpoint*.

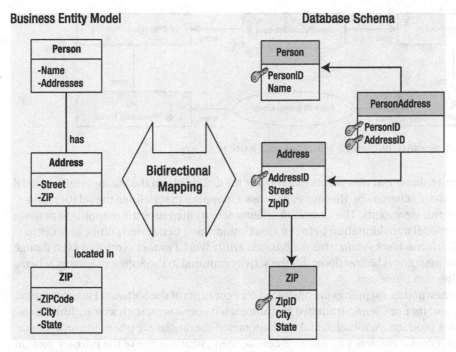

Figure 5-5. *Bidirectional mapping between business entity model and database schema*

This figure already indicates the mapping between the two models. So let's further assume that during development of our application we have created the business entity model. From there we can perform a transformation and derive the database schema from the business entity model by applying a set of rules:

- For each entity in the business entity model, define a table in the database schema.

- For each 1:n relationship in the business entity model, include the primary key of the parent table as a foreign key in the child table.

- For each m:n relationship in the business entity model, create an m:n table in the database, containing the two foreign keys of the related tables.

This is a simplified set of rules that ignores many issues, such as collection-based relationships like sorted lists or hashtables, but it should be sufficient for our purposes. If we now put everything into a Software Factory schema, we will come up with something like what you see in Figure 5-6. This figure was actually created using a custom Software Factory schema DSL, which we developed for the ISpySoft factory, and which we will cover later in this chapter.

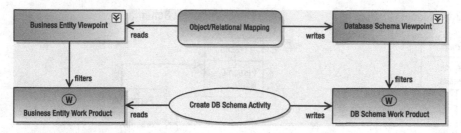

Figure 5-6. *Viewpoints, mappings, activities, and work products*

This figure shows two viewpoints that provide the definitions of the business entity model and the database schema. Furthermore, it shows a mapping that defines the relationship between the two viewpoints. The *Create DB Schema Activity* then uses the mapping to perform a model-to-model transformation between views conforming to the viewpoints, in order to derive a *DB Schema Work Product* from a *Business Entity Work Product*. Note that even though in theory the mapping is bidirectional, for the activity captured in the Software Factory schema only one direction is relevant.

Beside viewpoints, mappings are one of the core concepts of the Software Factory schema, as they support manual, semiautomated and automated operations, such as transformations, between work products. Automated and semiautomated operations are one of the most important ways to increase efficiency in software development, which is one of the primary goals of the Software Factory approach, as we noted in Chapter 1.

Models, Model Transformations, and Generators

 We touched on model-driven software development as one of the pillars of Software Factories already in Chapter 1. Because Software Factories use the concept of domain-specific languages, we need to drill down into more detail on this concept, and explain the mechanisms it uses, such as models, model transformations, and generators.

Domain-specific Languages

Let's continue with a discussion about DSLs. Back in Chapter 1, we gave you examples of some DSLs that you already use, such as SQL and WinForms. Domain-specific languages have been used for almost as long as computing has been around. They allow you to create models that can be used to capture, analyze, design, simplify, aggregate, and compare information about a particular solution in a specific domain. DSLs use a graphical or textual syntax. A graphical syntax often requires the use of a specialized editor. We distinguish two basic types of models:

1. *Formal models* use a formally defined concrete syntax to express metadata that adheres to a formally defined abstract syntax (a metamodel). This metadata can be used to support automation and other kinds of integration. Formal models can be compiled or translated into other artifacts.

2. *Informal models* are unstructured models such as sketches or other forms of documentation that do not allow for further automated processing.

The goal of DSLs is to efficiently represent specific problem sets, called *domains*. For example, imagine a subway map of New York City, as a practical example of a DSL. The subway map is a model of the subway system, created with a Subway Map language. The map only shows the relevant details that passengers need to get from one subway station to another. Taking this example a bit further, let's say you want to get from Penn Station to Grand Central. Consulting the subway map, you could easily find out that you should take lines 1, 2, or 3 to Times Square at 42nd street and change there to line 7, which would take you right to Grand Central. While this might seem to be a trivial example, it shows that using a special language with a high abstraction level is a powerful tool in managing complexity. On this subway map, complexities like street names, traffic lights, water lines, electric lines, restaurants and ATMs, are not shown, because they are not relevant to the passenger whose concern it is to get from point A to point B by subway.

Let's expand this example: say you wanted to go to a certain address in New York City, a place that is not shown explicitly on the subway map (because it only shows subway lines and stations). You would consult a street map, which is another model of New York City based on another DSL, in this case a DSL designed to support the discovery of addresses. By combining the two models, the subway map and the street map, you can first find the subway station nearest to your target address on the street map, then use the subway map to find the best way to get to that station by subway, and then finally use the street map to walk to your destination after getting off the subway.

You can think of DSLs in our Software Factory in the same way. DSLs raise the level of abstraction. They differ from other general-purpose modeling languages in the fact that they reflect the concepts found in particular domains.

Software Factories often use multiple DSLs, each capturing information about the application under development from a different perspective. At certain points, models based on these DSLs can interconnect, just as the street map shows subway entrances and the subway map shows the street names of the stations. The goal of using models based on multiple DSLs is to narrow the gap between a problem domain (e.g., getting from point A to point B) and a solution domain (e.g., riding the subway and walking).

By using DSLs, we can use the language of the problem domain, which allows us to get people involved in the development of the system who otherwise would not be able to participate in that process. For instance, domain experts usually cannot directly contribute to software projects because of lack of technical knowledge and software development skills. By providing modeling languages that contain the domain concepts, we enable them to directly contribute to the development of a product. This corresponds to the scenario shown in Figure 5-7.

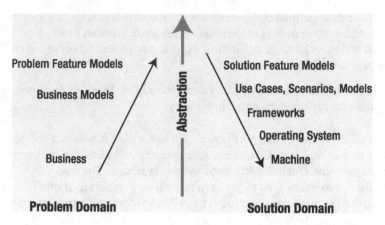

Figure 5-7. *Raising the level of abstraction with DSLs*

So what does it take to create a DSL? Every language, be it a third-generation language (like C++ or C#) or a specialized modeling language, consists of the concrete syntax, abstract syntax, and semantics.

While the notation (concrete syntax) is what the user of a language actually sees, the more interesting parts are the abstract syntax and the semantics. For example, most people, when they hear of UML, think of diagrams created with an editor like Rational Rose or Microsoft Visio. The abstract syntax is hidden within the implementation of the editor, and the semantics are revealed by the code generation or by the way people interpret the diagrams. Few people know that there is actually a textual representation of UML available.

Both representations, textual and graphical, are based on the abstract syntax, which in turn is defined through a metamodel. Very often we use a metamodeling tool to graphically define a metamodel. You can think of the model-metamodel relationship as analogous to the relationship between class and class instance (i.e., object). Figure 5-8 displays the metamodel hierarchy of DSL Tools that come with the Visual Studio 2005 SDK.

The M0 layer is the instance layer, which contains the objects being modeled, e.g., an activity in a workflow or a C# object. The M1 layer contains a model of those objects, created using a custom editor, e.g., a workflow diagram containing elements representing activities or a class diagram containing elements representing classes. The DSL used to express the model is defined in the M2 layer in the form of a metamodel or domain model. When you design a DSL using DSL Tools, you create the domain model using another modeling language defined in the M3 layer. The abstract syntax of that modeling language is called the meta-metamodel or the model of the domain model. This meta-metamodel is incorporated in DSL Tools. It contains primitive concepts like relationships, inheritance, embedding, and the like.

For each DSL, we define a metamodel that represents the abstract syntax. We then define the visualization of the concepts with the concrete syntax, meaning the shapes that are displayed for the concepts of our language and their relationships. This enables us to provide very specialized languages that can be used intuitively. With this knowledge in hand, we will show a Software Factory schema DSL as an example later in this chapter.

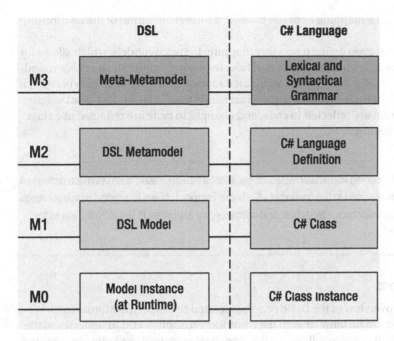

Figure 5-8. *DSL metamodel hierarchy*

■**Note** A model in the context of model-driven development is always defined by a metamodel, which is one level higher in the metamodel hierarchy. In Figure 5-8 we could create even more layers, or in other words, create a meta-meta-meta layer, and so on. In the case of DSL Tools, however, M3 is the highest level, as the model at the M3 layer can describe itself, or in other words, an M4 model would be expressed in the same language as an M3 model.

Model Transformations

In the introduction to the Software Factory schema, you already encountered a model transformation, namely a transformation from a business entity model to a database schema.
Software Factories use models of different aspects and different parts of systems, at different
abstraction levels. Mappings between viewpoints in the Software Factory schema support a
variety of operations between models, such as reference, trace, navigation, validation, analysis,
refactoring, and optimization. One type of operation, transformation, allows for deriving models,
often but not always at lower abstraction levels from other models, often but not always at higher
abstraction levels. This leads to the question, "What exactly are transformations?"

Generative Programming[3] defines a transformation as "an automated, semantically correct
modification of a program representation." In order for a transformation between two models

---

3. Krzysztof Czarnecki and Ulrich W. Eisenecker, *Generative Programming: Methods, Tools, and
    Applications* (Indianapolis, IN: Addison Wesley, 2000)

to be meaningful, we need a mapping between the two, a formal definition of the relationship between them.

In some cases, we can even define a two-way mapping between models, which allows for creating transformations in both directions. Therefore, two-way mappings can enable round-trip engineering, which is used to keep two interrelated models synchronized when one of the models changes. A good example of round-trip engineering is the Visual Studio Class Designer. Changes to a class diagram are reflected in code, and changes in code are reflected in a class diagram after synchronization.

■**Note** The relationship of mapping and transformation is such that a transformation is an operation performed across a mapping. Mappings are used in the context of a Software Factory schema to support a broader range of operations including trace, reference, navigation, and validation, as explained in the introduction to the Software Factory schema.

Types of Transformations

What follows is a quick overview of the basic concepts related to model transformations. We feel it is important for you to be familiar with the common vocabulary and to understand the basic concepts behind it in order to fully grasp the modeling aspects of the Software Factories methodology. Model transformations can be classified according to the abstraction level of their input and output models. Figure 5-9 shows the three different directions: vertical, horizontal, and oblique.

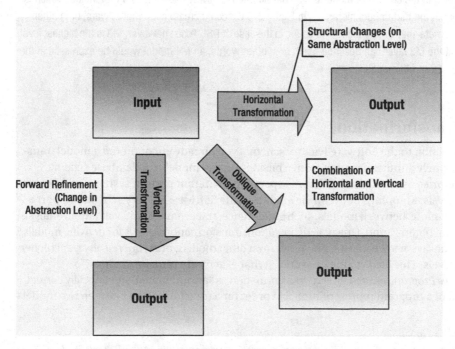

Figure 5-9. *Vertical, oblique, and horizontal transformations*

Vertical Transformations

Vertical transformations are refinements. They transform higher-level information into lower-level information. While the transformation might add additional information, it leaves the structural information of the input model intact. An example of a vertical transformation would be the generation of SQL DDL files from a model of business entities.

Horizontal Transformation

Horizontal transformations change the structure of the information, but the abstraction level stays the same. Horizontal transformations are typically used for model evolution where you can distinguish between refinements and optimizations.

Optimizations change the structure of the information in order to improve some of the characteristics of a model, like performance or memory consumption. While these changes are performed at the same abstraction level, often an optimization will make the resulting model harder to understand by humans.

Oblique Transformation

The combination of vertical and horizontal transformation is called *oblique transformation*. Compilers usually use oblique transformations: they perform a vertical transformation from source code to assembly code, and a horizontal optimization transformation, e.g., to make the program faster or the memory footprint smaller.

Generators

Transformations are merely operations based on mappings. Generators are the tools that execute transformations. Most generators require us to use some kind of mapping language in order to define the mappings across which they perform transformations. Generators take an existing input, such as a model, execute the transformation, and generate an output, which could be another model. As you can see in Figure 5-10, generators are classified into two groups: compositional and transformational.

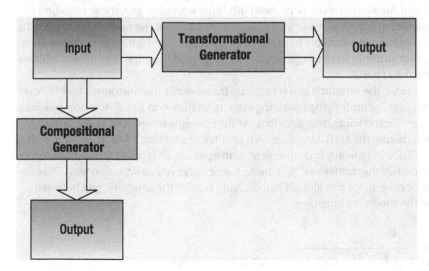

Figure 5-10. *Types of generators*

Compositional Generator

Compositional generators perform vertical transformations only. This means the generator does not change the structure of the input but adds implementation details.

Code generators are a special type of compositional generator. Many compositional generation technologies are available for Microsoft .NET technology, such as *brute force*, *CodeDOM*, and *Extensible Stylesheet Language Transformations* (XSLT). These three are described in great detail in *Code Generation in Microsoft .NET*.[4] Note, however, that only two of them are limited to code generation. XSLT is actually a general-purpose compositional generation technology that can be used for model-to-model transformations and for transformations involving other types of work products, such as SQL files and HTML files.

Another general-purpose compositional generation technology is provided by T4 templates that can be processed with the T4 template engine shipped with Microsoft DSL Tools. T4 templates combine templatized content fragments and control code that can traverse the inputs and control the generation of the desired outputs using the templatized content fragments. More information on T4 templates can also be found on the DSL Toolkit web site.[5]

Transformational Generators

Transformational generators are those that perform horizontal transformations or both horizontal and vertical transformations combined (i.e., oblique transformations). As mentioned earlier, most compilers fall into this category, since they perform vertical as well as horizontal operations in one or more steps transparent to the user.

Raising the Level of Abstraction

The main role of models in software development is to raise the level of abstraction. Why is this important for Software Factory development? In Figure 5-11, you can see the evolution of how models are used in different software development methodologies.

Box A of Figure 5-11 shows how CASE tools, in the late 1980s, tried to create software systems from models. The generic modeling tools had to bridge a large semantic gap between the requirements and the system level. Because of this large semantic gap, these tools had to generate large amounts of code and make a lot of assumptions about the underlying system. In most cases, the code generated was very hard to read and test, and ran with poor performance. Modeling languages oftentimes were too general or did not provide enough flexibility to address the business problems at hand.

One way to decrease the semantic gap is to create frameworks that introduce higher-level concepts by abstracting the underlying operating system, as shown in Box B. It is now possible to create domain-specific modeling languages that use the concepts introduced by these frameworks, e.g., by customizing the UML language with profiles or creating a DSL with Microsoft DSL Tools. Such a DSL will typically be implementation-specific, as it directly builds on top of the concepts provided by the framework. Still, using frameworks in combination with DSLs for model-driven development, we can already significantly reduce the semantic gap between requirements and the modeling language.

4. Kathleen Dollard, *Code Generation in Microsoft .NET* (Berkley, CA: Apress, 2004)
5. http://msdn.microsoft.com/vstudio/DSLTools/

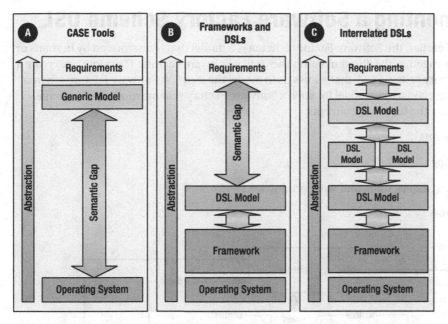

Figure 5-11. *Evolution of model use in software development*

The vision for model-driven development as proposed in the Software Factories methodology is two-fold. On the one hand, Software Factories propose to use interrelated domain-specific models at different levels of abstraction in conjunction with frameworks to raise the level of abstraction, as it is shown in Box C. This approach is very similar to how UML profiles are used in MDA. On the other hand, the larger vision of Software Factories is to use multiple interrelated work products at different levels of abstraction, supporting different aspects of the product.

That is the purpose of the Software Factory schema. It defines a set of interrelated viewpoints describing sets of interrelated views that get created during the course of building an application. Some of those viewpoints may be supported by DSLs, meaning that some of those work products will be models, but that's not the most important part of the story. The rest of the work products will use plain old code. And even when a Software Factory does use models, most of the operations involving the models will be mundane operations like analysis, reference, trace, navigation, and validation.

■**Tip** One of the key differentiators between Software Factories and MDA as proposed by the Object Management Group (OMG) is that Software Factories aim to be pragmatic and realistic, providing a way to integrate code and models effectively to support real-world software development, where a lot of the steps are not fully automatic. MDA, on the other hand, tries to make software development entirely automated using models and model transformations. The problem we see with a solely model-based approach is similar to the problems we experience with CASE tools that try to build real-world applications using nothing but models and try to generate all of the code with the push of a magic button.

Implementing a Software Factory Schema DSL

As explained earlier, the Software Factory schema is a model that is interpreted by humans or tools and ties together the different components of a Software Factory. Therefore, we create a Software Factory schema DSL that allows us to model the ISpySoft Software Factory schema. Figure 5-12 displays a metamodel for such a Software Factory schema modeling language, which supports the following concepts:

- Viewpoints

- Mappings

- Artifacts, assets, tools, and work products

- Activities

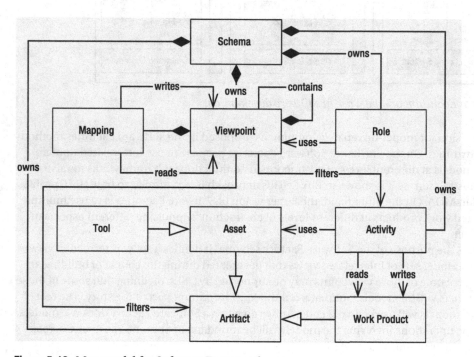

Figure 5-12. *Metamodel for Software Factory schema*

This metamodel is aligned with the notion of a Software Factory schema as introduced in *Software Factories*.[6] The actual Software Factory schema metamodel developed by Microsoft is much more complex than the one we use. For the purpose of our case study, we use this simplified metamodel, as it will make it easier for us to demonstrate the concepts behind the Software Factory schema and to actually implement a Software Factory schema DSL using Microsoft DSL Tools.

---

6. Jack Greenfield and Keith Short, *Software Factories: Assembling Applications with Patterns, Models, Frameworks, and Tools* (Indianapolis, IN: Wiley, 2004)

You can see in Figure 5-12 that the schema owns the artifacts, viewpoints, and activities. A viewpoint can contain other nested viewpoints and owns mappings between them. You can also see that assets and work products are artifacts and tools are in fact assets. Furthermore, activities use assets and work products as inputs in order to create or modify work products. A viewpoint then filters, or in other words selects, a number of related artifacts and the activities that produce the selected work products.

Using Microsoft DSL Tools

In the course of our ISpySoft case study, we decided to show two things: First of all, we use Microsoft DSL Tools to implement our own Software Factory schema DSL. Second, we demonstrate the *Software Factory Schema Browser*, which is a navigable developer help page that is created through generation from the Software Factory schema (actually it is XML generation). Based on the metamodel shown in Figure 5-12, we implement the Software Factory schema DSL, which requires the creation of three artifacts:

1. *Metamodel (created with the domain model editor)*: Defines the concepts of the language and the relations between them. In DSL Tools, the term *domain model* is used as a synonym for metamodel.

2. *Designer definition*: Describes how the concepts defined in the metamodel will be displayed in the model editor for the DSL, e.g., the graphical representation for each element and relation, decorators, etc. Furthermore, the designer contains specific validation logic in order to validate models for correctness.

3. *Installation package*: DSL Tools provide a project template for creating installation packages for custom DSL designers (the editors that you use to create DSL models). This makes distribution and deployment of your own DSLs a breeze.

The Domain Model Editor provides concepts like classes, properties, embedding (aggregation in UML), reference, and inheritance. Figure 5-13 shows the complete metamodel of our Software Factory schema DSL. Please note that we had to modify the original metamodel from Figure 5-12 a little bit in order to accommodate some of the constraints imposed by Microsoft DSL Tools at the time of writing.

Based on this schema metamodel, we need to create a matching designer definition that provides the basis for a graphical Software Factory schema editor, which is integrated into Visual Studio 2005. Even though at the time of writing no editor was available for DSL designer definitions itself, we expect that in the future it won't take long until we get such an editor, as it will greatly simplify the creation of DSLs.

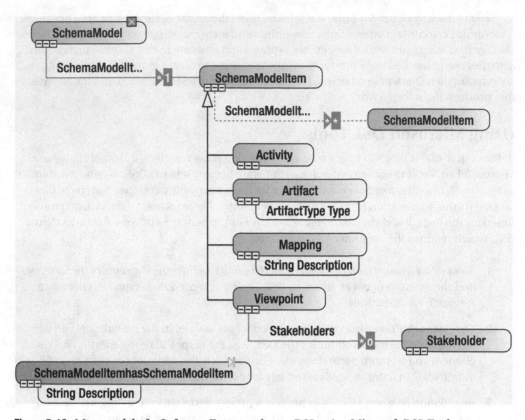

Figure 5-13. *Metamodel of a Software Factory schema DSL using Microsoft DSL Tools*

ISpySoft Software Factory Schema

Figure 5-14 shows an example of what this Software Factory schema DSL ultimately looks like. The figure is taken from the ISpySoft Software Factory schema and shows the high-level viewpoints of our factory. These high-level viewpoints contain the lower-level viewpoints as we described in Chapter 4. The five viewpoints shown in this overview representation of the schema are as follows:

1. Business (problem) viewpoint

2. Requirements (solution) viewpoint

3. Test viewpoint

4. Architecture viewpoint

5. Implementation viewpoint

You can also see the stakeholders concerned with a particular viewpoint shown as properties in the viewpoint shape. In addition to the viewpoints, Figure 5-14 shows you the *mapping* between different viewpoints, e.g., the mapping between requirements and architecture viewpoints. The mapping defines a *reads* relationship to the requirements and a *writes* relationship to the architecture viewpoint.

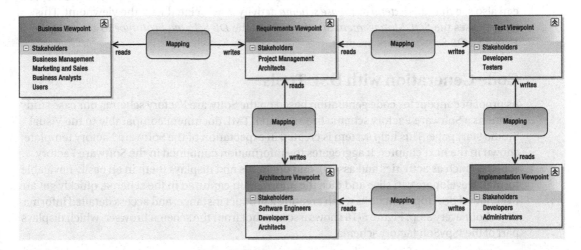

Figure 5-14. *High-level viewpoints of the ISpySoft Software Factory schema*

Let's now look at the implementation viewpoint in more detail. Figure 5-15 shows the drill-down with parts of the implementation viewpoint. In this more detailed diagram you can see not only the viewpoints and their mappings, but also artifacts (like tools, assets, and work items) as well as activities.

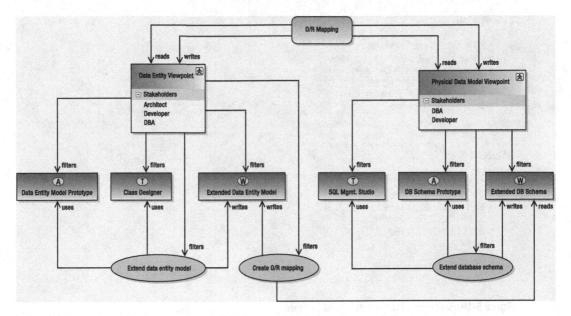

Figure 5-15. *Some detailed viewpoints of the ISpySoft Software Factory schema*

The *Physical Data Model Viewpoint* for our example filters three artifacts: the *SQL Management Studio* (which is a tool indicated by the "T"), *DB Schema Prototype* (an asset indicated by the "A"), and the *Extended DB Schema* (work product indicated by the "W"). Furthermore, you can also see that the *Extend database schema* activity is associated with the viewpoint. This activity uses the *SQL Management Studio* tool and the *DB Schema Prototype* to generate the *Extended DB Schema* work product.

Code Generation with DSL Tools

As proof of concept for code generation based on the Software Factory schema, our case study contains a Software Factory schema browser, an HTML document comparable to the Visual Studio start page. This help system is created in expectation of the Software Factory template, shown in the next chapter. It aggregates the information contained in the Software Factory schema (such as activities and assets), and organizes and displays them in an easily navigable format. Developers can slice and dice the information captured in the schema, quickly get an overview of development tasks when creating a product instance, and access detailed information about every step. Figure 5-16 shows a screenshot from the schema browser, which displays part of the ISpySoft factory schema.

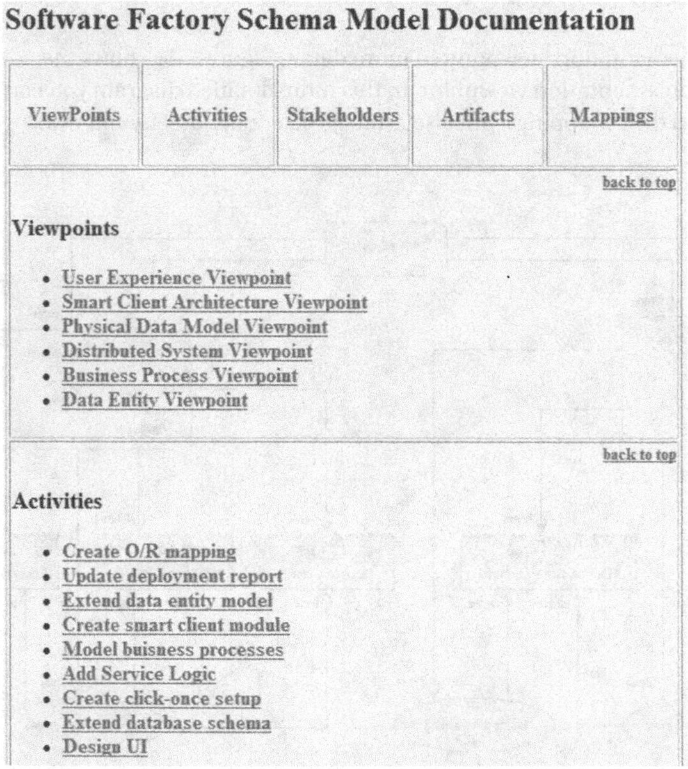

Figure 5-16. *Software Factory schema browser*

The schema browser basically consists of a large XML document that references an XSL style sheet, which transforms the XML into an easy-to-read and easy-to-navigate HTML page.

The generation of the XML document from the Software Factory schema model is performed using a T4 code template. T4 templates look somewhat similar to ASP code in that they contain template code mixed with directives for the code generator. Listing 5-1 shows a sample T4 snippet extracted from the ISpySoft factory with some explanations. The directives in the template traverse viewpoints and stakeholders in a SF schema model and generate the appropriate XML code. The generation task itself is a vertical transformation, as it transforms the SF schema model into XML code by adding information.

Listing 5-1. *T4 Template for Software Factory Schema Browser*

```
<# // Header information regarding input file, transformation engine
  and output file extension #>
<#@ template inherits=
  "Microsoft.VisualStudio.TextTemplating.VSHost.ModelingTextTransformation"#>
<#@ output extension=".xml" #>
<#@ SchemaModel processor="SFSchemaLanguageDirectiveProcessor"
  requires="fileName='ISpySoft.sfschema'"
  provides="SchemaModel=SchemaModel" #>
<# // Template code for XML output starts here #>
<?xml version="1.0" encoding="ISO-8859-1"?>
<?xml-stylesheet type="text/xsl" href="transformation.xslt"?>
<SFSchema>
  <ViewPoints>
<# // T4 directives for traversing the viewpoint nodes of the schema
foreach (object o in SchemaModel.SchemaModelItems) {
  if (o.GetType() == typeof(Siemens.SFSchemaLanguage.DomainModel.ViewPoint)) {
    Siemens.SFSchemaLanguage.DomainModel.ViewPoint vp =
      (Siemens.SFSchemaLanguage.DomainModel.ViewPoint) o;
    // now dynamically generate viewpoint nodes...
#>
    <ViewPoint ID="<#= vp.Id #>" name="<#= vp.Name #>">
      <Stakeholders>
<#
    foreach (Stakeholder s in vp.Stakeholders) {
      // ... and nested stakeholder nodes
#>
      <Stakeholder name="<#= s.Name#>" />
<#
    }
#>
      </Stakeholders>
    </ViewPoint>
<#
  }
}
#>
  </ViewPoints>
</SFSchema>
```

Summary

We have shown how the Software Factory schema forms the core of a Software Factory by tying all its components together. In the theoretical part of the chapter, you learned about model transformations and code generation. We applied this knowledge practically to create a DSL that allows us to model the SF schema and formally capture its content, followed by a simple example of how to generate XML from a model using Microsoft DSL Tools.

Our vision is that one day we will have a Software Factory for Software Factories. Such a toolkit would require a sophisticated Software Factory schema DSL. As we mentioned before, research in this area is going on, and we hope it won't take too long until we get such a tool.

The Software Factory schema is not a technique set in stone. The current ideas will undergo an evolutionary process of improvement and refinement, as is typical for a new paradigm like the Software Factory schema. Ultimately, it is also up to you to take this as a starting point and bring in your own ideas when using other Software Factories or creating your own. If you are interested in contributing to our DSL examples, please visit us at the `http://www.codeplex.com/Wiki/View.aspx?ProjectName=ISpySoft` web site.

Checkpoint

After this chapter, you should understand the following concepts related to the Software Factory schema:

- *Software Factory schema*: Enhances architectural descriptions after IEEE 1471-2000 with mappings, activities, assets, tools, and work products in order to provide a model that formally and coherently interrelates these concepts.

- *Application development process under Software Factories*: Several life-cycle activities are considerably different compared to a conventional development process, such as requirements analysis and implementation phase.

- *Domain-specific languages*: Allow for creating models that efficiently represent domains; can therefore raise the level of abstraction when used in software development.

- *Model-driven development*: Builds on DSLs, model transformations, and code generators

- *Microsoft DSL Tools*: Allow for creating your own DSL. Furthermore, integrate with a T4 template engine to allow for code generation.

CHAPTER 6

■ ■ ■

Software Factory Template: Application Core Assets

 The Software Factory template is a collection of customizable integrated assets such as guidelines, patterns, code samples, snippets, templates, wizards, class libraries, frameworks, designers, models, and configuration files that is installed on the application developer's computer. You can think of it as a big toolbox together with a context-sensitive instruction manual for building the applications targeted by a Software Factory. The Software Factory template and its content are specified by the Software Factory schema, so that the template can be considered an instance of the schema.

To continue the toolbox analogy, the Software Factory schema defines the relationships between items in the toolbox, the tools it contains, the products that can be built with this toolbox, the activities that need to be performed, and the execution order of the activities. For example, the toolbox may contain a saw, hammer, measuring tape, pencil, nails, and some wood. Furthermore, the toolbox also contains the blueprints for building different wooden chairs, and of course instructions about how to use the measuring tape, pencil, saw, hammer, and nails. The instructions, as given through the schema, would define that the user first should measure the wood (better twice!), mark it with the pencil, cut several pieces according to the selected blueprint, put the pieces together as described, and finally relax on the newly built chair.

Depending on how much you want to invest in such a toolbox, we could think of different versions. The basic and therefore cheapest one would contain a hacksaw, one type of nail, and a simple hammer. The most sophisticated toolbox, however, would be more like a completely equipped wood workshop with a storage area full of prebuilt parts for different chairs, a laser-guided precision saw, an electric staple gun, and other fancy equipment. Depending on the guidance and the automation that such a toolbox provides, it can greatly improve the productivity of anybody building chairs, and the quality of the same.

When deciding on what toolbox to buy, we certainly need to look at our goals and the best return on investment. If we only plan to produce eight individual chairs for our patio, we would probably invest in the basic toolbox rather than invest in a wood workshop. On the other hand, if our goal is to produce thousands of chairs, in different variations, that we want to sell worldwide, we would probably invest in a much more sophisticated solution, or toolbox.

Alright, enough of toolboxes, let's get back to real Software Factories. We can distinguish between two types of core assets that the Software Factory schema contains:

- *Application core assets (also called product assets)*: These assets provide the building blocks for product line members, such as platforms, frameworks, and other reusable components. These assets map to common and variable features of product line members as determined during product line analysis. While some of these application core assets can be used as is (e.g., frameworks that provide variability mechanisms), others are prototypical work products that will be modified and customized during application development (e.g., a prototypical data entity model that needs to be manually adapted to specific needs).

- *Development core assets (also called production assets)*: These assets are typically automation tools, wizards, templates, designers, guidelines, patterns, code samples, etc., that are integrated into a highly customizable development environment like Visual Studio 2005. They help propel application development through the process of assembling and configuring the variable parts of product line members, customizing of application core assets, and creating extensions to the product line.

Because we focus on the practical application of the Software Factories theory throughout the book, we dedicate two chapters to the Software Factory template. This chapter explains the creation of the ISpySoft application core assets, whereas the creation of the development core assets is covered in Chapter 7.

In the remainder of this chapter, we will go through a first iteration of filling the ISpySoft Software Factory template with application core assets. More specifically, we implement a vertical slice of case management functionality, which is representative of the business domain of ISpySoft. Starting with back-end web services, we especially focus on smart client technology where we create a shell application with the case management module provided as an extension.

We recommend that while reading through this chapter you open up the Visual Studio solution of our ISpySoft factory in case you'd like to get into more detail. Again, the complete reference implementation including documentation can be downloaded from the Apress Source Code web page.[1] Furthermore, we encourage you to join our CodePlex workspace[2] and participate as we and other people continue evolving the ISpySoft Software Factory.

Approaching the Software Factory Template

Let's take a minute to talk about the process of developing the Software Factory template. We recommend you follow an iterative approach in order to gain experience and to identify best practices while delivering business value as soon as possible. In each iteration, we implement and test additional assets as well as modify existing assets of the factory. As a result, we can identify more and more common functionality. The identified common functionalities can be factored out, and through continuous refactoring we can transform them into more generalized, reusable components that eventually become core assets of our factory.

So what do these iterations look like? Figure 6-1 shows the principle of how you can gradually increase skills and knowledge, as well as broaden the scope of the Software Factory template in an iterative way. In general, the process of building and extending the Software Factory template

---

1. Go to http://www.apress.com, access the Source Code page under Quick Links, and select "Practical Software Factories in .NET" from the drop-down list to start the download process.
2. http://www.codeplex.com/Wiki/View.aspx?ProjectName=ISpySoft

will be iterative on two levels. On the micro scale, these are the iterations while developing one product; on the macro scale, this will happen over the course of building multiple products with the factory.

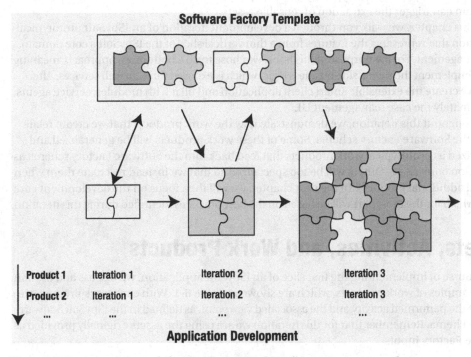

Figure 6-1. *Iterative approach for development of a Software Factory template*

Depending on your particular case, the initial fill rate of your Software Factory template will vary. In some cases, you might have a lot of existing applications from which you can extract reusable application and development core assets in order to populate a SF template. In such cases, you would probably be able to build applications right away that include many of the common features and at least some of the variable features.

In other cases, you might not have such a large number of core assets, e.g., because your existing applications are using older legacy technology. Therefore, you would typically start with building some prototypical applications that cover the most important common and variable features of the Software Factory under development in order to gradually produce reusable core assets.

In our ISpySoft case study, we initially start our Software Factory template with assets that were extracted from the defined Software Factory inputs. During each iteration of application development, we identify, extract, and refactor components and other building blocks that we add to our set of application core assets. These assets become part of the Software Factory template. In addition to a growing asset base of our Software Factory template, this also means that the Software Factory development team takes ownership of these new application core assets.

At the same time, we not only factor out reusable assets, but also identify patterns, best practices, and possibilities for automation that become part of the development core assets. With the best practices at hand, we can build first versions of guidance packages, wizards, or even DSLs with attached code generators. This continuous extraction and refactoring of application and development core assets is based on the Software Factory schema, which defines the assets, tools, work products, and activities necessary to develop an application with the factory. Each product will typically also bring new extensions to the product line, which then again can trigger the extraction of reusable assets.

In this chapter, we walk you through a development iteration of an ISpySoft prototypical application that represents the features from a thin vertical slice of the ISpySoft's core domain, case management. For the purpose of this book, we chose to do a bottom-up approach, meaning we first implement the server-side business logic, which is exposed through web services. Afterwards, we create the extensible smart client application and fill it with modules, service agents, and ultimately the case management UI.

Throughout this iteration, we demonstrate how the work products that we create relate back to the Software Factory schema. Some of these work products will be generalized and templatized as prototypical work products that feed back into the Software Factory schema as application core assets. Others will be too specialized so that we instead re-create them when we build additional products. In the next chapter, we will then focus on the development core assets, which for the most part will be based on the best practices identified during this iteration.

Assets, Activities, and Work Products

In the course of implementing the first slice of an ISpySoft application, we discuss and explain some examples of work products, which are shown in Table 6-1. With each work product, we describe the performed activity and the associated viewpoint, as defined in the ISpySoft Software Factory schema. Remember that for this iteration we are using the assets originally provided as Software Factory inputs.

Table 6-1. *Viewpoints, Work Products, and Activities*

Viewpoint	Activity	Work Product
Architecture Viewpoint		
Component structure viewpoint	Define web services. Define smart client modules. Define interactions between modules and services.	Informal web service descriptions Informal smart client module descriptions Communication diagram
Distributed system viewpoint	Define web service interfaces.	WSDL definition for web services
Control flow viewpoint	Define flow of control in smart client UI.	Sequence diagram for commands and events between UI, presenters, controllers, and services
Implementation Viewpoint		
Data entity viewpoint	Extend prototypical data entity model. Create O/R mapping.	Data entity model
Physical data structure viewpoint	Extend prototypical database schema.	Database schema

Table 6-1. *Viewpoints, Work Products, and Activities*

Viewpoint	Activity	Work Product
User experience viewpoint	Define UI layout. Implement UI parts.	UI sketch Shell, workspaces, smart parts
Solution structure viewpoint	Unfold smart-application template.	Smart-client solution structure in Visual Studio
Testing viewpoint		
Unit test viewpoint	Create unit tests for source code work products.	Unit tests

During this iteration, the implementation of a thin vertical slice, we make use of a number of core assets as they are defined by the ISpySoft factory schema. These core assets are shown in Table 6-2.

Table 6-2. *Core Assets Used in First Iteration*

Core Assets
Application Core Assets
Problem feature model, solution feature model
Framework provided by Smart Client Software Factory
Selected parts of the smart client reference implementations
Composite UI Application Block (CAB)
NHibernate O/R mapping library
.NET Framework, WinForms, ASP.NET
SQL Server
IIS/ASP.NET Development Web Server
Other reusable parts of existing ISpySoft applications
Development Core Assets
UML modeling tool
Custom configurator
Feature modeling DSL
ISpySoft Software Factory schema browser
Visual Studio 2005
SQL Server Management Studio
SCSF smart client solution template
SCSF recipes (contained in SCSF guidance package)
NUnit

Developing the Back-end Services

Based on the product line architecture developed in Chapter 4, the ISpySoft system could, in theory, run on one single PC, but typically multiple PC clients will connect to an application server from within an intranet. In future versions of the ISpySoft factory, there could even be a smart client for Windows Mobile 5.0, which would allow field agents to use their PDAs to make the ISpySoft system truly mobile. Regarding communication, the common denominator for these scenarios is SOAP web service technology, as it allows for easy protocol tunneling through corporate firewalls to provide access to remote clients.

The decision to use web services comes at a price: web services can have an impact on performance and architecture compared to other communication mechanisms for distributed systems such as COM+ or .NET Remoting. This is mainly because XML serialization and deserialization consumes precious CPU cycles. Furthermore, at this point in time, web services, for example, cannot yet take part in distributed transactions, at least not without considerable effort like manually implementing compensating transactions. However, as neither distributed transactions nor top-notch performance are a #1 requirement for ISpySoft, we chose a uniform approach using web services, which provide the greatest flexibility. For each back-end service, we need to implement the following work products:

- Data entity model containing the object-relational mapping for persistency in SQL Server 2005 database

- Business logic that orchestrates and performs operations on data entities

- Web service facade that exposes business logic as a web service and provides a coarse-grained interface (also called *chunky*, as opposed to a chatty interface with many small-grained transactions)

Data Entity Model and Object-relational Mapping with NHibernate

Figure 6-2 depicts the business entities related to case management, as there is the Case entity with its subordinated entities Evidence, Report, and Expense. Additionally, the User entity is required for a complete audit track (who added or modified what information when). Visual Studio 2005 Class Designer is a great help in developing the initial model.

This model was manually created as a work product during one of the very first iterations of product development using the ISpySoft factory, when there weren't many core assets developed. Afterwards this model was turned into a prototypical work product, which became an application core asset as specified by the Software Factory schema. Once integrated into the Software Factory template, it can quickly be customized and extended to an application's specific requirements.

The data entity model is persisted with the help of the object-relational (O/R) mapping technology NHibernate,[3] which is the .NET port of the well-known Java Hibernate project. NHibernate allows for annotating the data entity model with attributes that relate business entities to tables in the database.

---

3. http://www.nhibernate.org/

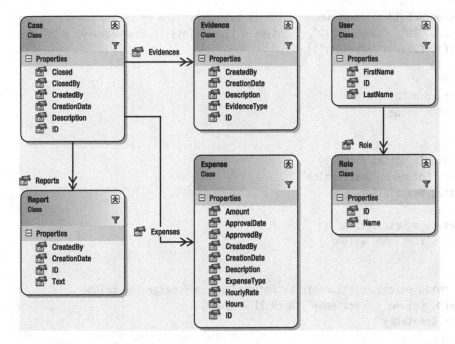

Figure 6-2. *Data entity model for case management*

Without going into details about advantages and disadvantages of other data access approaches, such as typed datasets, O/R mapping frameworks like NHibernate do not force developers to create suboptimal object models around an existing database schema, but rather allow them to design full-featured object models that support advanced relations between entities such as sets, lists, sorted lists, or dictionaries. Furthermore, when it comes to cascading updates and deletes, developers provide the necessary information in a declarative way, so that at runtime the O/R mapping layer will take care of most of this complexity.

Listing 6-1 shows what the annotated Case class looks like (the listing was shortened for demonstration purposes).

Listing 6-1. *Case Class Annotated with NHibernate Mapping Attributes*

```
// Maps the Case class to the Case table
[Class(0, NameType = typeof(Case), Table = "Case")]
public class Case
{
  int m_ID = 0;
  string m_Description = "";
  User m_CreatedBy;
  IList m_Reports = new ArrayList ();
```

```csharp
// Maps an object identifier, whose value is auto-generated by the database
[Id(0, Name = "ID", Column = "ID", TypeType = typeof(Int32), UnsavedValue = "0")]
[Generator(1, Class = "identity")]
public int ID
{
  get { return m_ID; }
  set { m_ID = value; }
}


// Maps a simple string property
[Property(0, Column = "Description")]
public string Description
{
  get { return m_Description; }
  set { m_Description = value; }
}


// Maps a child-parent relationship by indicating the foreign-key column
[ManyToOne(0, Column = "CreatedBy", NotNull = true)]
public User CreatedBy
{
  get { return m_CreatedBy; }
  set { m_CreatedBy = value; }
}

// Maps an unsorted parent-child relationship as list, lazy-loaded
[Bag(0, Cascade = CascadeStyle.All, Inverse = true, Lazy = true)]
[Key(1, Column = "CaseID")]
[OneToMany(2, ClassType = typeof(Report))]
public IList Reports
{
  get { return m_Reports; }
  set { m_Reports = value; }
}
}
```

Physical Data Model

Underneath the business logic and the data model sits a SQL Server 2005 database. Figure 6-3 shows the DB schema that represents the database equivalent to the data entity model as previously shown in Figure 6-2. Just as the data entity model before, this database schema was manually created as a work product during the first application development. Afterwards it was integrated into the Software Factory template as a prototypical work product that can be customized depending on the application at hand.

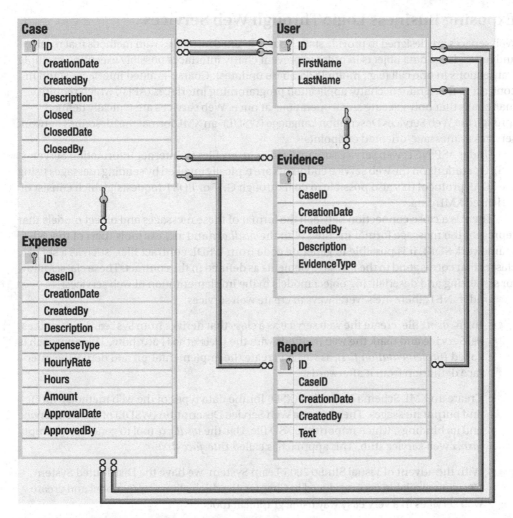

Figure 6-3. *Database schema for case management domain*

The ISpySoft database does not contain any stored procedures for Create, Read, Update, and Delete (CRUD) operations, which is often a recommended practice for database design with regards to encapsulation, performance, and security. While the ISpySoft database does not use stored procedures, there are several reasons why this is not necessarily a disadvantage:

- NHibernate dynamically creates SELECT, INSERT, UPDATE, and DELETE statements based on the mapping definition. Therefore, there is no need to manually create and maintain any SQL code.

- Performance-wise, once NHibernate SQL statements are executed for the first time, the execution plans for these statements are cached by SQL Server and therefore give a performance comparable to using parameterized stored procedures.

- Securing the database against misuse through other applications is not as much of a concern as it might be in the case of, e.g., large enterprise databases that are accessed by a multitude of applications and systems. All applications using the ISpySoft database are developed and tested by ISpySoft itself.

Exposing Business Logic Through Web Services

 Web services are designed to provide static, coarse-grained interfaces with methods that receive and return large data objects in order to prevent chatty interfaces possibly executing multiple transactions in one call (e.g., multiple database updates). Coarse-grained interfaces stand in contrast to fine-grained, chatty application programming interfaces (APIs), which require many calls that only execute small operations at once. Web services are typically defined through the Web Services Description Language (WSDL), an XML format that describes network services as message-oriented endpoints.

Under ASP.NET, web services are realized as *.asmx* files in Internet Information Server (IIS). Operations on the web service endpoints are typically invoked by sending messages using the SOAP protocol (it's also possible to do it through GET or POST requests), which consist of serialized XML data.

There is a close connection between the format of these messages and object models that represent the message format in code. With the *wsdl.exe* and *xsd.exe* tools (part of the .NET Framework SDK), it is possible to generate code from WSDL contract files, such as a set of classes that correspond to the message elements as defined in the contract. These classes allow for serializing and deserializing object models in the implementation of web services.

Under .NET, there are several ways to create web services:

- In an *.asmx* file, create the web service as a class that derives from System.Web.Services. WebService and mark the web methods with the [WebMethod] attribute. This approach is called *implementation first*, as we first create the implementation and derive the interface definition from it afterwards.

- Create an XML Schema Definition (XSD) for the data types of the web methods' input and output messages. Then create a Web Service Description (WSDL) of the web service and its bindings, which imports the XSD file. Use the *wsdl.exe* tool to generate an empty *.asmx* web service stub. This approach is called *interface first*.

- With the advent of Visual Studio 2005 Team System, we have the Distributed System Designer available (as introduced in Chapter 4), which allows us to model and create web services in a very easy way using graphical tools.

 ISpySoft web services, such as the case management web service, are not only accessed by ISpySoft client applications in the local office but also from agents using laptops in the field. Therefore, it is important to keep the number of web service requests small and transfer data in large chunks.

The ISpySoft case management requires some static data in order to be operative even when offline, such as lists of categories. Static data rarely changes, which means that there is room for optimization. Figure 6-4 shows the interface of the CaseMgmtWebService, which we use to demonstrate such an optimization.

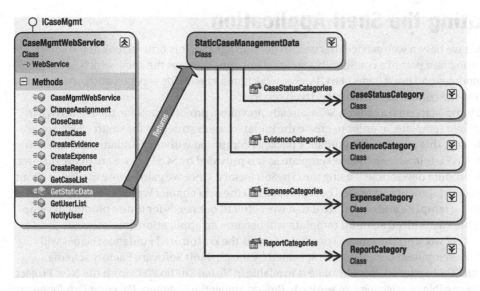

Figure 6-4. *Case management web service with coarse-grained interface*

The case management web service provides several methods in order to retrieve this static data, each requiring a round trip. In order to minimize the number of round trips that need to be performed by a web service client, one technique is to combine several fine-grained method calls into one. In this case, the GetStaticData method effectively returns the result from several web methods, such as the GetEvidenceCategories, GetReportCategories, and GetExpenseCategories methods. This is a simple example for the *Facade* pattern, which hides the complexity of subsystems behind a simple interface.

On the client side, the result of this web method call can then be transparently cached. The caching takes place after the initial call, which helps reduce the number of round trips even further and enables field agents to work offline.

The case management web service provides a set of common and variable features as specified during Software Factory specification. Regarding the variable features, such as customizable workflows, we will demonstrate the application of several variability mechanisms in the next chapter. Once the case management service is implemented, it becomes an application core asset of the ISpySoft factory. Over time, as ISpySoft builds additional product line members, it is likely that the case management web service will need to provide additional features. This will trigger the implementation of extensions that might also be refactored to become core assets, as described earlier.

What this means is that new functionality will usually first be implemented as a custom extension to the factory for a specific application. During or after a product development iteration, this functionality can be generalized and made reusable, and be integrated as a core asset.

Creating the Shell Application

Now that we have a web service that we can develop against, it is time to look at the smart client. The main part of a configurable smart client application is the shell, which at runtime loads modules and hosts items like UI views, work items, client-side services, and service agents providing the connection to back-end web services.

To jump-start such a project, SCSF already provides a project template, the *Light Weight Smart Client* template, in order to create the initial solution structure for smart client applications. In fact, this template is a guidance package composed with the Guidance Automation Toolkit (GAT). Initially, we use the template as it is provided by SCSF, as we are in the first iteration of product development using the ISpySoft factory. Once we gain more experience about product development and related best practices, in the next chapter we show how to configure this existing template and customize it so it will better fit our needs for future product development. This customized solution template will become an application core asset (a prototypical work product, to be specific), whereas the customized guidance recipes will become development core assets, as specified by the ISpySoft Software Factory schema.

With SCSF installed, this template is available in Visual Studio 2005 from the New Project dialog (accessible by selecting *File* ➤ *New* ➤ *Project*), under the *Guidance Packages Development entry*. A wizard guides you through the creation of the initial solution. Under the hood, GAT will execute solution and project templates to unfold the initial solution structure. Furthermore, the Light Weight Smart Client template will enable several other guidance assets for this particular solution, such as recipes that allow you to create additional modules and views (essential components of an SCSF smart client) to support further development.

In Figure 6-5, you can see the Visual Studio solution structure representing the first prototypical application based on the ISpySoft Factory. This solution includes back-end web services and components as well as the smart client shell application with related modules. Note that this solution represents the first ISpySoft application built based on the ISpySoft factory. During and after the first product development iteration, we will extract both application and development assets from this solution in order to gradually extend the Software Factory template with more refined reusable assets.

Note that this is part of consuming the SCSF factory. Back in Chapter 4, we consumed a number of viewpoints from SCSF and extended them to the ISpySoft factory. Now we consume and specialize the application and development core assets provided by SCSF.

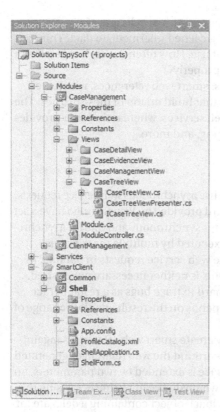

Figure 6-5. *Solution structure for the prototypical ISpySoft application*

Developing the Client-side Service Agents

 Smart clients are designed to perform well in web service environments. One of their great strengths is the ability to handle situations with limited network connectivity gracefully (e.g., slow, unreliable connection with frequent timeouts or no connection at all). However, this additional capability comes at the price of additional architectural implications and additional effort when creating the client tier of a distributed application.

Communicating with a web service typically happens through a client-side web service proxy, which can be, e.g., created using the *wsdl.exe* tool provided by the .NET Framework SDK (note that Visual Studio internally uses this tool to create web references). Unfortunately, without some kind of extension, this proxy falls short of a few features required for certain situations:

- Asynchronous web service calls do not have individual timeouts.

- Asynchronous web service calls are all executed in parallel. No support is provided for sequential asynchronous calls.

- There is no intelligent caching of incoming data or queuing of outgoing calls.

A design guideline for smart clients is to submit web requests asynchronously in order not to block the user interface, since invocations could take even several minutes. An alternative solution, which we do not recommend, is to send the web request from another thread. Unfortunately, this would put the burden on the developer to make sure the application is thread-safe.

Additionally, a smart client should always handle failing remote calls gracefully, e.g., by switching the application to offline mode or by returning cached intermediate data. This in theory even applies to applications designed for intranet use. How often does it happen that a server goes down or a network cable wasn't plugged in properly?

SCSF provides a twofold solution to these problems: smart web references, which are more advanced web service proxies, and service agents that build on top of these proxies. The former provides asynchronous, queued invocation of web services, whereas the latter provides functionality such as data conversion, transparent caching, and more.

Smart Web References

As stated previously, smart clients should most of the time use asynchronous web service requests. Web references created with the *Add Web Reference* wizard provided by Visual Studio have a set of duplicate methods for each web service method: one for synchronous and one for asynchronous invocation. Since asynchronous invocations are executed by multiple threads, it is possible, unless you take further precautions, to execute web service requests in parallel. In some cases this might be desirable, but for most cases this is neither necessary nor desired. Rather, if not applied correctly, this might lead to very hard to trace bugs as a result of race conditions, e.g., if the later web service call implicitly depends on the result or a state change of the former call.

Therefore, SCSF provides a wizard to automatically create smart web references (again, provided as a GAT recipe), which basically are wrappers around the web references generated by Visual Studio. Each method on the web service interface is extended by two parameters, an individual timeout and a callback. The result looks like what you see in Listing 6-2. Using this approach, smart clients can provide a timeout and a callback object containing a delegate for each individual invocation. Internally, a smart web reference queues calls to web methods and executes them sequentially.

Listing 6-2. *Extended Method Signatures for Smart Web Proxies*

```
// original method signature in web reference
public Case[] GetCaseList(string filter) {...}

// extended method signature in SCSF smart web reference
public void GetCaseList(int timeout, sting filter,
    GetCaseListCommand.CallbackType callback) {...}
```

Figure 6-6 shows the classes that participate in the smart web reference, to allow for serializing and queuing web service invocations. The core element of a smart web reference is a web service proxy class, which derives from ServiceProxy and exposes the extended web method signatures with timeout and callback. Incoming calls are stored in command objects, either with or without callback, depending on whether the web method returns a value or not. ServiceProxy contains a worker thread that sequentially submits the commands waiting in its command queue.

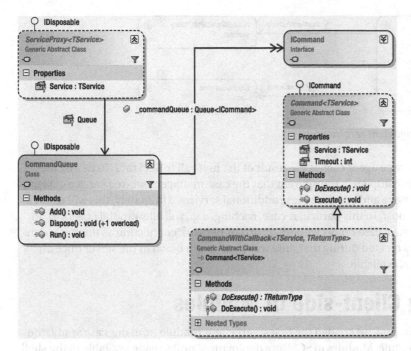

Figure 6-6. *Smart web reference*

Don't worry, you will not have to create all the wiring code for a smart web proxy. As stated earlier, SCSF provides a recipe that allows for creating these proxies at the click of a button. Should the interface of a web service endpoint change (yeah, we all know interfaces shouldn't change), it is a trivial task to re-create a smart web reference.

Service Agents

Service agents are yet another abstraction layer between client-side logic and web services. The name *agent* is derived from the fact that a service agent not only is a static adapter wrapping a web service, but also can, for example, provide client-side data entity models or "active" services such as caching or client-side persistency.

Remember how, for example, the GetStaticData of the CaseMgmtWebService returned a structure containing four collections of categories that are used to describe cases, reports, expenses, and evidence. A service agent allows us to expose a fine-grained API because it encapsulates the "translation" logic inside. Take a look at the CaseMgmtServiceAgent class in Figure 6-7. It exposes four methods: GetCaseStatusCategories, GetReportCategories, GetEvidenceCategories, and GetExpenseCategories. All four methods return parts of the data returned by the GetStaticData method from the CaseMgmtWebService (as shown earlier).

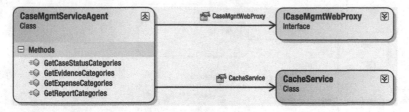

Figure 6-7. *Case management service agent*

Internally, the service agent caches the result of the first call to GetStaticData. For the smart client logic, it is completely transparent that the case management web service communicates with a web service and provides these additional services. Ultimately, this will result in a nice performance boost. In this particular case, caching, e.g., will allow mobile users to do their expenses or create a case report without a current network connection as the static data is cached. Any entries created during that time will be sent as a batch to the server once an Internet connection is available.

Developing Client-side UI Modules

Now we'd like to show how we created the first smart client module from our case study, the case management module. Modules in SCSF are deployment units, made available to the shell application using work items as containers. Each work item covers a certain aspect of business functionality and is made up of a collection of modular UI smart parts and service agents. SCSF prescribes that developers use the Model-View-Presenter (MVP) pattern when implementing UI views.[4] These UI widgets and their respective presenters can then be dynamically loaded into an extensible shell. The views' presenters communicate with other parts of the application, such as services and service agents, either directly or using events that can globally be published and subscribed to. Through this global event broker pattern and the service locator pattern modules can be kept independent from each other.

The steps required to generate an empty module are automated by the *Create Module* recipe provided with SCSF, just as previously with the *Light Weight Smart Client* template. The only information required is the location and the module name, which in this case is CaseMgmtModule. The GAT recipe finishes its work with a result page that displays further process instructions (see Figure 6-8). Initially, we used this and other recipes as they were provided by SCSF. However, after gaining experience about how to build modules and other items for use as application core assets, in a refactoring step these recipes were customized to the specific needs of ISpySoft and integrated into the factory as development core assets. We show you this step in the next chapter.

---

4. Here is a quick pattern reference: http://www.martinfowler.com/eaaDev/ModelViewPresenter.html.

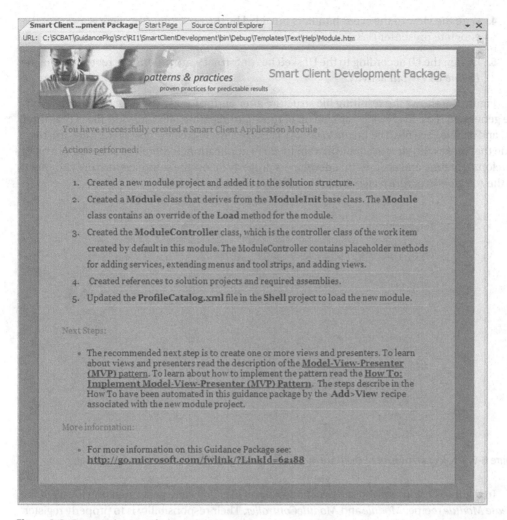

Figure 6-8. *Process instructions—next steps*

Model-View-Presenter Pattern for SCSF Views

After creating the empty case management module, we now use the *Create View* recipe, just as suggested by the guidance shown in Figure 6-8, in order to create the first view. Remember that views in SCSF smart clients follow the Model-View-Presenter pattern. In general, views are implemented using the following steps, as defined by the *Implement UI Parts* activity in the ISpySoft factory schema:

1. Create an empty view with its presenter using the guidance package provided by SCSF.

2. Define the interface implemented by the view so that the presenter can update the view (the presenter should be unaware of the concrete view class and only communicate through an interface).

3. Implement the presenter methods that handle events coming from the view.

4. Wire the view to the event handlers provided by the presenter (the view is aware of the concrete presenter class).

5. Design the UI according to the UI sketches (informal work products) created during the *Define UI Layout* activity.

Figure 6-9 shows the resulting file structure after performing the *Create View* recipe with the generated files. Every view is made up of three participating files: the view file, a presenter file, and an interface file. The *Create View* GAT package already creates most of the infrastructure code that makes the view available in a smart client application. It therefore saves quite a bit of development time and ensures that developers properly follow the solution structure as defined by the *solution structure viewpoint* in the factory schema.

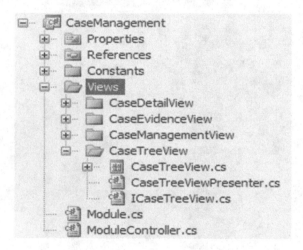

Figure 6-9. *Project structure of the case management module with views and presenters*

In Figure 6-9, you can also see two module-level files that were generated previously in the *Create Module* recipe: *Module* and *ModuleController*. Their responsibility is to properly register the module in a smart client shell application, publish and sign up for events, and make commands globally available.

Figure 6-10 shows the MVP implementation of one of the case management–related views, the *case details* view. Following the MVP pattern, the presenter communicates with the view through an interface. This pattern was chosen for separation of concerns, as it allows for easy UI-less testing, for example, as we describe at the end of this chapter.

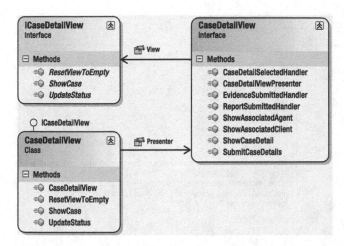

Figure 6-10. *Case details view following the MVP pattern*

Events and Event Publications in the Smart Client UI

Before we conclude this UI module discussion, we will talk about another great feature of SCSF (actually provided by the underlying Composite UI Application Block). One of the requirements for ISpySoft is that it can easily be extended with customer-specific functionality. One of the variability mechanisms that you already learned of are modules that can be loaded (almost) independently by a smart client application and that contain work items, controllers, smart parts, and others. The big question now is how independently developed modules can possibly communicate with each other, without having design-time references.

Views need a way to communicate with their hosting environment, the smart client application shell, and with views from other modules. Take a look the *case management view* in Figure 6-11, which allows for navigating the information associated with a case in a treeview-like manner. Upon changing the selection in the browser treeview (displayed in the middle), related detail information is displayed in the right-hand detail workspace. At the same time, the toolbar with context-sensitive commands changes accordingly.

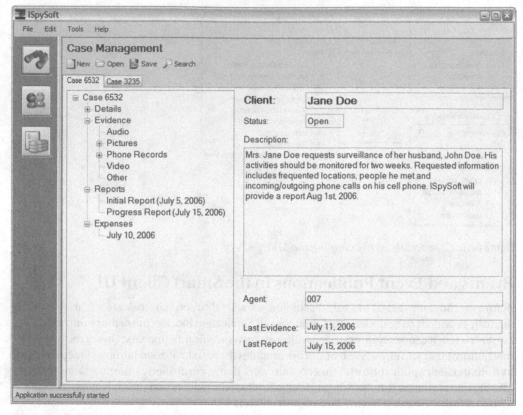

Figure 6-11. *Case management view*

The answer is a publish-subscribe mechanism, or as it is called within CAB, an event broker. Listing 6-3 shows how a global CAB event is published declaratively. It shows part of the presenter of the case management view, which publishes a global event that is fired whenever the user creates a new case. Any interested view or service can now subscribe to this event, even across modules and therefore assembly boundaries, without having design-time references. Furthermore, events can be published with different scopes such as global (accessible from other modules) or locally within one work item.

Listing 6-3. *Publishing an Event*

```
public class CaseMgmtViewPresenter
{
    ...
    [EventPublication(EventTopicNames.NewCaseEvent, PublicationScope.Global)]
    public event EventHandler NewCaseEvent;
```

```
public void NewCase()
{
  NewCaseEvent(this, new EventArgs());
}
}
```

On the other end, we have event subscriptions like the one in the ModuleController class, as shown in Listing 6-4. Subscribing to an SCSF event is as easy as annotating an event handler with the EventSubscription attribute, which takes the name of the event and the threading option as parameters. The threading option allows fine-grained control about how this event handler is invoked, e.g., it allows for creating multicast event handlers. In this particular example, ModuleController creates a CaseDetailsView, which allows the application user to enter the details of a new case. Then ModuleController adds the view to the work items and calls the Show method with the appropriate location in the shell.

Listing 6-4. *ModuleController Event Subscriber*

```
public class ModuleController : WorkItemController
{
  ...
  [EventSubscription(EventTopicNames.NewCaseEvent, ThreadOption.UserInterface)]
  public void NewCaseEventHandler(object sender, EventArgs e)
  {
    CaseDetailsView myView = WorkItem.Items.AddNew<CaseDetailsView>();
    WorkItem.Workspaces[WorkspaceNames.DetailWorkspace].Show(myView);
  }
}
```

The full sequence beginning with the button click to displaying the view is shown in the sequence diagram in Figure 6-12. While the flow of control is nothing exciting, it shows all the participating classes in the case of the NewCaseEvent.

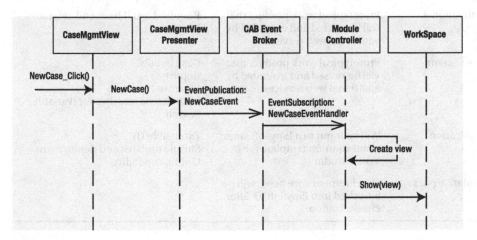

Figure 6-12. *Sequence diagram with participants in SCSF event*

Extraction of Core Assets

During the first iteration of product development, we extract a number of additional application core assets in order to populate the Software Factory template. Before we show what assets we extract, we need to point out that certainly not all work products that we created will be, or better should be, reusable. There is a certain cost involved with creating and maintain a reusable asset. Therefore, we need to use careful judgment of the involved cost to generalize the asset as a core asset of the factory.

For example, web services are great candidates for reuse because they should have been identified (ideally) from a business capability assessment. Data entity/schema may be reused as prototypical work products but have to be carefully versioned so they don't break the web service. There are a lot of considerations to identifying reusable assets, such as organizational and political considerations like who should be responsible for creating, maintaining, and versioning the asset.

To help us evolve the ISpySoft factory, Table 6-3 shows a list of things that either are already reusable assets or that can be used as input to build reusable assets for our ISpySoft factory in addition to the ones provided as Software Factory inputs. Application core assets typically have an m:n to relationship to solution features, which were determined during Software Factory specification. Variable features will either relate to optional assets (assets that are not used in every product) or to variation points in common assets.

Please note that this list is not yet complete, as we will continue covering the Software Factory template in the next chapter.

Table 6-3. *Core Assets Mapping to Solution Features*

Core Asset	Description	Addressed Solution Features
Case management web service	Provides case management business functionality to smart clients	Case administration Evidence documentation Power search Equipment requests (variable) Expenses (variable)
Data entity model	Prototypical work product that will be reused and extended by additional web services	Required by all back end-related features
Database schema	Prototypical work product that will be reused and extended by additional web services	Case details Report Expense (variable) Multimedia attachment (variable) Search
Shell application	Will be input to a ISpySoft smart client solution template for Visual Studio	Extensible UI Simple updates and deployment Offline capability
SCSF guidance package	Development core asset, will be absorbed into ISpySoft SF after customization	

Testing the Common Assets

 We want to emphasize that, when developing a Software Factory, you should follow the best practice to test early and to promote defense in depth. Core assets will be the foundation of many products. Any bug in core assets that is not found before application development might need to be fixed in many individual applications. Testing during product line development therefore becomes even more important than with one-off applications.

However, the good news is that since applications developed with a Software Factory are built on a number reusable core assets, bugs in these core assets need only be found once. While after building a number of products the increased reuse results in better quality, it requires additional effort in the development stages of a reusable asset. As with Software Factories in general, this higher up-front investment stands against the promise of more efficient development in the future and more reliable systems, as these are being built on top of already-tested components.

Unit Testing

 During our case study, we mainly placed emphasis on unit tests. Unit tests have many advantages, as probably every agile developer can confirm:

- Unit tests allow automated regression testing and continuous integration.

- Unit tests allow white-box testing (e.g., of internal methods).

- Unit tests support refactoring and code maintenance (very important for reusable assets).

- And last but not least, unit tests are a good reason to start test-driven development.[5]

Our unit testing tool of choice was NUnit[6] because we are familiar with it and it is freely available. We will not go into any further details about unit testing here as there is plenty of information available, e.g., on the referenced web sites. Please note that unit tests (and other tests) arise as work products, which then become assets just like the components that they were written for.

■**Note** If you are in the lucky situation to have a Visual Studio Team Suite Edition available, then you can also use the new VSTS unit testing. There is even an NUnit converter should you decide to start off with building NUnit tests but want to upgrade at a later point in time. VSTS unit testing is built into the Visual Studio IDE. Furthermore, VSTS unit testing provides direct life-cycle integration with other team system functionality (e.g., you can attach a defect to a work item and associate that work item with the unit test results).

---

5. http://www.testdriven.com/
6. http://www.nunit.org/

Interfaces and Testing

To top off the testing section, we want to share a good practice with you that allows for simplified testing of scenarios that cross boundaries between units, components, or even subsystems. Consider the scenario where you want to verify the functionality of a client-side service agent, which relies on a web service. Having to rely on the existence of a true web service for this test doesn't sound like a great idea. Not only would it considerably slow down this kind of test, but also it would introduce an external dependency for this test scenario.

The solution is to use interfaces whenever such boundaries are crossed. For this example, it means that the service agent will not work against a concrete instance of a web service proxy, but rather against an interface that is provided from the outside through dependency injection (yet another pattern).

By decoupling the service agent from a strong dependency to a web service reference, for testing we can now create a driver, which invokes the service agent, and a web service stub, which implements said interface and at the same time simulates the web service logic (driver and stub generation, yet another possibility to provide automation). When you start working with SCSF and look at the generated solution and project structures, you will notice that basically all intercomponent communication is performed through interfaces.

Another example for this driver-stub combination is given in Figure 6-13, which shows how a UI presenter can be unit tested without any actual UI. A unit test for a presenter will provide two test implementations, a driver for the view and a stub acting as a service agent used by the presenter (here *TestView* and *TestServiceAgent*). These test implementations are also often referred to as *mock objects*.

■Note Another possible alternative, although currently out of the scope of ISpySoft, would be to use the *Windows Communication Framework* (WCF, or codename Indigo) for communication. A reusable component becomes even more reusable in WCF, as it is a simple matter to change the communication method (one line) of the component without having to change any of the underlying plumbing. So as a best practice, we could take advantage of WCF whenever possible for ultimate communication agility.

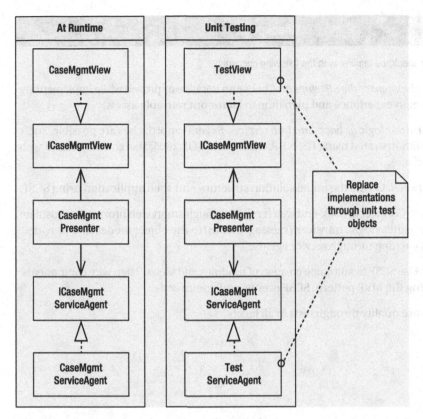

Figure 6-13. *Easy testing through use of interfaces*

Summary

In this chapter, we gave an introduction of how to harvest and implement some of the core assets required by the ISpySoft Software Factory in the course of actual product development. The activities that we performed, the work products that we built, and the reusable assets that we derived from these work products are all specified by the Software Factory schema.

We further demonstrated how SCSF provides a very flexible infrastructure framework for product line development. Regarding the architectural constraints imposed by using SCSF, developer guidance and automation in the form of GAT recipes greatly facilitated a good part of the recurring steps such as creating an initial solution structure or adding views. For now we used SCSF out of the box for the purpose of implementing some of the core assets. In the next chapter, we will truly consume SCSF, customize it, and make it an integral part of our Software Factory template.

Of course, there are lots of other core assets that need to be created in the course of our factory (such as the premium web services hosted centrally at ISpySoft). However, we felt demonstrating a thin slice of product development together with extraction of reusable assets and prototypical work products was most important in order to show how the Software Factory template can be built incrementally while providing real value as soon as possible.

Checkpoint

After this chapter, you should be familiar with the following concepts:

- *Iterative development of the SF template*: Choose an iterative approach while implementing products to gain experience and plan time to factor out reusable assets.

- *Exposing business logic as back-end web services*: Several approaches are possible, such as the one demonstrated using IIS, NHibernate, and SQL 2005. Use coarse-grained web service interfaces.

- *Smart client shell*: Create the initial solution structure and shell application using SCSF.

- *Service agents*: Connect to back-end web services through smart web proxies. Encapsulate client-side business logic, transform messages from/to the object model, and provide transparent caching through service agents.

- *UI modules*: Use SCSF to automate creation of modules and views. Then wire components together using the MVP pattern, SCSF events, and commands.

- *Testing*: Ensure quality through tests in all layers.

CHAPTER 7

■ ■ ■

Software Factory Template: Development Core Assets

 The product line members that we create with our Software Factory are assembled and configured from a set of core assets. These core assets provide all the common features and support for variable features that are specific to each application and in the scope of the factory. After having built a set of application core assets, as described in the previous chapter, we will now show you how to implement the development core assets for the ISpySoft factory.

Development core assets in a Software Factory include tools, guidance, and automation for the application developer to use during the application development process. These development core assets are packaged together with the application core assets and provided to the application developer through the Software Factory template. They are used during development to produce work products, as described by the Software Factory schema.

Based on our ISpySoft case study, we give two hands-on examples of development core assets: The first is contextual guidance and automation of Visual Studio 2005, a concept that you already used in the form of GAT packages and recipes during the implementation of the application core assets. The second example shows how we effectively address variability in a product line through domain-specific languages (DSL). Furthermore, we will cover these topics in this chapter:

- Background on guidance in context and automation

- Guidance Automation Toolkit (GAT)

- How to build a simple Visual Studio solution template with GAT (case study)

- How to identify application areas for DSLs

- Windows Workflow Foundation (WF)

- How to build a simple, long-running, interactive workflow (case study)

- Deploying the Software Factory template

█Note We could say that the GAT and DSL Tools are two down payments from Microsoft towards Software Factories. Therefore, we show how to incorporate these tools into our case study. As other tools become available, they could be incorporated in later iterations of Software Factory development.

Guidance and Guidance Automation

Providing and automating guidance is one means of exploiting economies of scope in the application development process. By guidance, we mean advice that helps developers know what to do, when to do it, and how to do it. Just as we can harvest and apply architectural assets that capture recurring structures in product line members, we can also harvest and apply guidance assets that capture recurring activities. Here are a few examples of recurring activities during application development:

- Setting up the development environment and initializing version control (e.g., by creating a new repository or a branch in an existing repository)

- Creating an initial Visual Studio solution populated with projects and source code files

- Creating a web service from a Web Services Description (WSDL) with stub and proxy classes

- Modeling a workflow

- Creating the participants of patterns (e.g., view, presenter, and interface source files in MVP)

- Building (compiling) and integrating the system

- Executing unit tests

- Packaging and deploying the application

Some these activities might occur only once in the life cycle of an application. However, in the context of product lines, these activities have to be performed for each and every application. By investing in guidance automation, we can exploit economies of scope throughout the development of multiple similar, yet distinct, applications.

The Basics

Guidance in context helps developers do the right thing at the right place and time in the context of a particular problem, much like a mentor. Often, guidance is contextualized by viewpoint, as viewpoints relate to clearly defined assets, activities, and work products. Simple forms of guidance are how-to documentation and comments in generated source code. A more advanced form involves automating this advice and providing it in the context where it is needed. This automated guidance will then enact actions or activities within the development environment to disburden the developer as much as possible when applying the provided advice.

Guidance often happens interactively and leaves room for variability. Here is an example: after the developer unfolds a Visual Studio project template to configure his development environment, the wizard displays a list of initial steps that need to be done in order to build an application. Within the list the developer would find actions like *Set Up Version Control* and *Add a New XYZ Component* to the Visual Studio solution. Through hyperlinks, the developer could start wizards for each of the activities.

The *Add a New XYZ Component* wizard could allow a developer to interactively pick from a number of features that the new component supports. Of course, these features stem from variabilities of the factory's underlying solution feature model.

Automation is the enactment of the provided guidance and occurs, for example, when the wizard automatically creates the initial project based on the provided information. In the following sections, we describe several not-so-obvious advantages and benefits that you can gain from investing into and applying contextual guidance and automation.

For a conventional one-off project, it is very difficult to plan for guidance or automation. The reason is that often the details of the application development process, and therefore the development activities, are not well known until the actual implementation phase. In contrast, if we look at the Software Factories paradigm, we can use the Software Factories schema as starting point. The schema helps us to identify the context and the activities in which the guidance applies and further enables us to automate this guidance.

The level of automation we implement will vary depending on the factory constraints such as time, budget, and scope, to name just a few. In the simplest case, we can provide specific documentation about the activities and the tools defined in the schema; a more advanced solution would provide semi- or entirely automated activities (e.g., based on a mapping between viewpoints) to produce certain work products. The automation and guidance for Software Factories are usually refined and extended in an iterative process, as is the Software Factories schema.

Incorporating Patterns and Best Practices

Patterns are generalized and proven solutions for known recurring problems in a defined context. Throughout a software project, many patterns can come into play, such as the Model-View-Presenter[1] (MVP) pattern, which separates the behavior from the GUI, or the dependency injection pattern,[2] which breaks dependencies between reusable components by injecting objects rather than relying on classes to create objects themselves. Other patterns used in the ISpySoft case study are Web Service Façades,[3] which provide coarse-grained interfaces to access subsystems in a uniform way, and the Service Locator pattern,[4] a derivative of the dependency injection pattern used in the smart client application to break dependencies of service consumers on services.

Some of the applied patterns might already be prescribed in the software architecture. Other patterns we discover during the planning phase of the Software Factory (e.g., when harvesting existing assets), during an iteration of building application core assets for the Software Factory template, or during application development.

More often than identifying patterns, though, we will be able to discover best practices. While patterns are generic solutions to problems, the best practices we find might only apply to a specific Software Factory, such as how to structure a Visual Studio solution effectively for ISpySoft product line members.

---

1. http://www.martinfowler.com/eaaDev/ModelViewPresenter.html
2. http://www.martinfowler.com/articles/injection.html
3. http://www.soaprpc.com/patterns/archives/000037.html
4. http://java.sun.com/blueprints/patterns/ServiceLocator.html

Members of a product line usually share most of these patterns and best practices. The goal is to relate these findings to activities as defined by the Software Factory schema, and capture and incorporate guidance as well as the best practices and patterns themselves in the Software Factory template. Therefore we can make this expert knowledge available to every application developer as guidance during application development, at the right time and in the correct context.

 During the first iterations of implementing application core assets for our ISpySoft factory template, we were able to identify a number of patterns and best practices; Table 7-1 shows some examples. Each finding describes how guidance could be provided (not necessarily in an automated way). Furthermore, we relate each pattern or best practice back to variabilities and extensions as defined in Chapter 3.

Table 7-1. *Patterns and Best Practices for ISpySoft Guidance*

Identified Item	Used in	Delivery	Supported Variability/Extension
Patterns			
Facade pattern.	Back-end web services expose coarse-grained interfaces acting as facades.	Provided as textual advice after creating a web service.	Additional web service as extension
Model-View-Presenter pattern.	Used in smart client applications to decouple UI from business logic.	Automation through GAT recipe that creates participating classes.	Extensible user interface
Factory pattern.	Provides a factory for NHibernate sessions (DB connections).	Readily provided as reusable component; additionally, textual instructions are provided.	Custom extensions to back-end services
Service Locator pattern.	Used in smart client applications to break dependencies between services and service consumers.	Provided as textual advice after creating a smart client module.	Shell application extensible with additional modules
Best Practices			
Make ISpySoft SF documentation available.	Software Factory schema browser.	Quick and centralized access from the IDE (e.g., as shortcut).	
How to build smart clients.	Build smart clients as prescribed by SCSF.	Integrate documentation from existing SCSF guidance.	Shell application extensible with additional modules
Decouple data models.	Define web service information models (message formats) independently from data entity models and provide transformation classes.	Provided as textual advice after creating an ISpySoft solution.	Shell application extensible with additional modules
In-project unit tests.	Use in-project unit test fixtures to allow for white box testing.	Provide unit test fixture template through GAT recipe.	

Boilerplating Code and Error-prone, Menial Activities

Software development is supposed to be fun and should consist of creating the interesting and unique features of a system. However, the truth is that much of a developer's time is spent on creating boilerplate code and wiring components together. Many of these steps need to be done repetitively while at the same time the boundaries of variation are limited and well known.

Today's IDEs already provide a great number of tools that help automate some of these cumbersome activities, such as the WinForms editor that easily allows us to assemble a UI and create event handlers. Another great example for automation of a boilerplate activity is Visual Studio's *Add Web Reference* wizard. This wizard queries a web service for its Web Services Description (WSDL) and then uses it to generate a client-side web service proxy with an object model. This proxy and its object model directly map to the messages defined in the WSDL contract (the service information model), which are exchanged with the web service. Writing this code manually could take anything from half an hour to multiple days, depending on the complexity of the web service interface.

Automation tools can come in multiple forms, e.g., as a stand-alone windows application, as a batch-capable command line tool, or as some kind of add-in for an IDE. Before Visual Studio 2005, it was a very cumbersome activity to extend Visual Studio with add-ins. However, VS 2005 now has an improved add-in mechanism. On top of that, other tools like the Guidance Automation Toolkit[5] make it easier to provide automation within the IDE for development activities.

During the development of ISpySoft-based applications, we ran across a number of recurring activities. Several examples are shown in Table 7-2 together with possible ways of automating the activity to make development more efficient. Depending on the frequency and complexity of such recurring activities, we can effectively prioritize them when planning for automation.

Table 7-2. *Boilerplating Activities in ISpySoft*

Activity	Frequency	Possible Automation
Set up VS solution structure for new product line member, create projects, reference core asset assemblies, etc.	Once per application	GAT recipe and VS template.
Create NUnit test fixture, include NUnit namespace, and annotate test fixture with attributes.	Frequently for any kind of component	Visual Studio template.
Create NHibernate entity class, include a number of namespaces, annotate class and properties with attributes, and look up documentation about NHibernate attributes.	Multiple times for back-end service extensions	Visual Studio template, mapping wizard accessible from the context menu of .cs files.
Create mapping code to transform data entity model to web service information model and vice versa.	Once per additional smart web reference	Provide mapping wizard that generates large parts of the mapping code.

---

5. http://lab.msdn.microsoft.com/teamsystem/workshop/gat/download.aspx

The Guidance Automation Toolkit

In the last chapter, we made first contact with GAT packages as we used them to create smart client projects, MVP views, and smart web references. Now it is time to show how you can create your own GAT packages to extend Visual Studio and offer guidance to application developers. The guidance is provided in a defined context, and developers activate the guidance through gestures in Visual Studio, such as by selecting a menu item in a context menu.

For example, consider a guidance recipe that modifies a single class by extending it with attributes. It can only be executed in the context of a class. The provided gesture is a context menu item, *Annotate with Attributes*, that only appears when right-clicking a class in Visual Studio Solution Explorer. When the developer clicks this menu item, the recipe executes a series of activities.

The Basic Components of GAT

Figure 7-1 shows the key concepts provided by GAT,[6] which are as follows

- The functionality of guidance packages is made up of recipes, actions, VS templates, and T4 text templates. Guidance packages are the top-level concepts of GAT and tie these parts together.

- Recipes automate repetitive activities that developers otherwise would have to perform manually. A recipe contains actions and defines the order in which they are executed. Furthermore, a recipe can contain other recipes and templates and make use of value providers like wizards and type converters in order to dynamically gather data.

  A recipe can either be defined as *single execution*, in which case it will disappear from menus and command bars after it was executed the first time, or *multiple executions*, in which case it can be executed over and over again. GAT provides two types of recipes:

- *Bound*: A (contextually) bound recipe is a recipe that is associated with a certain type of Visual Studio solution element, such as class files, projects, or solution folders. A recipe is associated with a solution element by first creating a reference of that recipe and then associating the recipe reference with the particular Visual Studio Solution element. Bound recipes can often be accessed from the context menu of the associated solution element.

- *Unbound*: An unbound recipe is not directly associated with a particular solution element. In order to use an unbound recipe, we have to create an unbound recipe reference that allows for greater control with the solution elements a recipe is associated with. For example, an unbound recipe reference could associate itself with a subset of C# projects in a solution or all solution elements whose name matches a certain pattern. The selection condition is defined in reference code written in C# or Visual Basic .NET, which allows for very complex selection conditions.

---

6. Find more information on the GAT at http://lab.msdn.microsoft.com/teamsystem/workshop/gat/intro.aspx.

- Actions are automation blocks used by recipes that invoke them. They accept input either from arguments gathered by the calling recipe using value providers or from output created by actions run earlier in the sequence.

- T4 templates consist of a combination of template parts and scriptlets (it kind of looks like ASP code). The scriptlets are expressions written in either C# or Visual Basic .NET and return text that is inserted into the enclosing template parts. The same template mechanism is used by code generators for Visual Studio's *DSL Toolkit*, as demonstrated in Chapter 5.

- Visual Studio templates are a Visual Studio extensibility mechanism used to unfold solutions, projects, or project items, and defined in XML format. GAT allows us to combine VS templates with recipes. Using GAT packages, we can further customize the creation of solutions, projects, and project items. VS templates defined in a GAT package are automatically added to the *Guidance Packages* entry in the *New Project* menu in Visual Studio and will be unfolded when executed from there.

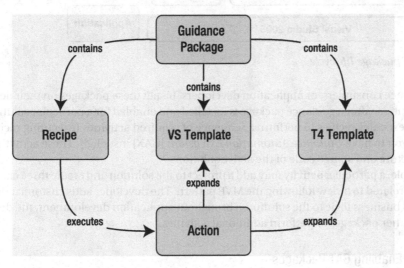

Figure 7-1. *Key concepts of GAT packages*

GAT Package Life Cycle

Figure 7-2 illustrates how a guidance package is created and used across the development life cycle. First, guidance authors, or in our case the Software Factory authors, use the Guidance Automation Toolkit to create guidance packages, which typically contain hooks into Visual Studio, UI elements (value providers) to capture additional information, templates, and automation code to generate some kind of output. After building one or more guidance packages, the guidance author distributes them in the form of a Windows Installer package.

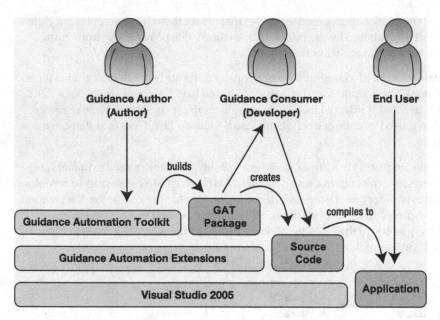

Figure 7-2. *GAT package life cycle*

The guidance consumers, or application developers, install these packages on their development computers. After a guidance package is installed and enabled for a particular solution, the developer executes recipes to perform a sequence of required activities (executing recipes only requires you to have *Guidance Automation Extensions* [GAX] installed). These activities affect the structure and source code of the active solution.

For example, a particular activity may add a project to the solution and create three classes in that project related to a view following the MVP pattern. The developer adds customizations and additional business logic to the solution. Throughout application development, the developer will use other packages to perform additional activities.

Installing and Enabling GAT Packages

Guidance packages map relatively easily to viewpoints in the schema. Therefore, if you build a guidance package for each viewpoint, the user can focus on a viewpoint by enabling the corresponding guidance package. Guidance packages can be enabled in two ways:

- Manually select and enable the recipes in *Guidance Package Manager* from the Tools menu.

- Unfold a Visual Studio project template, which programmatically enables the corresponding recipes.

In the context of a Software Factory template, the latter is the best option, as it activates the guidance transparently to the application developer.

■Note As a guidance author, if you want to install a GAT package on the same computer that was used to develop it, you must first unregister the development guidance package before you install the MSI. To do this, use the *Unregister Guidance Package* recipe (available in Guidance Package Manager when you have GAT installed).

GAT Recipes and the Software Factory Schema

As mentioned earlier, in the context of Software Factories, each GAT recipe will provide guidance and automation for one or more activities that were defined in the Software Factory schema. A good way to lead developers from one guidance step to the next is to display summary pages after each recipe with advice on what steps come next in the application development process or are related in other ways. In Figure 6-8 in the previous chapter, we saw such a summary page provided by SCSF.

In an advanced Software Factory, it should even be possible to generate such summary pages directly from the Software Factory schema. This guidance documentation would be similar to what we provide through the Software Factory Schema Browser, even though our proof-of-concept does not integrate directly into the IDE. For a product development environment, this documentation should appear right in the Visual Studio IDE.

ISpySoft GAT Packages

 It is now time to put this theory to work by implementing a GAT package for our ISpySoft factory. We start with a simple example, a GAT package that creates a solution structure in Visual Studio. After that, we explore how the template can be extended in order to provide us with the initial solution structure for ISpySoft applications. Finally, we show you how to create a context-sensitive recipe that is bound to projects in that particular solution. While these are all simple examples, they show the main concepts that are used to implement the ISpySoft GAT packages, which are part of the case study that you can download from the Apress web site[7] or the book's web site.[8]

The Smart Client Software Factory (SCSF) already provides a number of GAT packages. While developing our ISpySoft factory, we will absorb these GAT packages with their templates and recipes, such as creating a smart web reference, and customize them to make them fit for ISpySoft. The end result will be a seamlessly integrated set of guidance packages provided through the ISpySoft Software Factory template.

Unfolding a Simple Visual Studio Project Template

Guidance packages often include Visual Studio templates that appear in the *New Project* or *Add New Item* dialog box of Visual Studio. These templates generally appear under the category *Guidance Packages* in these two dialogs.

---

7. http://www.apress.com
8. http://www.ISpySoft.net

The easiest way to start a new GAT package is to use the *Guidance Package* template. A wizard captures some basic information such as the package name, caption, description, namespace, and author, as shown in Figure 7-3.

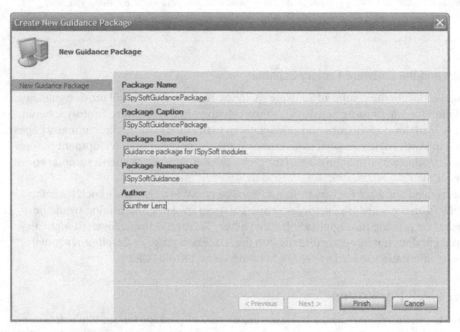

Figure 7-3. *New Guidance Package wizard*

Clicking the Finish button will result in the creation of the solution structure that is the starting point for your own guidance packages. This structure might look confusing at first glance, because the content is very comprehensive and contains many examples for different scenarios that enable you to quickly get familiar with GAT.

However, many of the examples provided by this template do not apply to the guidance we need for the ISpySoft factory. Therefore, we strip the initial guidance package template down to the bare minimum that is necessary. Figure 7-4 shows what our guidance package looks like. This is the baseline for our GAT package development that later will become part of the SF template.

In general, we recommend that whenever you start building a GAT package, you use the Guidance Package template. Even though you will have to take out all the items that do not apply in your case, the advantages are that you get the initial solution structure as well as the installer for your new GAT package.

Unfortunately, tool support to create and maintain GAT packages is still very limited. That means in the course of building GAT packages we won't get around some extensive editing of XML files, which contain all sorts of definitions, template code, and other information. To give you a bit of a head start for your own first tries, we picked three of the most important files and examined them a little more closely. On the positive side, the VS XML editor provides you with IntelliSense, as each of these XML files references an XML schema defining the template format.

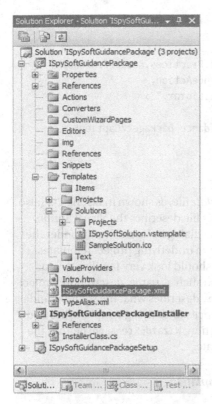

Figure 7-4. *Baseline ISpySoft guidance package solution structure*

The *ISpySoftGuidancePackage.xml* file is the central configuration file, and it contains definitions for the recipes provided by the guidance package, as shown in a stripped down version in Listing 7-1. After installation through the Software Factory template, the GAT runtime will read this file to provide recipes from within Visual Studio as guidance to the ISpySoft developer.

The only recipe in this simple example, `BindingRecipe`, is the obligatory binding recipe, which creates references of unbound recipes as launch points. Unbound recipes, unlike bound recipes, are not associated with any particular solution element. You would usually find actions in this section that create references of unbound recipes, but for the sake of simplicity we omit these for now. We will define more recipes and actions later when we extend this simple GAT package.

Listing 7-1. *ISpySoftGuidancePackage.xml*

```
<GuidancePackage xmlns="http://schemas.microsoft.com/pag/gax-core"
    Name="ISpySoftGuidancePackage"
    Caption="ISpySoft Guidance Package"
    Description="Guidance for ISpySoft modules"
    BindingRecipe="BindingRecipe"
    Guid="991a5cc3-141d-4bda-a8ae-4bb22232173e"
    SchemaVersion="1.0">
```

```
    <Recipes>
      <Recipe Name="BindingRecipe">
        <Types>
          <TypeAlias Name="RefCreator" Type="Microsoft.Practices.RecipeFramework.
                  Library.Actions.CreateUnboundReferenceAction,
                  Microsoft.Practices.RecipeFramework.Library"/>
        </Types>
        <Caption>Creates unbound references to the guidance package</Caption>
      </Recipe>
    </Recipes>
</GuidancePackage>
```

The next file we look at is the *ISpySoftSolution.vstemplate* file, as shown in Listing 7-2 (also take a look back at Figure 7-4, which displays this file). This file describes the Visual Studio solution template that you will later find in the *New Project* dialog in Visual Studio under the *Guidance Packages* entry. This file provides references to the underlying project templates. If you have ever used Visual Studio templates before, this should look very familiar to you.

The TemplateData node contains common information such as name, description, project type, and a default name. The TemplateContent section now describes what the solution folder structure really looks like. It defines directories and references underlying template files and projects that get copied into these directories. The last section, WizardExtension, defines the component that is used to unfold the Visual Studio template.

Listing 7-2. *ISpySoftSolution.vstemplate (Visual Studio Template)*

```
<VSTemplate Version="2.0" Type="ProjectGroup"
      xmlns="http://schemas.microsoft.com/developer/vstemplate/2005">
  <TemplateData>
    <Name>ISpySoft Solution</Name>
    <Description>ISpySoft Solution</Description>
    <ProjectType>CSharp</ProjectType>
    <SortOrder>90</SortOrder>
    <Icon>SampleSolution.ico</Icon>
    <CreateNewFolder>false</CreateNewFolder>
    <DefaultName>ISpySoftSolution</DefaultName>
    <ProvideDefaultName>true</ProvideDefaultName>
  </TemplateData>
  <TemplateContent>
    <ProjectCollection>
      <SolutionFolder Name="SampleFolder">
        <ProjectTemplateLink ProjectName="$ProjectName$">
            Projects\ConsoleApplication\ConsoleApplication.vstemplate
        </ProjectTemplateLink>
      </SolutionFolder>
    </ProjectCollection>
  </TemplateContent>
```

```
<WizardExtension>
  <Assembly>
      Microsoft.Practices.RecipeFramework.VisualStudio, Version=1.0.51206.0,
      Culture=neutral, PublicKeyToken=b03f5f7f11d50a3a
  </Assembly>
  <FullClassName>
      Microsoft.Practices.RecipeFramework.VisualStudio.Templates.UnfoldTemplate
  </FullClassName>
</WizardExtension>
</VSTemplate>
```

The last file that we examine is a project template as defined in the *ConsoleApplication. vstemplate* file, shown in Listing 7-3. We left this console application template in our initial example for demonstration purposes. After the TemplateData node (as shown in the solution template), the TemplateContent node defines the items that get unfolded at execution time of the project template, such as the ConsoleApplication.csproj project file. This project file furthermore contains project-specific settings like debug and release configuration information. With the *AssemblyInfo.cs* file, you see an example of how a project template references other project items.

You can run this example by following the instructions in *Intro.htm* (located in the GAT start menu), which explains how to build, install, and activate this basic guidance package. More information on the Visual Studio template format is available at the Microsoft MSDN web site.[9]

Listing 7-3. *ConsoleApplication.vstemplate (Visual Studio Template)*

```
<VSTemplate Version="2.0.0" Type="Project"
      xmlns="http://schemas.microsoft.com/developer/vstemplate/2005">
  <TemplateData>
    <Name>Sample Console Client</Name>
    <Description>Sample console application</Description>
    <Icon Package="{FAE04EC1-301F-11d3-BF4B-00C04F79EFBC}" ID="4547" />
    <ProjectType>CSharp</ProjectType>
    <SortOrder>20</SortOrder>
    <CreateNewFolder>false</CreateNewFolder>
    <DefaultName>SampleConsole</DefaultName>
    <ProvideDefaultName>true</ProvideDefaultName>
  </TemplateData>
  <TemplateContent>
    <Project File="ConsoleApplication.csproj" ReplaceParameters="true">
      <ProjectItem ReplaceParameters="true">Properties\AssemblyInfo.cs</ProjectItem>
    </Project>
  </TemplateContent>
```

___

9. http://msdn2.microsoft.com/en-us/library/6db0hwky.aspx

```
  <WizardExtension>
    <Assembly>
      Microsoft.Practices.RecipeFramework.VisualStudio, Version=1.0.51206.0,
      Culture=neutral, PublicKeyToken=b03f5f7f11d50a3a
    </Assembly>
    <FullClassName>
      Microsoft.Practices.RecipeFramework.VisualStudio.Templates.UnfoldTemplate
    </FullClassName>
  </WizardExtension>
</VSTemplate>
```

Extending the Visual Studio Project Template

This simple template example shows you how solution and project templates are integrated in GAT packages. From this baseline, we can derive an ISpySoft guidance package that enables us to create an initial solution structure for ISpySoft applications. In this first iteration of the Software Factory template development, an initial solution structure for an ISpySoft application will contain the following items:

- A WinForms smart client application

- One smart client module containing an empty view

- An empty service agent

- An empty back-end web service

- A template component for NHibernate business entities

- Template projects for common functionality and business logic

- References to application core asset assemblies

The ISpySoft solution template contains multiple initial folders, projects, and project items. Additionally, each project already contains references that point to libraries and assemblies that are required for each type of project. For example, each project contains references to the NUnit framework, UI module projects point to Enterprise Library libraries, and back-end projects reference the NHibernate assemblies required for database access. The final ISpySoft solution template is included in the download package of our case study, which is available from this book's web site or from the Apress web site.

Recipes and Actions Executing Text Templates

Now that we provided the initial project structure, the next step is to build additional guidance functionality in the form of recipes that developers can use at development time. These recipes can, e.g., be executed from the context menu of certain project items. As an exercise, we will extend the earlier example and create an *Add NHibernate Entity Class* recipe that provides the following functionality:

1. Add menu item *Add NHibernate Entity Class* to the context menu of projects and folders.

2. Provide a wizard that, upon execution of the recipe, asks the user for a class name and the name of the mapped database table.

3. The namespace of the generated class stub is automatically derived from the containing project and the path where the file will be placed.

4. Then, the recipe generates the class and NHibernate mapping attributes based on the information provided through the wizard.

This recipe will be used when developers extend the data entities in the back-end services. These data entities are mapped to database tables using NHibernate. The purpose of this recipe is to automate the recurring steps that need to be performed for each data entity such as including a number of namespaces, creating the class stub, inserting several NHibernate attributes, etc.

Furthermore, the file template used for this recipe contains some comments with code snippets for frequently used NHibernate mapping attribute combinations, such as for ID fields or one-to-many and many-to-one relations, in order to make the developer's life easier.

T4 Template

The first step in creating the *Add NHibernate Entity Class* recipe is to define a T4 file template that will unfold upon recipe execution, as shown in Listing 7-4. Note how it defines the three input parameters at the very top that will be used to generate the class file.

Listing 7-4. *NHibernateEntity.cs.t4 Template*

```
<#@ template language="C#" #>
<#@ property processor="PropertyProcessor" name="TargetNamespace" #>
<#@ property processor="PropertyProcessor" name="ClassName" #>
<#@ property processor="PropertyProcessor" name="TableName " #>
using System;
using System.Collections;
using NHibernate;
using NHibernate.Collection;
using NHibernate.Mapping.Attributes;
using NHibernate.Property;
using NHibernate.Type;

namespace <#= TargetNamespace #>
{
  [Class(0, NameType = typeof(<#= ClassName #>), Table="<#= TableName #>")]
  public class <#= ClassName #>
  {
    // ...
  }
}
```

Recipe Definition

In the next step, we add a recipe, called *AddNHibernateEntityClass*, to the *ISpySoftGuidance-Package.xml* file. You can see the first part of this recipe in Listing 7-5. This is an unbound recipe (the Bound tag is set to false) and requires a recipe reference that selects the appropriate solution elements for which this recipe will be available. A TypeAlias tag will allow us later on to use short names for external types, therefore making the XML code more readable. Additional information provided is the caption for the recipe, which will be shown in the project context menu, the Icon for the context menu entry, and the CommandBars in which the recipe will be available.

Listing 7-5. *AddNHibernateEntityClassRecipe, Recipe Definition*

```
<GuidancePackage>
  <Recipes>
    ...
    <Recipe Name="AddNHibernateEntityClass" Bound="false">
      <Types xmlns="http://schemas.microsoft.com/pag/gax-core">
        <TypeAlias Name="Evaluator" Type="Microsoft.Practices.RecipeFramework.
            Library.ValueProviders.ExpressionEvaluatorValueProvider,
            Microsoft.Practices.RecipeFramework.Library" />
      </Types>
      <Caption>Add NHibernate Entity Class</Caption>
      <HostData>
        <Icon ID="630" />
        <CommandBar Name="Project" />
        <CommandBar Name="Folder" />
      </HostData>
      ...
    </Recipe>
  </Recipes>
</GuidancePackage>
```

Recipe Argument Definition

In order to expand the class template correctly, the *AddNHibernateEntityClass* recipe requires several arguments that are passed on to the recipe, which is shown in Listing 7-6. The first argument is the CurrentProject name, which is automatically provided by the FirstSelectedProject value provider. The next arguments are ClassName and TableName, which need to be gathered via a UI wizard from the user. When collecting information from the user, this information needs to be translated to a system type by a type converter, which, in our case, is performed by the CodeIdentifierStringConverter. The TargetFile argument is automatically generated from the ClassName argument plus a .cs file name extension by the string Evaluator. The last argument, TargetNamespace, retrieves the default namespace from the previous CurrentProject argument.

Listing 7-6. *AddNHibernateEntityClassRecipe, Arguments Definition*

```xml
<Recipe Name="AddNHibernateEntityClass" Bound="false">
  ...
  <Arguments>
    <Argument Name="CurrentProject" Type="EnvDTE.Project, EnvDTE,
        Version=8.0.0.0, Culture=neutral, PublicKeyToken=b03f5f7f11d50a3a">
      <ValueProvider Type="Microsoft.Practices.RecipeFramework.Library.
          ValueProviders.FirstSelectedProject,
          Microsoft.Practices.RecipeFramework.Library" />
    </Argument>
    <Argument Name="ClassName">
      <Converter Type="Microsoft.Practices.RecipeFramework.Library.
          Converters.CodeIdentifierStringConverter,
          Microsoft.Practices.RecipeFramework.Library"/>
    </Argument>
    <Argument Name="TableName">
      <Converter Type="Microsoft.Practices.RecipeFramework.Library.
          Converters.CodeIdentifierStringConverter,
          Microsoft.Practices.RecipeFramework.Library"/>
    </Argument>
    <Argument Name="TargetFile">
      <ValueProvider Type="Evaluator" Expression="$(ClassName).cs">
        <MonitorArgument Name="ClassName" />
      </ValueProvider>
    </Argument>
    <Argument Name="TargetNamespace">
      <Converter Type="Microsoft.Practices.RecipeFramework.Library.
          Converters.NamespaceStringConverter,
          Microsoft.Practices.RecipeFramework.Library"/>
      <ValueProvider Type="Evaluator" Expression=
          "$(CurrentProject.Properties.Item('DefaultNamespace').Value)" />
    </Argument>
  </Arguments>
  ...
</Recipe>
```

Wizards for Gathering User Input

During execution of the recipe, the values for the two arguments ClassName and TableName need to be gathered from the user by a wizard UI. This wizard is defined in the GatheringServiceData section as shown in Listing 7-7. In this particular case, the wizard has two textboxes for the class name and the name of the mapped database table. When the developer executes the wizard, both values will be stored in the respective arguments as defined in Listing 7-6.

Listing 7-7. *AddNHibernateEntityClass Recipe, Gathering Data*

```
<Recipe Name="AddNHibernateEntityClass" Bound="false">
  ...
  <GatheringServiceData>
    <Wizard xmlns="http://schemas.microsoft.com/pag/gax-wizards"
        SchemaVersion="1.0">
      <Pages>
        <Page>
          <Title>Specify the new NHibernate Entity Class</Title>
          <Fields>
            <Field ValueName="ClassName" Label="Class Name" />
            <Field ValueName="TableName" Label="Mapped Table Name" />
          </Fields>
        </Page>
      </Pages>
    </Wizard>
  </GatheringServiceData>
  ...
</Recipe>
```

Recipe Actions

The *AddNHibernateEntityClass* recipe consists of two actions that are performed in sequence, as shown in Listing 7-8: generate the NHibernate entity class, and add it to the current project. The first action, CreateClass, uses the *NHibernateEntity.cs.t4* template (as shown in Listing 7-4) to generate the class by filling in the input arguments that were collected from the user and from Visual Studio. As mentioned earlier, T4 templates used in GAT follow the same syntax as the code generation templates used with the DSL Toolkit.

The T4 engine transforms the template into a string value that is made available to other actions through the output parameter Content. This output parameter is then used as one of the inputs for the AddClass action, which additionally requires TargetFile and CurrentProject as input, and attaches the generated file to the project.

Listing 7-8. *AddNHibernateEntityClass Recipe, Actions*

```
<Recipe Name="AddNHibernateEntityClass" Bound="false">
  ...
  <Actions>
    <Action Name="CreateClass" Type="Microsoft.Practices.RecipeFramework.
        VisualStudio.Library.Templates.TextTemplateAction,
        Microsoft.Practices.RecipeFramework.VisualStudio.Library"
        Template="Text\NHibernateEntity.cs.t4">
      <Input Name="TargetNamespace" RecipeArgument="TargetNamespace"/>
      <Input Name="ClassName" RecipeArgument="ClassName"/>
      <Input Name="TableName" RecipeArgument="TableName"/>
      <Output Name="Content" />
    </Action>
```

```
    <Action Name="AddClass" Type="Microsoft.Practices.RecipeFramework.
      Library.Actions.AddItemFromStringAction,
        Microsoft.Practices.RecipeFramework.Library" Open="true">
      <Input Name="Content" ActionOutput="CreateClass.Content" />
      <Input Name="TargetFileName" RecipeArgument="TargetFile" />
      <Input Name="Project" RecipeArgument="CurrentProject" />
    </Action>
  </Actions>
</Recipe>
```

Referencing the Recipe

We are almost done. But one important part is still missing. If you try to build, register, and activate the GAT package now, you will notice that you don't see the recipe in the context menu of any project or folder. The reason is that we did not define a reference to the recipe yet (remember, we are creating an unbound recipe).

Therefore, we need to add a few lines of code to the BindingRecipe that is executed when a developer enables a guidance package. This recipe will register all unbound recipes, which then become available in any solution.

Listing 7-9 shows the extended BindingRecipe element that will make the recipe available in the context menu of the project file and project folder (as defined in the recipe in Listing 7-5). Now when you build, register, and activate the GAT package from the Guidance Package Manager, you will see the new entry in the context menu of any project file and project folder.

Lisitng 7-9. *Unbound Recipe Reference*

```
<GuidancePackage>
  ...
  <Recipes>
    <Recipe Name="BindingRecipe">
      ...
      <Actions>
        <Action Name="UnboundAddNHibernateEntityClass" Type="RefCreator"
          AssetName="AddNHibernateEntityClass" ReferenceType=
          "ISpySoft.Guidance.References.AnyElementReference,
          ISpySoftGuidancePackage" />
      </Actions>
    </Recipe>
    ...
  </Recipes>
</GuidancePackage>
```

Reusing and Extending Guidance and Automation

In the previous sections, we showed you simple examples of how to create GAT packages that unfold Visual Studio Templates, define custom actions, bind recipes, use text templates, etc. So now is the time to step back to see whether we can reuse any existing guidance assets.

For example, we might be able to reuse parts of the Smart Client Software Factory with its viewpoints, core assets, and framework. It should be obvious that there is great potential for reuse of existing GAT recipes provided by SCSF. Because we are providing a factory for the vertical domain of private investigators, we can reuse many of the guidance assets provided by the horizontal SCSF after specializing and extending them.

The following list names a few recipes contained in the guidance package that are provided by the ISpySoft Software Factory template. Furthermore, each item indicates whether it was derived from an SCSF recipe.

- Create a new ISpySoft solution, create the initial smart client shell form, and reference assemblies that provide basic services such as logging, caching, and security (derived from the Guidance Package template and the SCSF *Create Light Weight Smart Client* recipe).

- Create a module (subapplication) project that plugs into an ISpySoft shell (derived from the SCSF *Add Module* recipe).

- Create smart web proxy project that connects to a back-end shell (derived from the SCSF *Add Smart Web Reference* recipe).

- Create empty back-end web service and reference the typically required assemblies.

- Create deployment project for back-end services.

- Create empty NHibernate entity class.

- Create factory class for data entity with standard methods such as GetByID, Save, Delete, etc.

- Create empty NUnit test fixture.

This concludes the guidance and automation part of this chapter. As always, you can find the full implementation in our ISpySoft case study available for download.

Variabilities and Domain-specific Languages

 Now we will get to a different aspect of how to support variabilities in Software Factories, namely through DSLs. You have already been exposed to two ISpySoft DSLs, the feature modeling language and our Software Factory schema DSL. While those two were used for implementation of our factory itself, DSLs are an even more powerful means to model variabilities during application development.

DSLs are a good way to support developers in areas that go beyond plain configuration or manually writing source code. As shown in Figure 7-5, Czarnecki explains variability using graphs that represent the space of variability. Depending on the complexity of variability, he differentiates between the following ways to select a subgraph of features:

- *Path through a decision tree*: Decisions are made top down, from general to detail. Typical examples for top-down decision trees are installation wizards, project templates, etc. This method is typically applied in sequential decision processes.

- *Subtree of a feature tree*: Here we select and deselect whole branches of a graph representing the variability. Our problem and solution feature models are a good example for this.

- *Subgraph of an infinite graph*: As an example, consider business processes within an enterprise. All the possible business processes form the infinite graph. It is impossible at Software Factory development time to account for all the possible processes. This is exactly where DSLs come into play because models created with DSLs can cover the wide range of variation represented in the infinite graph.

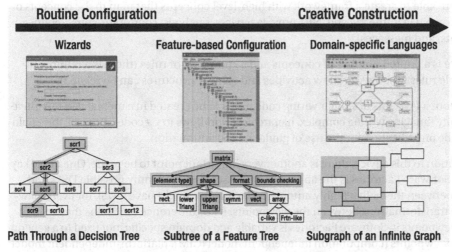

Figure 7-5. *Variability explained using graphs (courtesy of Krzysztof Czarnecki)[10]*

■**Tip** We could extend Figure 7-5 at the right of domain-specific languages with some interesting points such as frameworks, libraries, templates, patterns, guidelines, and raw coding.

So what are the indications that you could potentially use a DSL to capture variabilities? To answer this question, let's first consider the example of a Software Factory for an enterprise application involving workflows that are based on business processes. The solution feature model developed during the planning phase includes workflow-related concepts like actors, data entities, services, events, notifications, tracking, long-running processes, and asynchronous notifications. On top of that, these workflows should be highly configurable.

10. Krzysztof Czarnecki, "Overview of Generative Software Development," *Unconventional Programming Paradigms: International Workshop UPP 2004*, vol. 3566, *Lecture Notes in Computer Science*, eds. J.-P. Banâtre et al. (Berlin/Heidelberg: Springer-Verlag, 2005), pp. 313–328

The result is that during development of core assets, items like data entities, services, or transaction support can readily be implemented as core assets, but the creation of workflows, the wiring, needs to be done during development of the individual application. Of course, you can already guess the solution to this problem, which is to introduce a DSL such as the BizTalk Orchestration Designer or the Windows Workflow Foundation. We will soon get to this point, but let's first finish the indications for applying DSLs:

- Most important: the domain is *well understood* and domain experts are available (in our case, we have business analysts that define the business processes that are the basis for the workflows). In contrast, domains that are poorly understood, highly variable, or undergoing rapid technology churn are generally poor candidates for automation using DSLs.

- We are able to create a framework with high-level concepts that map to the concepts of the domain (e.g., the WF and .NET provide services, methods, control structures, entities, events, and messages).

- There is a limited number of concepts and a known set of rules (there is a number of simple rules for how workflow activities and control structures can be related).

- Without a DSL, lots of similar wiring code needs to be created in a menial and repetitive activity (imagine writing complex, hierarchical workflows in C# code). Even so, this could also be an indication for the use of guidance and automation.

In addition to this advice, there is another very important point to be made. One of the key benefits of Software Factories is the ability to use the schema to identify possible DSLs and mappings between them. In a highly automated factory, we might have a DSL for every viewpoint, with transformations between the viewpoints. A key difference to MDA is the fact that the set of viewpoints in Software Factories is variable and domain specific, not fixed to a generic set of three viewpoints (computation independent model [CIM], platform-independent model [PIM], and platform-specific model [PSM]) for all product families as it is defined by MDA. In fact, the Software Factories methodology was developed to enable working with DSLs, in the same way that RUP was developed to be the methodology for working with UML. The reason we spend a lot of time on the nonmodeling aspects of Software Factories is because software development involves much more than just modeling, a fact that MDA does not address.

However, keep in mind that DSLs require greater up-front investment than other types of development assets. Still, even though it might sound difficult to create a DSL, designing one yourself is probably easier than you might think, as domain experts are already familiar with most of the concepts that a DSL is supposed to represent.

For the remainder of this chapter, we will look into the Workflow Foundation, a very flexible DSL that allows us to model workflow and state models.

■**Note** The curious reader will probably ask whether the Workflow Foundation DSL was developed using the DSL Toolkit that we used for our DSLs. Surprisingly, the answer to that question is no. However, the work on the Workflow Foundation was started from an early version of the same code base.

Windows Workflow Foundation

The Windows Workflow Foundation allows us to model workflows using a graphical designer that is integrated into Visual Studio 2005. It allows us to build applications with configurable workflows (even configurable at runtime) that are based on activities and declarative rules that combine and link these activities. WF workflows are completely extensible, as developers create their own activities implementing domain-specific functions; it is even possible to create new control constructs, such as a do...while loop. As there are other in-depth books[11] and articles[12] available on Workflow Foundation, we will keep this introduction pretty short.

■**Note** At the time of writing, there was no official abbreviation for the Workflow Foundation that was owned by Microsoft. Reading through related blogs, we found that WF was chosen to be the "unofficial" acronym. Therefore, throughout the rest of this book, we sometimes will refer to Windows Workflow Foundation with WF for the sake of briefness.

Without a workflow DSL, we would have to manually write workflows, sequences, or state machines in code. Any future changes might require a lot of tedious manual rewriting of boiler-plating code. With WF, the high-level workflow concepts are preserved and available in a visual form that also allows for easy communication among team members and stakeholders. WF workflows can either be expressed declaratively in Extensible Application Markup Language (XAML) or be written imperatively as code, e.g., using C#.

■**Note** XAML is widely used in Windows Vista and is also an essential building block of the Windows Presentation Foundation (WPF, code name Avalon). There it is used to declaratively describe a UI with the goal being to separate GUI definition from presentation logic. More information can be found at the MSDN web site.[13]

Unlike other DSLs that require code generators to transform models into executable artifacts, WF actually comes with its own runtime engine, or in other words, WF workflows are directly executable. Figure 7-6 shows the high-level architecture. Windows Workflow Foundation always requires a host process, which can be WinForms or ASP.NET applications, or even Windows services, just to name a few. At the hosting layer, WF provides services such as persistence, timers, or transactions. The runtime then is responsible for loading and executing workflows. WF offers three different types of workflows:

---

11. Paul Andrew et al., *Presenting Windows Workflow Foundation, Beta Edition* (Indianapolis, IN: Sams, 2005)

12. http://msdn.microsoft.com/msdnmag/issues/06/01/windowsworkflowfoundation/ and http://msdn.microsoft.com/msdnmag/issues/06/03/cuttingedge/

13. http://msdn.microsoft.com/windowsvista/about/

- *Sequential workflows*: This type allows for modeling deterministic workflows with a limited amount of branching and choices. A good example is a fulfillment process for orders that follow a predefined sequence, such as inventory allocation, billing, picking, packing, and shipping, where only little derivation from the standard workflow happens.

- *State workflow*: Rather than following sequences, this type allows you to define states. Depending on the state, only certain transitions into other states are allowed. In general, state workflows are used for indeterministic processes, such as a help desk trouble ticket that might make the round several times among the submitter and first-, second-, and third-level support before the ticket can be closed.

- *Office workflow*: This type specializes on the document life cycle, processes based on documents and knowledge workers. It tightly integrates with the next version of Office, Office 12.

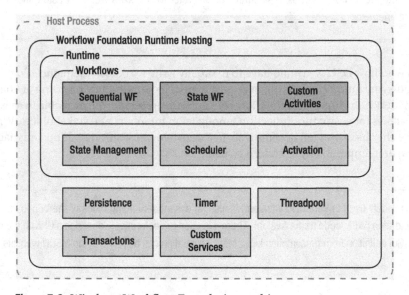

Figure 7-6. *Windows Workflow Foundation architecture*

Plans by Microsoft are to make Windows Workflow Foundation an integral part of Windows, and therefore make it available to every application that requires any kind of workflow support. This will not only allow us to deploy applications without a large WF redistributable, but furthermore, it will ensure that this promising technology will consequently be driven forward in the near future, e.g., as part of WinFX.[14]

---

14. http://msdn.microsoft.com/winfx/

Customizable Expense Approval Process in ISpySoft Using Windows Workflow Foundation

Now let's take a look into how we can put Windows Workflow Foundation to work for our ISpySoft factory. Back in Chapter 3, in our discussion of the Software Factory specification, we decided that we needed configurable workflows for case management (cases with evidence and reports) as well as for expense management. Consider a two-person office compared to an installation with 100 employees. Management's demands from each of these customers clearly will be very different. Using WF and a set of prebuilt activities and events will allow us to customize these two workflows and implement the desired business rules graphically. For the purpose of this book, we chose to demonstrate the *expense approval workflow* that you already saw in Chapter 4 as an example for the *business workflow viewpoint*. So, here is a rough list of scenarios that we need to support:

- Approve expense upon submission (trivial case).

- Require approval if above a certain amount.

- Require approval for items of a certain expense category.

- Require approval by one or more people (manager, finance department, CEO).

- Notify financial department upon approval.

- Notify submitter upon approval or rejection.

- Submit reimbursement for approved expenses to payroll.

Once an expense report is submitted by a smart client user, the back-end expense management web service starts an expense approval workflow that will process this expense report. The workflow runtime will execute this workflow, which performs the necessary actions on the expense, and make the correct decisions based on the workflow definition until the workflow is finished. Even though the approval workflow is a mix of human and computer action, the number of choices and branching logic within most workflow instances will be fairly limited. Therefore, a sequential workflow is a better choice than a state workflow in this case.

Figure 7-7 shows the asynchronous nature of this workflow (the three Wait... activity boxes). It could be days between the time when a field agent submits an expense and when her manager asks for the list of expenses that need to be approved. A web server would quickly run out of resources if it had to process hundreds and thousands of long-running workflows while keeping them all in memory. Therefore, WF supports persisting the state of idle workflows into a SQL Server workflow state database and unloading them from memory. When the time has come to resume, WF will automatically load workflows including their state into memory and continue processing them.

So how does the expense approval workflow (EAW) tie into the business logic of its ISpySoft back-end service? EAW needs to interact with the expense management business logic in the back-end as well with users connected through web services.

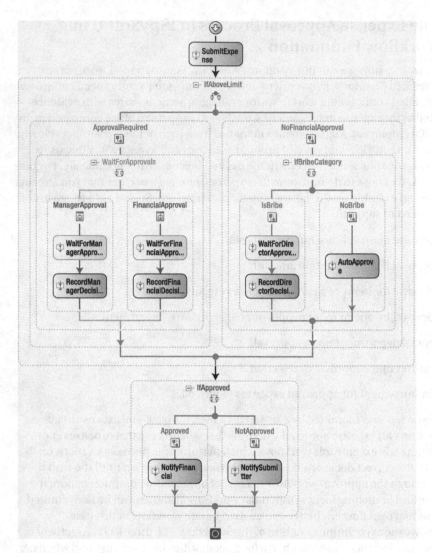

Figure 7-7. *Simple workflow (taken from ISpySoft case study)*

Interaction with business logic is straightforward, as the workflow will simply invoke one or more business logic methods; in the context of Software Factories, we could use pre- and post-conditions to automate them. However, interaction with users is by nature asynchronous. From the perspective of a workflow, EAW will actually listen to events triggered by users' actions such as ApproveExpense. To visualize this link, Figure 7-8 shows a possible sequence of an approval workflow (also based on the simple workflow shown in Figure 7-7). Clearly it shows the idle periods in the workflow lifeline. During these idle periods, workflows can potentially be unloaded by the WF engine, persisted to SQL Server, and reloaded upon the next event coming from the user.

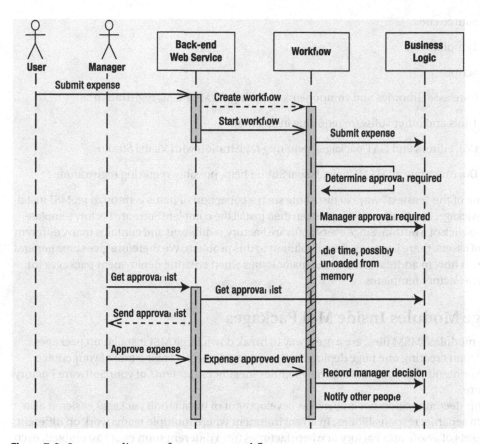

Figure 7-8. *Sequence diagram for expense workflow*

This completes our short excursion into the application of DSLs to tackle variabilities in the application development process. In the next chapter, we will show how the application developer actually customizes a workflow and how we separate customizable workflows from prebuilt core assets. As always, please take a look at the implementation of our ISpySoft case study to find out more about how we integrated Windows Workflow Foundation into our Software Factory.

Packaging and Deployment of the Software Factory Template

Before application developers can start building new applications using a Software Factory, the template needs to be made available to them. Unfortunately, this can potentially pose a major problem, as the template itself consists of a collection of many inhomogeneous items that all need to be installed correctly into a developer's development environment. The following is a sample list of assets that can be included in a SF template:

- Source code

- Templates

- Scripts

- Core asset libraries and components requiring COM or GAC registration

- Tools and other software requiring installation

- DSL editors and GAT packages requiring registration with Visual Studio

- Documentation, HTML help, Visual Studio help, possibly requiring registration

One of the "easiest" ways to distribute such a collection of items is through an MSI instal-lation package. Application developers can then install the complete Software Factory template with the click of a button. Since every Software Factory is different and contains many different kinds of assets, there is no one-fits-all solution to this problem. We therefore give some general advice on how to address some of the major issues when creating deployment packages for Software Factory templates.

Merge Modules Inside MSI Packages

Merge modules (MSM files) are a great way to break down large MSI installation packages. Rather than creating one huge deployment project with the packaging tool of your choice, we recommend that you create merge modules for subcomponents of your Software Factory template.

This decomposition not only makes development of installation packages easier, it also helps to separate responsibilities. In an environment where multiple teams work on different core assets of a Software Factory or where factories from different sources are assembled, each team would be responsible for creating a merge module that correctly installs these core assets on a developer's computer. These merge modules are then included in one common MSI package that allows for installation with one click. Another benefit is that you can separate the UI from the back-end installation logic of a merge module, allowing the person who assembles the merge modules into an MSI to provide a single UI for the entire installer.

Please keep in mind that merge modules might cause problems in the future when patches or new versions need to be deployed. There is no way to distribute an updated merge module by itself; this always requires that the containing MSI package is rebuilt and redistributed. However, in the Software Factory scenario that we described, this situation should not be much of an issue, as both merge module and MSI package are under your control and probably are only distrib-uted in-house.

Installing Third-party MSI Packages

Sooner or later you will find yourself in the situation where your Software Factory template requires third-party tools that in turn come as MSI packages. While it is possible to spawn new processes from within a running MSI installation, by design, Windows only allows one current installation at a time (who would ever want two installations changing the system state at the same time anyway).

The only practicable solution to this limitation is to use a setup bootstrapper approach, as shown in Figure 7-9 (also check out this article on The Code Project[15] about a bootstrapper). The Software Factory template MSI package and all the other third-party MSI packages are included in the setup bootstrapper. Upon installation, the bootstrapper will install one MSI package after the other and will check for correct installation of each of these packages.

Figure 7-9. *Bootstrapper approach*

The approach of using a setup bootstrapper and multiple MSIs also allows for replacement, removal, or repair of individual software packages from the *Add or Remove Programs* dialog, a feature that might come in handy when individual tools that are part of the SF template need to be updated.

Deployment Projects with Visual Studio 2005

VS 2005 comes with two project types that are of special interest in regards to the Software Factory template: Setup Projects, which create MSI packages, and Merge Module Projects, which create MSM merge packages (shown in Figure 7-10). These two project types allow you to easily create deployment packages by including project output from other projects located in the same solution. Furthermore, Visual Studio 2005 takes care of external assembly dependencies by automatically including the referenced assemblies in the setup. With regards to the Software Factory template, if the functionality and flexibility provided by these two deployment project types is not enough (e.g., it is difficult to deploy a database with an MSI from a VS deployment project), you always have the option to use more flexible third-party installer authoring tools.

---

15. http://www.codeproject.com/dotnet/dotNetInstaller.asp

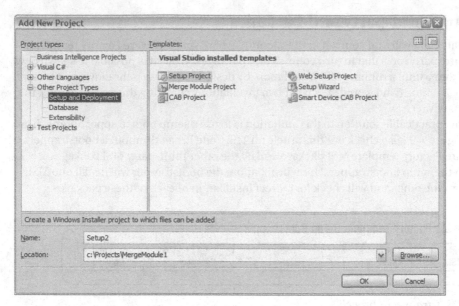

Figure 7-10. *Visual Studio deployment projects*

Summary

In this chapter, we showed two important concepts of how to support developers in their activities to implement product line members. One was guidance and automation, the other domain-specific modeling. Both concepts can be used to support the configuration and assembly of core assets, to implement product line variabilities, and to create extensions to the Software Factory. Together with the development of application core assets, as discussed in the previous chapter, this represents a coherent strategy for building a Software Factory template that can be packaged and installed into the development environment of application developers.

Our main goal in the past two chapters was to highlight the close relationship between the Software Factory schema and the most important aspects of the Software Factory template. Through our case study we provide a proof of concept with concrete examples of how this actually can be realized. Even though we were only able to touch briefly on each topic, with the provided references you should quickly find further in-depth information.

For ISpySoft, the Software Factory template concludes the development of its Software Factory (at least the first iteration). This finally allows us to build the first ISpySoft product line member and start reaping the benefits that the investment into the Software Factories approach promises.

Checkpoint

After this chapter, you should be familiar with the following concepts:

- Identify patterns and best practices learned during core asset development.

- Use guidance and automation in order to automate creation of boilerplating code and encapsulate patterns and best practices.

- Create Visual Studio solution and project templates, integrate them into a GAT package, and define recipes to provide automation.

- Find indications for the use and development of a domain-specific language.

- Apply Windows Workflow Foundation to support variability in Software Factories through highly customizable workflows.

- Create a packaging and deployment strategy for the Software Factory template.

CHAPTER 8

■■■

Product Development

Figure 8-1 shows how Software Factories are built and consumed, as we introduced way back in Chapter 1. While all the previous chapters described Software Factories from the perspective of the Software Factory author, on the left-hand side of the figure, we now switch over to looking at Software Factories from the perspective of the factory consumer, shown on the right-hand side of the figure.

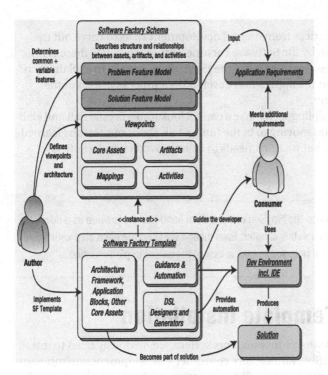

Figure 8-1. *Software Factory overview*

In this chapter, we will show you how a specific application, or product line member, is developed using the ISpySoft Software Factory that we planned, designed, and developed throughout our book. Because of the up-front investment in a factory, we should experience a payback in the form of a productivity and quality boost with each of the applications that the Software Factory consumer develops. Using the application process that we captured in the

Software Factory schema and the core assets packaged in the Software Factory template, building applications should now be a matter of mostly assembling and configuring components together with implementing additional features that are not provided by the factory.

At the time the ISpySoft factory was being implemented, the ISpySoft marketing team already negotiated with one of the existing customers, Private Eye Investigators (PEI), to be pilot customer for the first Software Factory–based ISpySoft product. So let's see how the ISpySoft application developers use the provided factory to efficiently produce a customized application tailored to PEI's needs.

We will guide you through the activities we perform and work products we produce in order to deliver the PEI-specific application:

- Software Factory template installation

- Application specification

- Application architecture

- Application implementation

- Application deployment

We explicitly focus on the differences from one-off development so as to carve out the benefits that you will potentially gain by the Software Factories approach. Since there is no one-size-fits-all development process, we mostly use the ISpySoft case study to explain each activity. Therefore, keep in mind that the application development process using another factory could be significantly different.

At the end of this chapter, as an epilogue, we take a careful look into a crystal ball and elaborate where we see Software Factories moving to in the future, talk about our lessons learned during our case study, and discuss what we think needs to be improved to make Software Factories a real success.

■**Tip** We strongly recommend that you keep the ISpySoft case study at hand that we provide as a download from the Apress web site while reading through this chapter. Even though we illustrate each step with figures and code listings, in case of questions it will help you to take a look at the actual implementation.

Software Factory Template Installation

 Before we can start building the Private Eye Investigators system, we obviously need to install the SF template, which prepares the Software Factory consumer's development environment for assembling, configuring, and customizing the PEI application. In the case of the ISpySoft factory, the SF template is deployed as an MSI package and can be installed (and uninstalled) easily.

The ISpySoft factory has several prerequisites in regards to tool and library support. The following list shows some of the required software that needs to be installed up front (for a complete list, please refer to the installation instructions provided with our downloadable case study):

- .NET Framework 2.0

- Visual Studio 2005, Version 8.0

- Visual Studio 2005 SDK (contains DSL Tools)

- Guidance Automation Extensions (GAX)

- Windows Workflow Foundation (WF) Version 1.0

- Internet Information Server

- SQL Server 2005

The bootstrapper that installs the Software Factory template checks for these prerequisites. If any of them is missing, it will point the user to the location from which the missing software can be installed. Figure 8-2 gives an overview of the components that make up the installed Software Factory template. After successful installation, the development environment is extended and configured to allow for efficiently producing applications that are in the scope of the ISpySoft factory.

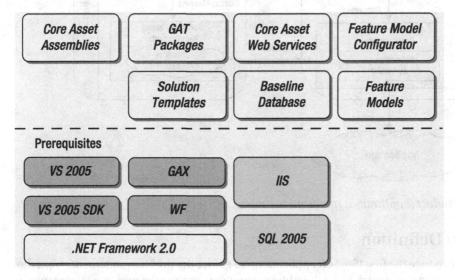

Figure 8-2. *Configured development environment*

Private Eye Investigators Application Specification

 We use the application development process as defined in Chapter 5 to specify the PEI application. Therefore, let's revisit the overview of the application specification process shown in Figure 8-3. The figure guides us through the specification process of the new PEI application in the context of the ISpySoft Software Factory.

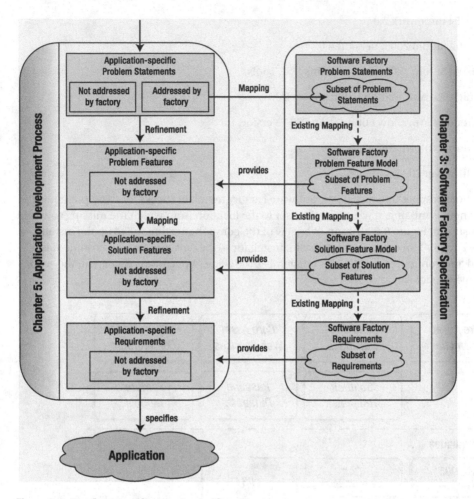

Figure 8-3. *Product (application) specification process*

Problem Definition

 In order to produce the first ISpySoft application, we gather the problem statements from the PEI customer. We then match the PEI problem statements against the problem statements addressed by the ISpySoft Software Factory and harmonize the terms used to describe the problems. Therefore, we can group the result of the problem statement matching process into two categories:

1. *Problem statements addressed by the ISpySoft factory through problem features*: Examples are "Need to manage customer data" and "Need an efficient way to approve expenses of agents through supervisors or CFO, depending on the expense amount and type."

2. *PEI-specific problem statements*: These problems are not addressed by the ISpySoft factory and need to be solved through extensions mapping to PEI-specific problem features, such as "After a case is closed, PEI needs to archive this case."

Table 8-1 shows a number of problem statements that we selected. Each of these statements either relates to variabilities in the factory or will result in custom extensions to it. To further clarify, we also list a number of problem features related to each statement.

Table 8-1. *PEI Problem Statements*

PEI Problem Statement	PEI Problem Features
Expenses of field agents need to be approved by supervisor or CFO, depending on the amount and expense type.	Expense report. Approve/reject expense. Notify supervisor and other people. Approval business process.
Reports for case status are available to supervisors and management.	Reporting. Case reports (cases, agents, evidence, expenses, duration). Restrict access.
After closing a case, print reports for archive.	Bulk printing. Reporting.
After a case is closed, the final bill needs to be sent to a client with a request to pay the full balance within 14 days.	Send invoice. Adjust balance.
Reminders are sent to clients who did not pay by the due date.	Calculate due date. Send reminder. Flag account as defaulting.
Financial department needs to keep track of revenue, cost, and expenses.	Reporting. Financial reports (monthly, quarterly, yearly). Restrict access.

In order to capture and refine the application-specific problem features for the PEI application, we simply reverted to a notation that we are already familiar with: feature models. Just as we did in Chapter 3, we start with high-level features and iteratively refine them. However, there is one difference: instead of doing domain analysis, where we identify common and variable features for a whole domain, with PEI we only focus on additional problem features that need to be addressed through extensions. As a result, you won't see any optional features in such an additional feature model.

Coming back to the problem statements that we elaborated for PEI, we can see that many of them relate to providing statistical reports, analyzing data, and printing these reports, or in other words, common reporting functionality (not to be confused with expense or case reports). This need for reporting functionality was not discovered during the initial domain analysis through ISpySoft, as none of the analyzed customers had requested it before. Based on these initial high-level problem features, we created a PEI-specific problem feature model as shown in Figure 8-4, which contains a number of problem features that address these reporting needs. This problem feature model is a work product created during the requirements specification activity, as prescribed by the underlying Software Factory schema.

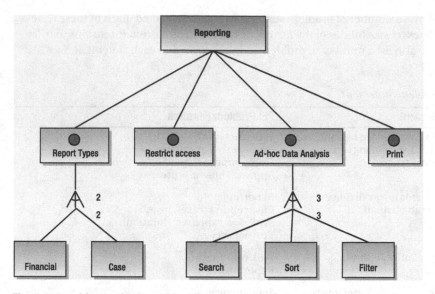

Figure 8-4. *Additional PEI problem features from reporting domain*

Another reason why we use feature models to capture additional features is consistency with the models provided by the factory. We will be able to use these additional feature models as input for iterative Software Factory evolution. In the case of the reporting features, we envision that the feature model will later be integrated in the factory so that other product line members can take advantage of these features as well. We anticipate the reporting features probably will become optional once we integrate them into the factory. Using feature models right from the start will make this transfer and Software Factory evolution step more efficient.

EXISTING REQUIREMENTS SPECIFICATIONS

The problem definition can be paraphrased as the process of identifying the problems that a particular application is going to solve. This process is fairly similar to the definition of the problem domain, as described in Chapter 3. The major difference is that instead of searching for problems of a whole domain, we are gathering business problems for the specific application that we are going to build.

However, in some cases a partial or complete set of requirements for an application might already exist, e.g., when replacing an existing application with a product line member. You might be tempted to take the requirements specification of the original application as a starting point. The problem that arises is that requirements specify solutions to the problems and do not state the problems themselves. In the case of a factory, the solution is already specified through solution features, requirements, a product line architecture, core assets, and prototypical work products. Therefore, you will need to either directly match the existing requirements to those provided by the Software Factory or, if the former is not possible, reverse-engineer the original problem statements to perform a harmonization in the problem domain rather than in the solution domain.

Solution Definition and Requirements Specification

Just as in Chapter 3, once the additional problem features are captured, we need to provide solutions for those problems. Again, these solutions can (but don't have to) be captured using a solution feature model that allows us in the end to map problem features to solution features. Again, this is another work product that we created as prescribed by the Software Factory schema.

Looking at Figure 8-5, which shows the application-specific solution features for PEI, you can see that we will in fact create a new reporting module on the client side that plugs into the modular smart client UI, and a reporting web service on the server side that the smart client communicates with.

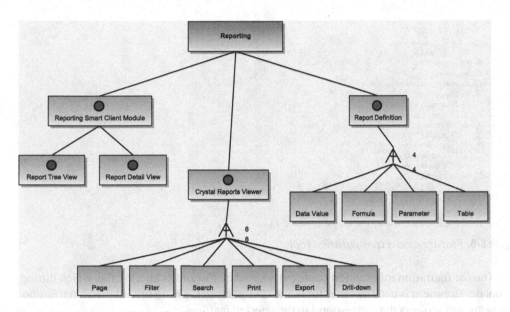

Figure 8-5. *Additional PEI solution features from reporting domain*

We then attach constraints and conditions to these capabilities to specify the requirements of the PEI system (remember that requirements consist of capabilities, conditions, and constraints). Therefore, we achieve requirements traceability for PEI's extensions just as before with the requirements of the Software Factory itself.

Selecting Variable Features

The feature model configuration tool that we introduced in Chapters 3 is shown in Figure 8-6. It is part of the Software Factory and was installed into the application development environment as part of the Software Factory template. Using the feature model configuration tool, we now can select the variable features that apply to the PEI application.

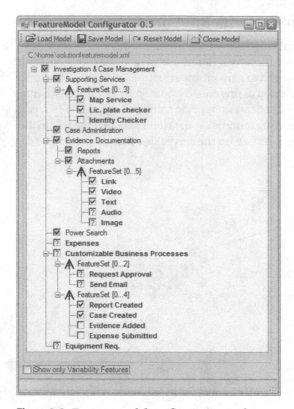

Figure 8-6. *Feature model configuration tool*

The configuration information collected is saved by the tool as an XML file, which during actual development is used by other tools and GAT packages, e.g., to unfold the Visual Studio solutions and projects that correspond to the selected features.

Private Eye Investigators Application Architecture

Depending on the particular Software Factory, the product (or application) architecture will be predetermined to a large part through the product line architecture captured in the Software Factory schema. Typically, this product line architecture is supported through architectural frameworks and other core assets, which predetermine the individual product architecture even further.

Custom feature extensions to product line members often also mean an extension to the product architecture, as we will show in an upcoming example. Therefore, when developing an instance of a product family and designing its architecture, it is generally necessary that we revisit the product line architecture provided by the factory in order to verify that it supports the new requirements of the application.

The question now is, How can we address the selected variable features from a configuration during application development? Back in Chapter 4, we introduced variability mechanisms in a product line architecture together with examples from the ISpySoft factory. In some cases, the variability is well understood and bounded so that we can use simple configuration files, feature models, or DSLs, for example. In other cases, the variability may be complex, poorly understood, or unbounded, and therefore needs to be handled with straight and manual coding. In between these extremes, the application developer can rely on prototypical work products such as templates that need to be customized or filled with implementation.

Because of these reasons, it should be clear that each individual application will typically have a unique product architecture within the constraints given by the underlying product line architecture. This also holds true for product-specific extensions that need to be based on the extension points provided by the Software Factory.

 Now we'd like to take a look at the architecture of such an extension. For the PEI reporting features, we chose to use Crystal Reports for ASP.NET. Crystal Reports provides a web control that acts as a report viewer and can be integrated in ASP.NET web pages. In order to display a web page inside a smart client application, the reporting UI module hosts a web browser control that requests a web report from the back-end server via HTTP. Figure 8-7 visualizes the flow of control when the user requests a report:

1. In a smart client application, the user opens the reporting UI.

2. The reporting module requests a list of reports from the reporting service agent.

3. The service agent checks whether the report list is cached. If not, the smart web proxy is invoked.

4. The smart web proxy asynchronously forwards the request to the web service via SOAP.

5. The web service retrieves the report list from the database. The result gets sent back to the client.

6. The smart web proxy notifies the service agent, which in turn triggers an event in order to update the UI. The user then picks a report from the list.

7. The hosted web browser control requests the web report through report.aspx, a web page that contains the Crystal Reports web control and that is hosted on the back-end web server.

8. Report.aspx queries the database based on the report definition, and the parameters provided in the query string renders the report as HTML and returns it to the client.

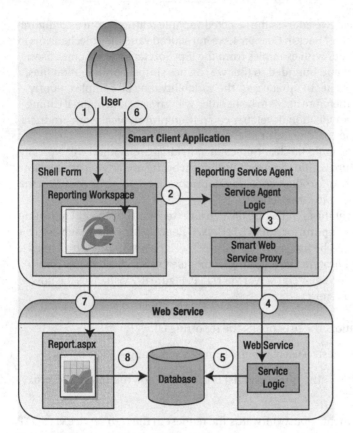

Figure 8-7. *PEI reporting architecture*

The PEI reporting example shows how we integrated a new feature into the existing architecture by creating a new service agent and a new UI module, both extension points provided by the product line architecture captured in the Software Factory schema. We extended the architecture as we introduced the possibility to provide data not only through web services, but also through readily rendered web pages. A web browser control allows us to seamlessly integrate this content into a smart client workspace.

Private Eye Investigators Application Implementation

Once the specification and architecture for the PEI application is available, the application developer can start with the actual implementation (note that in reality this would be an iterative process). Here we will see additional payback for the invested time and effort that we put into developing the ISpySoft Software Factory, its core assets, and automation parts.

Unfolding the Visual Studio Solution Template

The ISpySoft application developer starts implementing the PEI application, or any other ISpySoft application, by unfolding the solution template provided by the Software Factory template in order to create an initial Visual Studio solution, which is prepopulated with a number of projects (depending on the provided feature model configuration), such as the smart client shell project. At the same time, it has already preconfigured most of the references and dependencies to the core asset libraries installed by the template. This solution structure is a work product described by the solution structure viewpoint in the ISpySoft SF schema.

Customizing Back-end Workflows

The ISpySoft product line architecture prescribes how back-end workflows can be customized. As an example, we show how the expense management workflow is adapted to the requirements of PEI. The overall expense management functionality is split into three assemblies as follows, where the participating classes are shown in Figure 8-8.

1. *ExpenseWorkflowInterfaces.dll* provides the IExpenseWorkflowService interface, which is annotated with the ExternalDataExchange attribute. Methods defined in such an interface can be invoked by workflows, e.g., by CallExternalMethod activities, whereas events act as value providers to HandleExternalEvent activities. The separation of workflow service interfaces into separate assemblies eliminates strong dependencies between workflow definitions and business logic.

2. The *ExpenseManagement.dll* contains the underlying business logic except the expense workflow itself. The ExpenseManagement.dll is a core asset and is therefore deployed through the SF template in binary form (as a DLL).

    This assembly also provides the ExpenseWorkflowService, which is an implementation of the IExpenseWorkflowService interface. At runtime an instance of ExpenseWorkflowService is registered with the workflow runtime in order to make it available for communication with workflows.

3. The actual expense workflow is defined in a separate assembly that references *ExpenseWorkflowInterfaces.dll*. The Software Factory template provides a trivial default workflow as a prototypical work product, which is then customized according to PEIs needs. Keeping workflows independent from underlying workflow services allows for customizing workflows even after deployment to a customer site.

In the previous chapter in Figure 7-8, we already showed what the expense workflow could look like. Upon building and packaging the deployment project for the back-end services, the workflow assembly will be included in the installation package. However, one issue still remains: looking at the dependencies of projects, we see that neither the expense web service nor ExpenseManagement.dll is aware of our customized workflows. This is because the former two are core assets and built in the course of the Software Factory template, whereas the workflow assembly is only supplied at application development time.

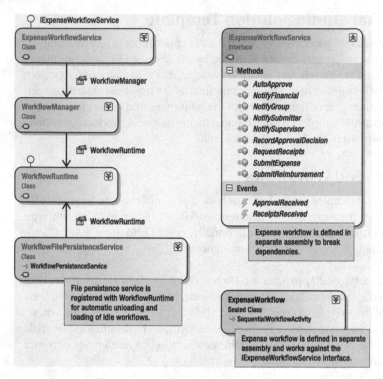

Figure 8-8. *Participants in customizable workflows*

The solution is to make the expense management web service dynamically load this custom assembly at runtime. The workflow runtime then uses reflection in order to find the type of workflow that needs to be created. The required settings are stored in the web service's configuration file and can therefore be changed at any time after application deployment.

Note Throughout this chapter, we draw a clear line between core assets provided by the SF template and extensions that are manually implemented in the form of source code. Reusable core assets are typically provided as compiled assemblies that prevent developers from making unplanned changes and only allow extensions through prescribed mechanisms.

Core assets are part of the Software Factory and therefore under the responsibility of Software Factory architects. While it often might be easier to "make a quick fix" in a reusable asset during application development, not adhering to the distinction between core assets and extensions will quickly lead to many different versions of the same component, making bug fixes and the implementation of new features cumbersome and error prone, and ultimately leading exactly to the problems of one-off projects that we are actually trying to solve.

Creating a New Web Service

In addition to the functionality provided by the ISpySoft core assets, PEI requested an additional reporting feature. This feature will require additional business logic in the back-end together with a reporting web service that exposes it. The requested reporting functionality will require us to work in five different places:

- *Database*: Create additional tables to store metadata about reports and related data.

- *Data entity model*: Enhance the model to accommodate additional information.

- *Business logic*: Create a new manager class that provides the reporting functionality.

- *Web service*: Expose business logic as a web service to smart clients.

- *Web page*: Make reports accessible as an .aspx page hosting a Crystal Report web control.

For the most part, this work does not differ from the implementation of back-end services that became core assets and were developed in the course of the Software Factory template. However, now developers can use several GAT recipes provided by the template in order to reach their goal quicker.

- Create a new web service stub including a manager class (determined as a best practice) and a reference to data access library.

- Create a new data entity and corresponding factory class providing the standard factory methods GetByID, GetAll, Save, and Delete.

- Create an ID property for data entity that relates to the unique key in the corresponding database table.

- Create a property of a given type that maps to a corresponding database column.

Listing 8-1 shows the *Report* business entity after executing some of these recipes. Much of the NHibernate wiring code is done automatically and therefore makes business entity creation a breeze.

Unlike most other core assets, which are made available as compiled assemblies, we decided to make the data entity model available for application development as a C# project containing the full source code. The reason is the lack of a simple extension mechanism for NHibernate data entity models that would allow creating new entities and extending existing entities (e.g., add new properties and add new object relations) while building on a readily compiled assembly.

Listing 8-1. *Report Entity Class Built with ISpySoft Recipes*

```
//****************************************************
// This file was created using the ISpySoft Software Factory template.
// It will not be regenerated and therefore can be modified manually.
//****************************************************
using System;
using System.Collections.Generic;
using System.Text;
using NHibernate.Mapping.Attributes;
```

```
namespace ISpySoft.Backend.DataAccess.DomainModel
{
  [Class(0, NameType = typeof(Report), Table = "Report")]
  public class Report
  {
    int m_ID = 0;
    string m_Name = "";
    string m_Url = "";

    [Id(0, Name = "ID", Column = "ID", TypeType = typeof(Int32),
          UnsavedValue = "0")]
    [Generator(1, Class = "identity")]
    public int ID
    {
      get { return m_ID; }
      set { m_ID = value; }
    }

    [Property(0, Column = "Name")]
    public string Name
    {
      get { return m_Name; }
      set { m_Name = value; }
    }

    [Property(0, Column = "Url")]
    public string Url
    {
      get { return m_Url; }
      set { m_Url = value; }
    }
  }
}
```

Regarding deployment, the web service and any attached business logic will get packaged into the back-end installation package, as will the other core asset web services provided by the template. Packaging and deploying a customized database, however, becomes trickier.

The ISpySoft core assets contain a SQL script that will create a new database during application deployment. While this script is installed together with the Software Factory template in order to set up the development environment, developers are not supposed to modify this file, as it is a core asset and therefore under control of Software Factory architects. Instead, developers will create a change script, which gets executed after the initial creation script to accommodate eventual changes and extensions. For the PEI application, this change script will create the additional tables and columns for reporting metadata.

Creating a New Module

What's left to complete the PEI reporting functionality is the UI part that plugs into the smart client shell. The reporting feature actually consists of three different parts: reporting module with multiple reporting views, reporting service agent, and reporting smart web proxy. The efficiency gains when implementing this additional functionality mainly come from the contextual guidance provided through GAT recipes and templates, as the following list shows:

- Generate smart web proxy (100% generation)

- Service agent project template

- UI module project template

- Create view (following the MVP and dependency injection pattern)

As a little eye candy before we move on to product deployment, Figure 8-9 shows the result of all our hard work, the additional reporting UI integrated in the smart client shell application.

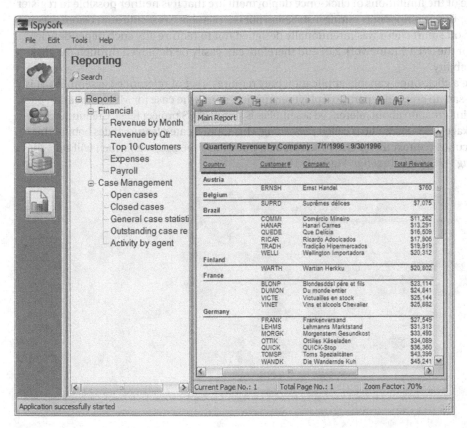

Figure 8-9. *Reporting module*

Private Eye Investigators Application Deployment

We are almost done with building our first ISpySoft application, for which we showed how to configure and customize the variable parts and how to extend it with new functionality. As the final step, this application needs to be packaged into installer packages and shipped to Private Eye Investigators for deployment.

Each ISpySoft product line member will require an individual installation package because different additional components and dependencies will need to be included depending on the product. Furthermore, deployment is split into two packages, one for the back-end server installation and one for smart client installation on the users' PCs. We now show how the ISpySoft factory helps to streamline the deployment process for the PEI application.

Smart Client Deployment

Back in Chapter 4 when we designed the ISpySoft architecture, we decided on click-once deployment for the smart client part of the system and to use automatic or forced updates.

Some of the limitations of click-once deployment are that it is neither possible to register services or COM components during installation nor is it possible to execute any custom actions. The ISpySoft smart client was intentionally designed not to require any such dependencies (except for the .NET Framework 2.0) and therefore can easily be deployed through the click-once capability.

Since a click-once-capable application only requires a set of referenced assemblies, it is not necessary to create a separate deployment project as it is the case for MSI installation packages (the information about referenced assemblies is stored in VS project files). Creating a click-once package in Visual Studio is called *publishing*. This sophisticated feature hides behind the inconspicuous context menu entry *Publish* of application-type projects, which will start the *Publishing Wizard* as shown in Figure 8-10.

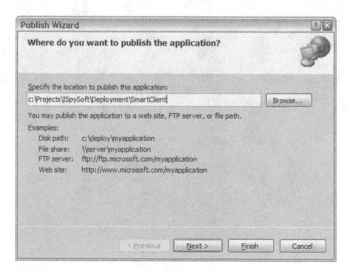

Figure 8-10. *Click-Once Publishing Wizard*

In order to make the build process more efficient, The ISpySoft template provides a GAT recipe, *Build Deployment Packages*, that combines the creation of smart client and back-end deployment packages into one click.

Back-end Deployment

Unlike the smart client with its few dependencies, the back-end services require a full-blown installation, as they have a number of dependencies, such as SQL Server 2005 or Windows Workflow Foundation, and require additional custom installation steps, such as creating a database or configuring IIS. Therefore, MSI installation packages are the way to go for back-end deployment.

Even though each application based on the ISpySoft factory includes different individual components, all the installation packages also share a number of settings and included components, which are identical in each installation package:

- Core asset components containing common features, such as the case management UI module
- Checks for prerequisites (software that needs to be installed beforehand on the client machine), e.g., .NET 2.0 or Windows Workflow Foundation
- Database script and possibly a change/extension script
- Setup wizard screens, e.g., for the installation folder or the database server name

In order to make developers more efficient when creating back-end installation packages, the solution template provided by ISpySoft already contains a prefilled setup project as a starting point. It is then up to the developer to include any additional web services, components, and other dependencies in the installation package. This MSI installation package is then included in a bootstrapper, which checks the prerequisites and performs additional installation steps, such as the creation of the ISpySoft SQL database. As mentioned previously, the ISpySoft guidance provides the *Build Deployment Packages* feature, which simplifies the deployment process.

Summary

This brings us to the end of the custom ISpySoft implementation for Private Eye Investigators. After many chapters of designing and building core assets, we were finally able to put our Software Factory to work.

In our PEI example, we first demonstrated the specification phase of a product line member. While a real-world Software Factory will certainly require some more sophisticated requirements engineering techniques, the basic idea of configuring variable features and defining extensions to a product will still apply. During the implementation phase, we then used this configuration to build a first product in a highly prescriptive process that over time and after multiple feedback cycles into the factory will provide even more automation. New functionality was built as prescribed by the product line architecture and integrated using well-defined extension points.

In real life, now two things would happen: first, more applications would be developed with the Software Factory, and second, the factory would continuously need to be extended and evolved as new requirements come along and the targeted domain changes. No matter what, having built a flexible and extensible Software Factory should allow us to tackle these changes at much greater ease (and much fewer sleepless nights) than it was possible before with conventional one-off projects.

Checkpoints

In this chapter, we showed you how the Software Factory approach effectively automated the development of ISpySoft applications throughout the following life-cycle phases:

- *Product specification*: Define the product using the configuration tool to select and dese-lect optional features. Add requirements for features that are not covered by the factory. Use the same techniques as when identifying the factory requirements (problem and solution feature models).

- *Product architecture*: Develop the architecture according to the product line architecture as prescribed by the Software Factory schema. Use extension points for product-specific extensions and verify their architecture for conformance with the product line architecture.

- *Product implementation*: Build the application by assembling and configuring core assets. The main focus is on product-specific extensions.

- *Product deployment*: Use installation package templates as a starting point and customize deployment packages.

A Look into the Crystal Ball

In our ISpySoft case study, we demonstrated many technologies and tools that are available today and are successfully used in software development. Nevertheless, in many areas of our ISpySoft Software Factory we had to improvise using existing tools or even build our own tools, such as the Software Factory schema DSL or the feature model configurator. What we can see is that for each of the four pillars of Software Factories, there are tools and techniques available. But these tools and techniques are more or less isolated applications. The Software Factories schema tries to fill the gap in between by relating these concepts, but it will require a new generation of tools to enable a seamless Software Factories experience, both for the Software Factory author as well as for the Software Factory consumer. You can compare this with the evolution of other development tools that we use today such as source control, IDE, testing, and defect tracking, which began as stand-alone tools but over time became seamlessly inte-grated into tool suites like the Visual Studio 2005 Team System.

In this final section of our book, based on our experience in developing a Software Factory, we want to identify necessary improvements and other opportunities that will help making Software Factories a success story. Therefore, we would like to take a quick look into the crystal ball and share with you what we think will be ahead of us. Alternatively, you could think of this as the high-level problem statements for Software Factory tools that we pass on to development tool vendors as input for future tooling strategies.

In our opinion, the best way to do this is to distinguish between short-term goals, which have a horizon of maybe 1 or 2 years, and long-term goals, which could be as far away as 10 years.

Short-term Goals

The most value at this point we would get from tools that help us in implementing and integrating the Software Factory schema as it is the core concept of any factory. Even simple tool support like the Software Factories Schema DSL that we developed already greatly improves the experience of developing a Software Factory. But we certainly can envision more sophisticated tools to model Software Factory schemas that could become a key to the industry adoption of Software Factories.

Software Factory Schema

In our case study, we demonstrated a DSL that allowed us to model a factory schema. With this rudimentary DSL we were able to document the schema and produce useful help files for the application developer. While this was great for demonstration purposes, in reality you would need a much more sophisticated tool to capture the wealth of information that makes up large-scale Software Factory schemas.

To draw an analogy, for example, you can capture requirements in an Excel spreadsheet. However, with an increasing number of requirements, this Excel spreadsheet will outgrow its initial purpose, and more capabilities will be required such as requirement traceability, easy browsing, status information, concurrent working, etc. You could switch over to something like Rational Requisite Pro, which provides a user-friendly UI optimized for capturing requirements and many other features like requirement analysis. Underneath the hood it is based on a repository for storing the captured data.

Similarly, you would need a Software Factory author-friendly tool for modeling Software Factory schemas (not necessarily in a graphical way), with a schema repository that is based on the SF schema metamodel. Such a Software Factories schema modeling tool should not only support the creation of the schema, but furthermore should support us in identifying and capturing the viewpoints, assets, and activities that are required to produce work products (e.g., by providing viewpoint libraries and other templates). It would combine architectural aspects as well as development process aspects, and allow for integration with other tools by providing access to its model repository for data exchange, such as with GAT packages or code generators.

Our last comment on the schema concerns viewpoints and mappings. At this point in time we can only define mappings as textual descriptions. In order to make use of such a powerful concept, we will need a formal definition language, which we use to define mappings and operations across mappings, as described in Chapter 5. Only then will we be able to provide broadly applicable tools that can understand mappings between viewpoints and perform meaningful operations across them.

Tool Integration and Horizontal Factories

With more and more emerging horizontal factories, we see yet another possibility for integration. Imagine you are sketching the high-level architecture of an enterprise application using a tool like the Distributed System Designer. At the same time you are already capturing information about the different systems (e.g. web service, WinForms client) of such an enterprise system.

It should now be possible to attach horizontal Software Factories to each of these systems, such as the Smart Client Software Factory or the Service Software Factory.

When it comes to the implementation of such a system, a developer would not have to create a new project manually. Rather, based on the system diagram, the developer would unfold the horizontal Software Factories that are attached with each of these parts, while using information that was previously captured. Instead of having to decide which project type to create for each of the applications, the developer would then use one or more templates and GAT recipes to create the initial solution structure of such a system, similar to what we did in Chapter 6 when we built a prototypical smart client application to harvest common assets.

We used the Distributed System Designer as a concrete example for demonstration purposes, but it should be clear that we can just as well apply this vision to other tools typically used in the early phases of software design.

Further Tool Support

As we mentioned earlier in this book, you can consider the DSL Tools and the Guidance Automation Toolkit as a first down payment from Microsoft towards the Software Factories vision. While these tools do not specifically support factories, they still are a great step forward due to their support of model-driven development, contextual guidance, and automation, as required for effectively building products with Software Factories.

On the authors' side, picture a feature modeling and configuration tool tailored to Software Factories. While there are already some tools around, such as the Eclipse Feature Modeling Plug-In,[1] what is missing is a tool that seamlessly integrates with Visual Studio, and specifically with the life-cycle management capabilities of VSTS.

GAT already provides great flexibility when creating guidance in the form of recipes. However, it should be possible to graphically orchestrate actions and recipes for certain tasks using a modeling language, similar to the way we capture workflows with the Workflow Foundation today.

Regarding model-driven development with DSL Tools, we are currently missing a number of concepts that we think are crucial to make this product a success. Diagrams based on DSL Tools with a large number of items quickly become unmanageable because diagram and model are tightly coupled and allow no partitioning. A first improvement would be the support for containers that will allow for creating modeling languages with a hierarchical representation and drill-down capabilities.

Second, in order to make large models even more manageable, DSL Tools would need some sort of model repository that allows for partitioning models and storing models independently of their graphical representation. Diagrams would then become selected views onto the underlying model, showing only a subset of elements.

Last but not least, we would like to see a mapping and transformation mechanism that helps us specify relations between different but interrelated DSLs in order to create automated and semiautomated model-to-model transformations.

Long-term Goals

Besides the immediate improvements that we think need to be addressed to spark the wider adoption of Software Factories in the industry, we would also like to share our vision for Software Factories tool support over a longer time frame.

---

1. http://gp.uwaterloo.ca/fmp/

Software Factory Supply Chains

The release of horizontal factories like the *Smart Client Factory* and *Service Factory* by the patterns & practices group at Microsoft is great news. This gives us hope for continuing strong support for Software Factories by Microsoft in the future. These two horizontal factories both have a broad scope that allows for consumption by a range of more specialized factories. As the knowledge and experience with Software Factories builds in the developer community, we will see more horizontal and possibly vertical factories become available for building Software Factory supply chains.

To successfully build supply chains, we will need a set of standards (or de facto standards). We can think of several areas where standards will be required, such as model and data formats (e.g., for the SF schema), model and data exchange, and tool interaction. Without such standards, it will be difficult to effectively assemble larger factories from smaller ones or to provide any nontrivial tool integration. The goal for us is to be able to assemble a Software Factory by extending and customizing components and factories from different sources efficiently, possibly with tool support.

Development Process Support

Currently, Visual Studio Team System (VSTS) probably is the best integrated platform supporting software development processes on the Windows platform. By providing customizable processes, roles, and guidance, it allows for managing the complete life cycle of applications. At the same time, a core concept in Software Factories is the definition of the application development process for product line members in the schema. Therefore, VSTS would be an ideal candidate for integration with other Software Factory tools in order to support such application processes defined through Software Factories.

The unfolding process of a Software Factory template could create a number of work items in VSTS that resemble the activities from the development process that need to be completed in order to build a particular application, as specified by the schema. Every work item would be annotated with additional information such as description of the work products that need to be produced (manually, semiautomated, or automated) or links to guidance in context.

Software Factory for Software Factories

Once the development community gains more experience with Software Factories, then we can start thinking about a factory for Software Factories. In the long term, we hope to see a development environment supporting factory life-cycle management by integrating necessary tools and providing us with a seamless Software Factory authoring experience. We can think of this in a similar fashion to what we saw with the release of Visual Studio 2005 Team System, which integrates different life-cycle tools in the domain of software development today.

Such a platform would support us in defining, building, and deploying factories using horizontal factories, frameworks, tools, and other assets as building blocks. Based on such a factory, it would also be possible to provide templatized work products for creating Software Factories in particular domains, e.g, problem and solution feature models for the Enterprise Resource Planning (ERP) or the Customer Relation Management (CRM) domains.

Parting Thoughts

We hope you enjoyed reading through this book as much as we enjoyed writing it. This is an exciting time to see how the theory of Software Factories turns into practice, as working prototypes are developed and the first consumable Software Factories become publicly available.

We also hope that all of us in the software development community will over time accomplish the goals stated previously in order to shape this new generation of tools that integrates the four pillars of Software Factories. Based on the experience of the past, this will be absolutely critical to the success and the broad adoption of Software Factories in order to industrialize software development.

APPENDIX

■ ■ ■

Software Factory Development: Checklist

The following checklist will help you get a quick overview when planning and building your own Software Factory projects. It summarizes the major deliverables, relates them to the tools that might be used, and provides a reference to the chapter where we cover the deliverable. Please keep in mind, though, that this list is a recommendation based on our experience and the ISpySoft case study, and serves as a starting point. The Software Factory paradigm defines only the Software Factory schema and the Software Factory template as mandatory deliverables; all other deliverables and activities are optional and need to be defined and tailored to the specific needs of your own factory.

Deliverable	Description	Modeling Language/Tools	Chapter
Software Factory Definition			
Software Factory overview	Provides the business case for the Software Factory project.		2
Software Factory vision	Defines a short and precise (~25 words) overall goal of the factory. The success of the Software Factory project is measured against the vision.		2
Software Factory inputs	Assets mined from existing systems that can be reused or made reusable for the factory.		2
Application constraints	Nonnegotiable requirements that are known up front and imposed by the environment on the products that will be built with a factory. Also called product constraints.		2
Factory constraints	Nonnegotiable requirements that are known up front and imposed by the environment on the product development process itself. Also called production constraints.		2

Deliverable	Description	Modeling Language/Tools	Chapter
Stakeholder description	Describes the different stakeholders and their interests in the Software Factory project.		2
Application context	Defines the context in which the Software Factory's products will be used.	Context diagram/UML tool	2
Factory context	Defines how the Software Factory fits into the overall organizational and development environment.	Context diagram/UML tool	2
Domain glossary	Lists the most important concepts in the targeted business domain and facilitates communication between the different stakeholders of a factory.		2

Software Factory Specification

Deliverable	Description	Modeling Language/Tools	Chapter
Domain model	Model of the targeted business domain. Typically derived from the domain glossary.	Entity model, static structure diagram (approximation)/UML tool	3
Problem statements	Describe the business problems that we want to solve with the factory.		3
Problem feature matrix	Relates business problem statements with high-level business problem features.	Spreadsheet/Excel	3
Problem feature model	Refines problem features, determines commonality and variability of the problem domain.	Feature model/feature modeling tool	3
Solution feature matrix	Analyzes the solution features of existing applications.	Spreadsheet/Excel	3
Solution feature model	Refines solution features, determines commonality and variability of the solution domain.	Feature model/feature modeling tool	3
Prototypical (scoped) feature models	Feature models scoped according to constraints such as budget, time, factory constraints, customer requests, marketing decisions, priority, relevance, and experience.	Feature modeling tool	3
Requirements specification	Refines features from solution feature model into well-defined requirements by adding conditions and constraints to the capabilities described by features.	Possibly integrated in feature modeling tool	3

Software Factory Schema

Deliverable	Description	Modeling Language/Tools	Chapter
Software Factory schema	Captures the product line architecture, design, and application development process of a factory. Relates all the different parts of the SF schema.	SF schema DSL/SF schema editor	4, 5

Deliverable	Description	Modeling Language/Tools	Chapter
Viewpoints	Address the concerns of different stakeholders and describe different aspects of the architecture and design of a product line. Provide a separation of concerns and are hierarchically organized.	SF schema DSL/SF schema editor	4
Definitions of work products	Define which work products need to be created in order to build a product line member.	SF schema DSL/SF schema editor	4
Mappings	Define relationships between viewpoints, allow for operations such as reference, navigation, validation, or query.	SF schema DSL/SF schema editor	5
Activities	Add information about how work products will be built (e.g., which tools and assets to use).	SF schema DSL/SF schema editor	5
Assets	Describe existing components, libraries, frameworks, documentation, how-to's, etc., that are used to build the work products for a product line member.	SF schema DSL/SF schema editor	5
Tools	Describe tools that are used to build the work products for a product line member.	SF schema DSL/SF schema editor	5
Software Factory Template			
Software Factory template	Installable package that contains the core assets, tools, and automation packages described in the SF schema.	VS 2005, Visual Studio 2005 SDK, DSLs, GAT, GAX, etc.	6, 7
Core assets	Product line–specific frameworks, libraries, components, libraries, frameworks, documentation, how-to's, etc.		6, 7
Prototypical work products	Templatized work products that conform to their associated viewpoint and that will be refined, customized, and extended during activities as defined in the SF schema.	Tools and languages according to related viewpoint	6, 7
GAT guidance packages	Provide guidance in context and guidance automation to developers during application development.	GAT, GAX	7
Product line–specific DSLs	Domain-specific languages used, among others, to model variabilities in a product line.	DSL Tools	5, 7
Other tools	Any software tool that will be used during application development.		6, 7

Deliverable	Description	Modeling Language/Tools	Chapter
Product Line Member/Application			
Configuration	Configured feature models with selected/deselected variable features.	Feature model configurator	5, 8
Work products	Building blocks of product line member, implemented according to SF schema.	VS2005, DSLs, etc.	8
Extensions	Implemented functionality that originally was not covered by the Software Factory.	VS2005, third-party products, libraries, services, etc.	8

Index

You Need the Companion eBook

Your purchase of this book entitles you to its companion eBook for only $10.

We believe this Apress title will prove so indispensable that you'll want to carry it with you everywhere, which is why we are offering the companion eBook for $10 to customers who purchase this book now. Convenient and fully searchable, the eBook version of any content-rich, page-heavy Apress book makes a valuable addition to your programming library. You can easily find, copy, and apply code—and then perform examples by quickly toggling between instructions and the application. Even simultaneously tackling a donut, diet soda, and complex code becomes simplified with hands-free eBooks!

Once you purchase this book, getting the $10 companion eBook is simple:

1. Visit **www.apress.com/promo/tendollars/**.

2. Complete a basic registration form to receive a randomly generated question about this title.

3. Answer the question correctly in 60 seconds and you will receive a promotional code to redeem for the $10 eBook.

2560 Ninth Street • Suite 219 • Berkeley, CA 94710

eBookshop

THE EXPERT'S VOICE™

Offer valid through 1/17/2007.